Advance Praise for *Analysis of Genuine Karate 2*

Hermann Bayer once again provides fresh perspectives and prudent explanations of the complex developments of karate-jutsu into karate-do and into sports-karate. He not only dares, in his seventies, to successfully add a combat karate system from scratch up to black belt to his thirty years of karatedo training, but he assesses his training observations and experiences with analytic acumen and astute research.

> —Noel Smith, Hanshi 9th Dan Yamashita International Budo Association, Kyoshi, 8th Dan Shorin Ryu, Shorinkan, head coach for the US karate team (1973 to 1978), USA Karate Hall of Fame Inductee (1976)

All who are serious about knowing more concerning the early life protection methods developed on Okinawa, and how they've "morphed" since then to become the karate-do many know today, will applaud this latest work by Dr. Bayer. I found it to be just as important to the future of genuine Okinawan karate as his first book, if not more so. This well-researched, comprehensive blend of history, philosophy, martial culture, and informed opinion educates our judgment when it comes to the reasons practitioners are rarely exposed to more than a glimpse of "genuine karate" these days, on Okinawa or elsewhere. This book fills numerous gaps in our understanding of that which we seek to learn and share. It provides thoughtful perspectives and honest appraisals—all with the intention of helping us steer a "true course."

> —William "Bill" Hayes, Hanshi, 9th Dan Shorin Ryu, Shobayashi-Kan, Major United States Marine Corps (retired), Karate Masters' Hall of Fame and American-Okinawan Karate Association Hall of Fame Inductee, award-winning author of *My Journey with the Grandmaster: Reflections of an American Martial Artist on Okinawa*

Supported by historical and socio-cultural facts, scientific analysis, and public records, Bayer examines how Japan reinterpreted Okinawan karate to best serve its own nationalistic agenda. Through his collective analyses he quantifies karate as an industry and reveals a complex and convoluted evolution, aptly illuminating the motivations behind various stakeholders.

> —Patrick McCarthy, Hanshi 9th Dan, ranks in jujutsu, judo, Yamaneryu kobudo, and Japanese swordsmanship; martial arts researcher, historian, and best-selling author. Director of the International Ryukyu Karate Research Society, Canadian Black Belt Hall of Fame Inductee (2012)

Once again, the author, Dr Hermann Bayer, invites karateka around the world to look at their art through the lens of reality rather than myth. His dedication to budo karate is clear, but that enthusiasm is put to one side as he burrows further into the legends, propaganda, and misinformation entrenched in modern-day karate, a field of study and practice where many students and teachers regularly mistake fiction for fact and place imagery over substance. As with his first volume, a level of discomfort while reading this book should not be unexpected. The book challenges the reader to examine their beliefs, and that alone makes the work a valuable tool in the learning of karate. I wholeheartedly recommend this book to anyone making a serious study of karate.

> —Michael Clarke, Kyoshi, 8th Dan Okinawan Goju-Ryu, award-winning author of *The Art of Hojo Undo, Shin Gi Tai*, and others

The first source for you to learn more about your karate. *Analysis of Genuine Karate 2* is second to none!

> —Kris Wilder, 6th Dan Goju-Ryu, black belt taekwondo and judo, USA Karate Hall of Fame Inductee (2018), award-winning author of more than twenty marital arts books, including *The Way of Kata, The Way of Sanchin Kata*, and others

Analysis of Genuine Karate 2 follows the first volume nicely. This is an insightful look at the multiple directions modern karate is taking based on the historic roots discussed in the first volume. An excellent reference for anyone interested in the history of karate and the directions it is currently moving toward.

—Raymond "Gene" Adkins, Renshi 6th Dan Shorin Ryu, Shorinkan

Dr. Bayer's *Analysis of Genuine Karate 2* expands on and develops a further analysis of the concepts and relationships of karate-jutsu, karate-do, and sports-karate. Drawing on an anthology of publications, educational materials, people, places, and concepts, Dr. Bayer furthers his analysis of what he has termed "Genuine Karate," discussing how it evolved, retreated, and is reinventing itself. Volume 2 is a wonderful exploration of his research and findings and his relevant exploration of Okinawa's "Gift to the World"—Okinawan karate.

—Ted Jacobson, Renshi, 6th Dan Shorin Ryu, Shorinkan

Analysis of Genuine Karate 2 is a book that reflects a love, devotion, dedication, and level of knowledge that in my opinion is comparable to, if not exceeds, anything that has been published on the topic.

—Bernard N. Curry, PhD, LCSW, CSOTP, CCTP, university professor

Analysis of Genuine Karate 2

Analysis of GENUINE KARATE 2

Sociocultural Development, Commercialization, and Loss of Essential Knowledge

Hermann Bayer, Ph.D.

YMAA Publication Center
Wolfeboro, NH USA

YMAA Publication Center, Inc.
PO Box 480
Wolfeboro, NH 03894
800 669-8892 • www.ymaa.com • info@ymaa.com

ISBN: 9781594399244 (print)
ISBN: 9781594399251 (ebook)
ISBN: 9781594399268 (hardcover)

This book set in Adobe Garamond and Source Sans.

All rights reserved including the right of reproduction in whole or in part in any form.
Copyright © 2023 by Hermann Bayer
Edited by Doran Hunter
Cover design by Axie Breen
Photos by author unless otherwise noted
Charts and graphs by author unless otherwise noted

20230511

Publisher's Cataloging in Publication

Names: Bayer, Hermann, author.
Title: Analysis of genuine karate 2 : sociocultural development, commercialization, and loss of essential knowledge / Hermann Bayer, Ph.D.
Description: Wolfeboro, NH USA : YMAA Publication Center, [2023] | Includes bibliographical references and index.
Identifiers: ISBN: 978159439244 (print) | 978194399268 (hardcover) | 9781594399251 (ebook) | LCCN: 2023936612
Subjects: LCSH: Karate--Japan--Okinawa Island. | Soldiers--Training of--Japan. | Karate--Foreign influences. | Jiu-jitsu--Japan--Okinawa Island. | Karate--History--Errors, inventions, etc. | Karate--Philosophy. | Karate--Economic aspects. | Karate--Study and teaching. | Martial arts--History. | BISAC: SPORTS & RECREATION / Martial Arts / General. | HISTORY / Asia / Japan. | SPORTS & RECREATION / History.
Classification: LCC: GV1114.3 .B392 2023 | DDC: 796.815/3--dc23

The authors and publisher of the material are NOT RESPONSIBLE in any manner whatsoever for any injury which may occur through reading or following the instructions in this manual.

The activities physical or otherwise, described in this manual may be too strenuous or dangerous for some people, and the reader(s) should consult a physician before engaging in them.

Neither the authors nor the publisher assumes any responsibility for the use or misuse of information contained in this book.

Nothing in this document constitutes a legal opinion nor should any of its contents be treated as such. While the authors believe that everything herein is accurate, any questions regarding specific self-defense situations, legal liability, and/or interpretation of federal, state, or local laws should always be addressed by an attorney at law.

When it comes to martial arts, self-defense, and related topics, no text, no matter how well written, can substitute for professional, hands-on instruction. These materials should be used for **academic study only**.

Printed in USA.

CONTENTS

Foreword by Noel Smith, Hanshi 9th Dan   vii
Introduction: Structure of the Text, Research, and Analysis   xi
   Content and Structure of This Text   xi
   Methods and Analysis Used   xv
   Excurse: Quantitative and Qualitative Research Characteristics   xviii

Chapter 1: Why Different Terms Are Needed for Today's Versions of Okinawan Karate-jutsu, Japanese Karatedo, and Sports-Karate   1
   Classic Okinawan Karate-jutsu   3
   Old-Style Japanese Karatedo   9
   Modern Sports-Karate   13

Chapter 2: Did Karate-jutsu Originate in Okinawa or in China? A Contribution to Historic Reasoning in Martial Arts History   19
   Throughout History Foreign Knowledge Has Been Integrated into Existing Knowledge   22
   China Is the Birthplace of Ch'üan fa, Japan Is the Birthplace of Bu-jutsu, and Okinawa Is the Birthplace of Karate-jutsu   24
   Is the Proposed Reasoning Plausible?   26
   Summary of Chapter 2   27

Chapter 3: Japan's Assertion of Okinawan Karate—How a Subcultural Intangible Heritage Is Used as a National Cultural Symbol   29
   Okinawa's History Creates Unique Socio-Cultural Conditions   30
   Assertion of a Subcultural Symbol as a National Cultural Symbol   33
      The First Reason for Japanization of Okinawan Karate: Japan's Preparations for War   36
         Budo and Karate as Means to Create an All-Embracing Warrior Spirit   38
         Karate as One Way to Secure the Human Raw Material for Pre-War Japan's Armed Forces and to Demonstrate Socio-Cultural Superiority   42
      The Second Reason for the Japanization of Okinawan Karate: Japan's Cultural Integration Efforts   46
         Conformity and Group Orientation in Japanese Culture   47
         Senpai Seniority as Social Mechanism to Integrate Karate into Japan's Martial Arts Tradition   48
   Summary of Chapter 3   52

Chapter 4: The Metamorphosis of an Ancient Fighting Art into Athletic Showmanship   55
   Sports-Karate: The Commercialization of Karatedo and Its Consequences   57
      Consequence One: The Loss of Essential Knowledge   62
         Offensive Moves Were Changed into Defensive Ones   66

Systematic Knowledge about Nerve Strikes and Grappling Came to Be Patchy ... 69
Excurse: A Psychological Perspective on Itosu Anko Sensei's Motivation to Teach Karate to Kids ... 72
Consequence Two: The Initial Unity of Kata and Kumite Separated into Unconnected Sport Disciplines ... 79
Kumite's Changed Role and Purpose in Sports Karate ... 81
Kata's Changed Role and Purpose in Sports-Karate ... 86
Consequence Three: The Modern Misconception about Avoiding a Fight at All Costs ... 90
Karate-jutsu's Initial Moral Code ... 93
Modern Alterations to Karate-jutsu's Initial Moral Code ... 95
Summary of Chapter 4 ... 107

Chapter 5: The Path to Mastery in Karate: Growing into Higher Levels of Understanding of Karate-jutsu ... 109
Three Core Components of Mastery ... 112
Advanced Stage of Holistic Perception and Insight ... 112
Advanced Level of Knowledge and Understanding ... 114
"Automatic" Application of Insight and Knowledge ... 118
Milestones on a Path toward Mastery ... 120
"Inductive" versus "Deductive" Learning in Karate-jutsu ... 122
Sensei Correct Errors and Blunders, Mistakes You Have to Correct Yourself ... 125
No More True Mastery in Today's Changed World? ... 129
Summary of Chapter 5 ... 131

Chapter 6: The Outlook—What Will Happen to Karate in the 21st Century? ... 133
"Arts and Crafts Movement" Following Industrialization Offers a Historic Blueprint ... 133
Today's Karate-jutsu Movement Is the Countercultural Response to Karatedo's Industrialization ... 136
Postwar Industrialization and Commercialization of Japanese Karatedo ... 137
The "Back to the Roots" Karate-jutsu Movement as Countercultural Response ... 141
The Resulting New Market Structure ... 144
Sports-Karate Remains the Prevalent Type ... 144
Karatedo Perpetuates Japanization's Lasting Budo Impact but Will Incorporate Some Rediscovered Karate-jutsu Elements ... 145
A Group of Dedicated Karate-jutsu Curators Secures the Art's Genuine Points of Reference ... 155

List of Abbreviations ... 159
Explanations of East Asian Terms ... 161
List of Photos (P), Tables (T) and Graphs (G) ... 171
References ... 173
Index ... 183

FOREWORD BY NOEL SMITH, HANSHI 9TH DAN

For some years now, we have been seeing new and growing interest in understanding karate as it was intended to be, beginning at its birthplace, Okinawa. Karate originally arose as a martial art that aimed at protecting oneself and others. Yet senior practitioners who studied the art on Okinawa some sixty or seventy years ago point out that much of today's karate may have lost its suitability for self-protection as it no longer contains the essential classic ways.

Okinawan *ti*, as the art was called in the local language (i.e., *te* in Japanese; both terms meaning "hand") before its name change into Japanese *kara-te* (empty hand), is a complex art. It is composed of several martial methods that go beyond simple punching—grappling, limb and head manipulation, throwing, joint locking and joint straining, nerve striking, and more—in addition to the unity of its martial, mental, and spiritual components. It takes a long time and much persistence to learn and to understand, which makes this art less attractive for those looking for easy achievements recreationally or athletically. Moreover, karate, as it was intended to be on Okinawa, neither was, nor is, freely and completely shared with all non-Okinawans. Specifically, those outwardly "small" nuances in moves, which make all the difference to success in a fight, were not taught to all, not in the past and not today. Hence, karate did not become mass market in its classic Okinawan form. Karate became mass market through modified Japanese karatedo styles, and when I compare what we learned sixty years ago to today's mainstream karate, I see significant contrasts to how it was taught to me and others back in the day.

I learned *Shorin Ryu* karate on Okinawa as a self-defense art from Hanshi Judan Shugoro Nakazato in the 1960s, first while stationed on the island and then while living there with my Okinawan wife. Thereafter, I continued to train with O'Sensei Nakazato every year until his passing in 2016, and after that with his son, Hanshi Judan Minoru Nakazato. Training was always based on the mindset of fighting an actual fight, and it produced a deep understanding of body-weight-power transfer into direct, short, hard, effective moves. The reality of combat and its logic were the leading ideas for every training session in O'Sensei Shugoro Nakazato's dojo and in other Okinawan dojo at that time. When we actually fought, which we did with full force in the evenings, we used the most direct, fight-ending kata techniques, instead of trying to re-engineer new complicated kata applications.

A group of Okinawan and Western students like myself, for decades close to their Okinawan sensei and now in their upper seventies and their eighties, preserved and taught this mental and spiritual combat mentality as their leading idea of what karate was intended to be at its birthplace of Okinawa: the self-defense art of karate-jutsu. However, it is obvious that newer concepts beyond classic self-protection better match the demand of what younger generations are looking for today. Though classic Okinawan karate always contained the unity of physical, mental, and spiritual development, newer Japanese karatedo versions, favoring meditative, self-development, health, and athletic aspects over combat skills, seem to better fit that bill. Consequently, today many karateka of all ranks have no realistic fighting experience anymore and use a different logic to learn and to teach the art.

So, where does this leave us? Should we better understand the old or invent something new? Or both? Well, it depends. On the one hand, there is "right" and "wrong" karate in terms of the logic of combat and moves for the purposes of self-*protection*, which would favor better understanding the old. But, on the other hand, this perspective involving "right" and "wrong" dissipates when health, spirituality, and character development are pursued for the purposes of self-*perfection*; then individual effort becomes the purpose of training, and a karateka's personal path to improved health and character replaces the initial self-defense logic. That way, by inventing something new, karate-jutsu evolved into its modern karatedo- and sports-forms as it did, based on the new leading ideas and noble intentions of the art's reformers.

Those modern recreational karate philosophies, with their interpretations of the art based on self-development, meditation, and athleticism, need to be understood and respected in their uniqueness instead of melting it all together with the classic ways. We are fortunate that Hermann Bayer does just that in his book *Analysis of Genuine Karate 2: Socio-Cultural Development, Commercialization, and Loss of Essential Knowledge*. Following *Analysis of Genuine Karate: Misconceptions,*

Origins, Development, and True Purpose, this analysis clarifies the background and intentions behind today's classic and modern karate versions, without putting one form above another. It reveals their differing purposes and identifying characteristics, and it leaves the choice of the karate type one wants to pursue to the reader. In the end, all of us karate enthusiasts are united in our dedication to upholding and disseminating the art.

Presenting substantially more than just an overview, the text further explains *why* karate developed as it did. It sheds light on the art's Okinawan origin and on the cultural settings, the political intentions, and the social mindsets during the decades in which it moved from secrecy into public practice and competition sports. It shows how socio-cultural conditions formed today's karate styles and prevents these key influences from falling into oblivion. We read about Japan's prewar reinterpretation of karate as part of the country's nationalistic agenda, and we find keen thoughts about the art's postwar industrialization and the loss of essential classic knowledge prompted by both developments. On top of that, the analysis discloses vital yet underrated truths about mastery, about karate's initial moral code, and about the current rollback to the art's Okinawan roots.

I highly recommend this comprehensive and captivating exploration of karate's past and probable future not only to all of us martial artists, but to everyone who is interested in Southeast Asia's history and sociocultural evolution.

Noel Smith, Hanshi, 9th Dan *Kobayashi Ryu*
USA Karate Hall of Fame 1976
Head Coach of the USA's national karate team 1973–78

INTRODUCTION: STRUCTURE OF THE TEXT, RESEARCH, AND ANALYSIS

Deeply humbled by the positive reactions and the appreciative reviews of *Analysis of Genuine Karate—Misconceptions, Origins, Developments and True Purpose* (in this text referred to as "Volume 1"), and supported by my *Kobayashi Ryu* sensei's enduring encouragement to dive deeper into specific aspects of modern karate's misconceptions and developments, I brought my research and the additional thoughts I developed over the last years into the text before you.

You being familiar with the thoughts presented in Volume 1 would be of advantage, but that is not a specific "prerequisite." Though this new text refers to some of that content, I now look into further aspects of karate's socio-cultural development, its commercialization and related loss of knowledge, and my following conclusions stand alone.

To continue the approach appreciated by many readers in Volume 1 of illustrating karate's socio-cultural developments and possible misconceptions with practical examples and documenting photographs, hands-on practical examples and photographic illustrations are included here in Volume 2 as well.

Volume 1 of *Analysis of Genuine Karate* ended with the request to use different terms for today's three completely different karate versions to help characterize them and clearly distinguish them from each other—and this is exactly where Volume 2 starts.

Content and Structure of This Text

Chapter 1 introduces the three different terms of karate-jutsu, karate-do, and sports-karate, which represent today's three karate versions; it gives the reason why these terms should be used, and it points out the fundamental differences among the three variations. Using different terms is the first step to avoid one of the most fundamental misunderstandings today: the assumption that "karate is just karate." The terms presented here are combined with the hope that the entire karate world finally decides to stringently use these different terms for the different versions of the art we all love.

In Chapter 2 the analysis moves on to endorse karate-jutsu as a genuine Okinawan martial art and not as a Chinese one—though foreign knowledge and skills from China were integrated—thus trying to shed some additional light on its nebulous historic roots. The current status of research is best described by nineteenth-century mathematician Henri Poincaré, quoted by Sensei Patrick McCarthy in his Facebook group: "Science is built upon facts as a house is with stones; however, the mere collection of facts is no more a science than a heap of stones is a house." Using the well-established hermeneutic-heuristic way of historic reasoning, Okinawan karate's "heap of stones history" is in this chapter transformed into meaningful understanding; the method for accomplishing that is explained further below and later in the text. The basic line of argumentation in Chapter 2 was considered worthy enough to be prepublished in Okinawa by Miguel Da Luz in his bilingual Japanese/English karate newsletter.

Chapter 3 retraces the strategic and political intentions behind Japan's assertion of Okinawan karate by neglecting its subcultural roots and claiming it as its own martial art, going several steps beyond our analysis as presented in Volume 1. Here, in Volume 2, we focus on Japan's strategy of using its Japanized karatedo to encourage a nationalistic-militaristic warrior spirit as part of an all-out spiritual and physical mobilization to prepare the nation for war. I am honored that some thoughts in this Chapter 3 were considered worthy enough to be presented by me at the 2022 Martial Arts Studies Conference in Lausanne, Switzerland. In this chapter references are made to Japan's culture of conformity, which carries the risk of misconceptions for foreigners, and I once again call for the highest sensibility when talking about Asian cultures through a Western lens. Hence my comments in Volume 1's preface are unaltered in force: looking at Eastern cultures does require more than intellectual understanding; it calls for open-minded holistic-hermeneutic avenues of reasoning, explaining, and interpreting, with broad perception, empathy, and emotional intelligence. Therefore, despite having developed these social skills as a professional coach, and despite having gone to great lengths to be objective in my arguments and conclusions, I cannot completely exclude bias, and I do apologize in advance for any misunderstanding or misinterpretation.

Since the Japanization of Okinawan karate-jutsu that transformed it into karatedo meant changing an antique fighting art not only into a new form of meditative athletics, but also into a new recreational form as a competitive sport, Chapter 4 specifically highlights the main implication the postwar commercialization of karatedo had for the way the art is practiced today. We look at sports-karate's separation of the initial unity of *kata* (sequences of fighting moves against imagined opponents) and *kumite* (fighting actual opponents), as well as at the newly invented interpretations of these two components. *Kata* and *bunkai/kumite* used to be the two essential pillars of karate in traditional training. This unity was completely torn apart and morphed into two separated sports-karate disciplines, which are substantially different from the genuine forms and which are separately performed and independently judged at tournaments.

This chapter also includes considerations about Itosu Anko Sensei's psychological motivation for teaching karatedo to young children and thereby adds an additional explanation to the commonly accepted one that Itosu Sensei wished to support Japan's militarization at that time. This psychological consideration points out his underlying, nobler intention beyond militarism in a way that has never been done before in any martial arts literature.

The chapter furthermore contains reflections on the moral code of the martial arts. A look back at Matsumuro Sensei's writings of more than two hundred years ago—or more than two thousand years ago with respect to their Chinese source—reveals that martial arts were initially understood as a value-neutral tool and weapon to maintain and restore peace, and that the specific code or moral guidelines for how to use this tool, how to handle this weapon, was developed separately, outside of the art, not within the art. Hence, the principle of not to move or attack first, for instance, was not a moral code within the art; it is a modern invention, and I explain why and how its interpretation today bears significant risk for misconceptions and for improper applications.

Practicing *kata* and *kumite* in unison in its traditional way once generated those legendary karate authorities, by Westerners sometimes called "masters" or "grandmasters," even "great-grandmasters", who we all admire and learn from. Consequently, in Chapter 5, we deal with the question that fascinates not only me but anyone who takes up this difficult art in a serious way, the question of what characterizes and establishes "mastery"—and this not only in the field of the fighting arts. What are the core components of mastery, in whatever area of expertise—in an occupation, in the arts, in crafts, in sports, or in any other field? We all are baffled by the seemingly effortless and spontaneous actions and reactions of a master, which are always spot on and are often called "intuitive." So, one question to be answered is whether masterly capability epitomizes an inherited ability, a God-given competence, a talent that someone has and another one does not have. And if not, if one can actually learn it, what path leads to it? By combining the relevant findings and explanations generated in sociology, social psychology, holistic developmental psychology, systems science, and cybernetics, we find the germane answers, and we are able to characterize the path to mastery adequately—which at the same time allows us to identify and clarify some common misunderstandings about "talent versus persistent practice."

Finally, in Chapter 6 a prognosis of karate's development in the twenty-first century is presented. Looking at the example and blueprint of the evolution of other traditional arts and crafts, their industrialization with a following counterculture, i.e., the example of the so-called "Arts and Crafts Movement," allows us to identify the most probable path toward the ultimate market structure of the art and craft of karate. A parallel existence of three different karate variations today is obvious, and the size of these variations will be defined by the demand for them in modern societies. Sports-karate will without a doubt remain the largest category. It is well on its way to establishing a new karate category of its own, as far away and as separated from its origin as the sports of javelin-throwing or fencing are away from their martial origins some centuries ago. The second large group will be karatedo, but I want to take the opportunity to suggest that some rediscovered karate-jutsu elements, which—as pointed out by the countercultural movement against karatedo's industrialization—were neglected after the time these Japanized styles were created, will eventually be integrated into old-style karatedo. This prognosis is supported by obvious jutsu incorporations in this sense within the Japanese karatedo style I train in, as well as by discussions with style headmasters and sensei, and by internet and print publications over the past years. Such a development brings the Japanized old-style karatedo versions closer back to their martial origin, whereas pure karate-jutsu will be preserved as an ancient relict and point of reference by a group of dedicated curators.

The question remains whether these three karate categories are seen differently by the public, as it is the case with common handcrafted versus mass produced physical goods which are closer to everyone's daily experience, or whether they are only seen differently by insiders. I do hope that the text before you, in combination with Volume 1, allows a comprehensive general clarification in this sense for everyone and helps to establish the use of three separate terms for the art's three unalike versions.

The chapters in this Volume 2 are written to be read independently of each other in the order of your preference, which of course means that one or the other brief explanation or background information has to be given more than once. This kind of overlap, however, is kept to its barest minimum.

Methods and Analysis Used

The benefit of using examples, photographs, and illustrations that enhance the message was pointed out in feedbacks to Volume 1; this approved approach is used here too in Volume 2 to illustrate my reasoning. When using practical examples from my training experience I refer to *Shorin Ryu*, the supposedly oldest Okinawan (and thus worldwide) karate system, in Chibana Choshin Sensei's *Kobayashi* version as prototype for karate-jutsu as I did in Volume 1. And I refer correspondingly to *Doshinkan* karatedo, the supposedly purest successor of Toyama Kanken Sensei's *Shudokan* (not to be confused with Funakoshi Sensei's *Shotokan*), as prototype for old-style Japanese karatedo.

Both approaches, *Doshinkan* karatedo and *Kobayashi Ryu* karate-jutsu, touched me deeply, helped me to understand better, and have their specific role in my personal development. I am grateful to have had and to still have the honor and privilege to study the most genuine versions of these Okinawan and Japanese karate systems, as I had and still have the rare opportunity to train with Hanshi and Kyoshi who were directly taught by the most senior authorities and creators of both systems. This has allowed me the chance to identify authentic forms and practices in both karate paths as valid representations of genuine Okinawan karate-jutsu and of old-style Japanese karatedo. However, I am neither authorized to speak for either of the two organizations in any official or unofficial capacity, nor do I intend to. *My position is the neutral-analytic one of independent research.*

I am still strongly convinced that Okinawan karate-jutsu approaches,

Image 1: Jutsu and Do Are Both Inseparable Components of the Whole of Karate

like classic *Shorin Ryu*, and Japanese old-style karatedo approaches like *Doshinkan*, i.e., those without competitive sports application, may merge into an overarching martial, spiritual, and mental unity (see Image 1)—as long as Japanese karatedo does not lose its combat orientation and application, which implicitly existed in *Doshinkan* karatedo in the 1980s. It was clearly embodied in Ichikawa Isao Sensei's powerful *kata* execution I had the honor to witness and to learn from. It is my opinion that this combat basis, though it always remained a part of the style, became less significant when some of Hanshi Ichikawa's influential followers prioritized holistic meditative and health-related aspects, and started to prefer the art's Zen-based meditative character development over its martial purpose. Since 2019, however, under Hanshi Fujimoto-Stock Masako's new leadership, in every training session I had the privilege to attend, there were strong indicators of her intention to point out the martial aspect and to rebalance *Doshinkan's* karatedo's path of character development with karate-jutsu's fighting applications.

Two years have passed since Volume 1 was launched, years during which I, now in my mid-seventies, thoroughly kept up (and still maintain) my strict training regimen of practicing karate daily and of attending at least three 90-minutes empty-hand and *kobudo* training-sessions every week. My insight, however, remains limited, as it always will be. My thoughts and conclusions are based on my personal level of understanding and I am in no position to claim that my opinions are as relevant as the ones contributed by anyone else who studied martial arts for several decades. Having said that, I trust that my academic socio-cultural research background and my analytic skills as a scientist—in combination with my current level of understanding—allow some fruitful perspectives.

In terms of the specific approach I use to find explanations, the method scientists call "qualitative research" (explanation below) comes in handy, since there are basically no written records about karate's early history, before Matsumura Sokon Sensei, available. I use exploratory techniques that are able to describe and to interpret socio-cultural and historic phenomena which cannot be exactly measured. Such techniques are "holistic" in nature, which means in English, that they are based on the idea that "the whole is more than the sum of its parts." In this sense, we find plausible answers to historic questions when discovering a pattern by combining a socio-cultural analysis with references to analogous occurrences either in history or in other socio-cultural fields which show a comparable configuration (Gill 2020; Gilje 2020).

The comments in this last paragraph bring us to research methods. If you, Dear Reader, are a *karate practitioner*, you may be mainly interested in the core messages of the text and you perhaps care less about the scientific background to get to those. If so, feel free to skip the following Excurse. Colleagues and readers primarily interested in history, or those in the academic field, however, definitely want to know more about the scientific basis of this study; and, since we are addressing these groups as well, it may be wise to comment on our approach in order to allow transparency and to position our qualitative research within the range of scientific methods.

* * * *

Excurse: Quantitative and Qualitative Research Characteristics

The scientific field is not as homogenous as one may assume. In fact, there is a conflict to be found which sometimes elevates into a clash of beliefs and even antagonism. I am talking about the (supposed) contradiction of "quantitative" versus "qualitative" research and its related "intersubjective verifiability," which is, in English, the impact of the methods used on the scientific research's requirement that other researchers can confirm the findings of their colleagues, that they get the same results when they use the same methods. Fulfilling this requirement is quite different between qualitative and quantitative research (Creswell 1994) and can be seen as a huge advantage of the latter, because quantitative research is based on the statistical analysis of more or less precisely measured numerical data which are accessible or replicable.

Qualitative research on the other hand is dealing with topics that cannot be measured as easily. This kind of research is mostly used in the social sciences and humanities disciplines to gain an understanding through observation and interpretation. It is an exploratory technique that deals with complex social, socio-cultural, and historic phenomena where data are missing or which are impossible to be measured exactly. Thus, the results presented by this kind of research depend on the analytic capabilities, skills, and thought processes of the researchers involved. Fellow researchers can confirm the findings of their colleagues, or get the same results, if they share the same lens, if they use comparable analytic approaches, if they share comparable analytic skills and thought processes.

And there the conflict is rooted . . . when results of qualitative research are presented, they may trigger a quasi-automated response from the quantitative researcher group of being "speculation" because of its probable lack of hard facts and data. The other way round, quantitative research may face the critique of "reductionism" or oversimplification from their qualitative researcher colleagues, because it does not include any un-scalable phenomenon. Jokingly speaking, in qualitative research a human being would be characterized as a combination or synthesis of body, soul, intellect, and emotions—the last three difficult to measure—whereas in quantitative research a human being would be seen as a combination or synthesis of easily measurable amounts of water, chemicals, minerals, fat, electric currency, and protein.

Obviously I cannot resolve these kinds of basic philosophical questions which deal with the challenge of how to correctly acquire knowledge and how to differentiate between true and false. These so-called "epistemological" questions and their possible answers are heatedly discussed in philosophical departments for decades (Seiffert 1971a, pp. 1-11). However, I dare to suggest that a possible solution is rooted in the fact that both research methods complement each other; that they are not mutually exclusive but mutually interdependent. In scientific terms, using dialectical thinking[1] (Seiffert 1971b, pp. 199-217), both approaches define each other in contrast, and form a new overarching unity, like night and day form a unity of time, yin and yang form the well-known holistic circle.

Hence, dialectically speaking, qualitative and quantitative research are the thesis and its antithesis which, when combined, form a new synthesis at an elevated level of insight and understanding. In this view, hermeneutic-heuristic case studies, which is qualitative research, may over time even provide the empirical raw material which then amounts to statistically relevant empirical support as quantitative research.

---

1. Dialectic thinking, formulated by the German philosopher Georg Wilhelm Friedrich Hegel, allows some parallels to some East Asian way of reasoning, where contradicting issues define each other by contrast, cannot exist without each other, and form an overarching entity together. Accordingly, in dialectic thinking a contradicting thesis and antithesis may lead to a new synthesis of higher quality.

Chapter 1

Why Different Terms Are Needed for Today's Versions of Okinawan Karate-jutsu, Japanese Karatedo, and Sports-Karate

Many may think that "karate is just karate"—but nothing can be farther from the truth. As Sensei Walter Dailey, 10th Dan *Shorinji-Ryu*, already stated 1996 in *Bugeisha* magazine's premiere issue, karate in its various forms resembles a "fruit salad," where it, as "one says is an Art or way of life (*budo*), another says it's a Self-Defense (*bu-jutsu*), another says it's a Sport, and another Business" (Dailey, *Bugeisha* 1996, Issue#1, p. 3). But, guess what; all these views are correct in their specific sense, all these variations are indeed mixed into today's "karate fruit salad"— they simply address different versions of the art. This creates an unfortunate misconception, because the same term "karate" is confusingly used for all these completely different karate-types and thereby suggests that unalike kinds would be alike.

In all other Japanese martial arts we see different terms in use for their different types; especially for their initial *koryu* [traditional] martial use and for their modern sports derivatives.[1] For karate, however,

---

1. See Volume 1, pp. 84ff. For instance, there is the term *ju-jutsu*, for the original combat martial arts version used by samurai in ancient Japan, and there is the different term *judo* for ju-jutsu's modern sports variation.

this is not the case; we do not see comparable different terms, but *the same term "karate" is used for all of the art's currently practiced three dissimilar varieties*; which are:

1. Classic *Okinawan [combat] karate-jutsu*, the genuine and lethal version which was created to protect oneself and others in violent situations.[2] This martial art was developed at least 500 years ago, some say more than 1,000 years ago (e.g., Funakoshi 1973, p. 3), and was called *Te* [hand] at that time at its birthplace on the Ryukyu Islands, and later karate-jutsu.[3] The genuine Okinawan combat art "is not a kind of striking to be incorporated into another fighting system . . . This is an independent style of martial arts, called karate-jutsu and is particular to Okinawa" (Motobu 2018, p. 19).

2. "Old-Style"[4] *Japanese karatedo*. This Japanized version transformed combat karate-jutsu into recreational athletic gymnastics with a meditative component, as a *budo* art, as a general way of life. Though karatedo still focusses on powerful execution of martial moves, yet hitting air instead of opponents, it concentrates on mental, spiritual, and health related character- and personality-development—including newly incorporated philosophical, Zen-based undergirdings which typify all mainland Japan *budo* arts. These philosophical components were not a part of Okinawan karate-jutsu and neither was Zen Buddhism the island's traditional belief system; that was ancestor worship (more details on this later). Japanized karatedo was created on mainland Japan in the 1920s, kicked off by Funakoshi Gichin Sensei's teachings—in other words 500 to 1,000 years after the creation of *Te* on Okinawa (Volume 1, pp. 21ff). "Before that time I think it was safe to say that almost no one had any knowledge

---

2. Funakoshi Gichin Sensei speaks of *Goshin*-Karate [karate for self-protection] in this sense (in Wittwer 2014, p. 193; Footnote 377).

3. For additional reasoning about Okinawa being the birthplace of karate see Chapter 2 "Did Genuine Kara-Te Originate in Okinawa or in China? A Contribution to Historical Reasoning in Martial Arts History."

4. Strictly speaking, there is no "traditional" Japanese karate, only a traditional Okinawan one, because the Japanized karatedo versions on the mainland were developed less than 100 years ago—which is a rather short period of time in the millennia-old history of martial arts. We use the term "old style" here to further distinguish earlier, pure Japanese non-competition karatedo versions from later, newer, Japanese competitive sports-karate derivatives developed after WWII. Old-style karatedo is called *"Budo*-Karate" too by some researchers (Wittwer, 2014, p. 193).

of karate-jutsu" (Motobu 2018, p. 19). In other words, during all the centuries before the 1920s, *Te* was unknown on the mainland. Strangely enough, however, today "the world knows karate as a Japanese sport, but it is far more likely that it is a 'Japanified' [*sic*] foreign sport created during a time of strong militaristic nationalism" (Swennen 2006, p. 2).

3. Modern *sports-karate* was created after WWII in the 1950s (Corcoran 2012),[5] in other words even some decades after mainland Japan's creation of non-competitive—here called "old-style"—karatedo. Some authors split this sports-karate version further into the two sub-categories of "competition karate" and "fitness karate" (Wittwer 2014, p. 193).

Hence, in order to clearly distinguish today's three different karate types, we use these above three different terms, which are further explained below, and we will empirically illustrate some of the essential differences between these three karate types by using the practical example of looking at a karateka's body positions when performing *kata*.

Classic Okinawan Karate-jutsu

The term *classic karate-jutsu* refers to the genuine, 1,000 year old, *Okinawan self-protection* version of karate, a lethal local fighting art for self-defense.

Sensei Bruno Ballardini, 7th Dan *Shorinji Ryu Zentokukai*, an author, university professor, and president of the Italian Association for the Research on Ancient Karate, justified the choice of this term in his feedback to an earlier draft of this text, explaining that "before the famous 1936 meeting between the masters of Okinawa, in which it was decided to adopt the writing 空手 (it is read 'karate') to replace the writing 唐手 (it is read "tode," but it can be pronounced 'karate' as well), the discipline was called tode-jutsu and later it was called karate-jutsu. Thus the genuine Okinawan self-protection version should be

---

5. Sensei Roy Roitman, 5th Dan *Shotokan* and President of the Israel Shotokan Association, shares in his feedback to a draft of this text that "competition sport actually started at Waseda 1952, as they wanted to bring more students to practice karate. This was told to me personally by Sensei Tetsumo Ohshima ... Captain of Karate Club in Waseda 1952-55." (A clarification: in this organization, *Godan* is the highest-achievable rank and hence would be comparable to the highest rank in other styles.)

called tode-jutsu or karate-jutsu to distinguish it from the Japanese karatedo."[6]

To be consistent with the use of terms in this text, the initial and genuine form of the art is here exclusively named as karate-jutsu [空手術]; we do not use the other terms which were also in use before 1936, and which may be used by other authors today, like *ti'gwa* [手小], *te/ti/di* [手], *toudi/todi/tode* [唐手; sometimes, as on this book's front cover, with the addition of the "jutsu" kanji].

Though there are strong efforts and distinguished proponents trying to preserve karate-jutsu in its traditional version today, and though we see a remarkable movement back to the original forms over the last two decades, combat oriented karate-jutsu has slowly faded after WWII into a smaller fragment of worldwide practice. The reason for its reduced importance is karate's all-embracing and overwhelming Japanization, or, as Sensei Bruno Ballardini calls it "Shotokanization," even on Okinawa itself (more about this in Chapter 4). At this point we want to highlight the challenge that a precious ancient heritage "is slowly being dispersed. . . classical karate is not a simple object but a complex one, extremely rich, composed of several complementary disciplines, it is not suitable for everyone, it cannot become mass market, and therefore it cannot be simplified. This is the great dilemma faced by Okinawan karate today. . . It is possible that in some schools the most ancient teachings are still handed down only to the oldest students, but from what some friends who go to Okinawa every year tell me there is no guarantee of this. I believe instead that the last school leaders who knew classical karate are dead and have left their legacy to a few senior Western students" (Ballardini on Facebook 2021, n.p.).

However, we need and want to tread very lightly here and avoid even the slightest form of unintentional Western hubris, because we actually don't know whether Sensei Ballardini's assumption is accurate. One can simply speculate here, and it is equally probable that Okinawan masters do not want to share karate-jutsu's hidden concepts and true combat abilities with Westerners anymore. As mentioned in Volume 1 (pp. 71f), asking an Okinawan master to share secret lethal techniques may be an ineffective, perhaps even an inappropriate

---

6. Sensei Ballardini's statement refers to the transcript of the 1936 meeting, which was published by several translators; in this text the one by McCarthy (2018, pp. 185-200) is used.

approach, born out of a Western thought process. Sharing these concepts works the other way round when a karate master chooses one individual or a small group of his students who then *in secrecy* are taught the deeper aspects of karate up to *Okuden* level, i.e., up to the level of full life protection capabilities (Hayes 2018, p. 88).

According to this line of thought, how can one assume to penetrate the art up to *Okuden* level, after having trained with a master for a couple of years, while stationed on Okinawa, or while visiting a *honbu* dojo every now and then—or even if visiting annually—when such a learning process takes decades of guided training (see Chapter 5, "The Path to Mastery")? Many of the secrets of Okinawan karate-jutsu are not passed on because of language misunderstandings and because the majority of Western (and Asian) students does not stay long enough, i.e., decades, in direct contact with a master, and the specific trust building student-teacher symbiosis of *uchi deshi* [live-in student] and master basically does not today exist. It did exist, however, including one or the other Westerner too.[7] So, "believing that this heritage is extinct today and that nobody is able to teach it anymore is a serious mistake dictated mostly by superficiality or ignorance. Many of the last heirs of karate-jutsu have passed on, but many are still alive and have already left their legacy to older Okinawan and Western students" (Ballardini 2021a, p. 9). It has to be stated though that, in Sensei Dan Smith's words, "due to reversion in 1972 there were few if any of

---

7. In addition to my sensei, Noel Smith (see Foreword here and Volume 1, pp 43f), Sensei Dan Smith, the US-chief instructor of *Shorin Ryu Seibukan* (http://www.seibukanusa.com/), may serve as an example. He lived and studied on Okinawa, training daily for many hours under Shimabukuro Sensei, and became a friend for decades to the Shimabukuro family, which is the family currently preserving the karate-jutsu system passed on from Kyan Chotoku Sensei to Shimabukuro Zenryo Sensei. The latter passed it on in its entirety to his son Shimabukuro Zenpo Sensei who started to train at the age of nine. Sensei Dan Smith studied with Zenryo Sensei before his passing in 1969, and with Zenpo Sensei for the past fifty-three years. Thus Sensei Dan Smith, who understood the *Uchinaguchi* terms related to his training (*Uchinaguchi* is the island's native language), learned in a different way compared to most other American soldiers, who were stationed in Okinawa for a couple of years—the usual tour was eighteen months for the army, thirteen months for the marines, and up to four years for the air force—then left and visited their *honbu* dojo sporadically thereafter. Both daily in-person instruction with a headmaster for many years as well as having a basic understanding of training-related terms in the local language are of utmost importance, since all karate-jutsu knowledge was passed on without written references and without a specific terminology in *Uchinaguchi* for jutsu techniques and concepts. All the terms and most applications we use today are Japanese inventions and re-creations (see Chapter 4 for more details).

Americans who trained to a meaningful degree while living on Okinawa. The decline on the emphasis the Okinawan teachers put on karate-jutsu aided in the decline of the pre 19th century combat methods that would be taught in the dojo. This decline was fueled by the influence the Japanese fast paced culture had on the island society that had historically moved at a slow pace. Reversion brought a faster pace of life and less time for adult males to continue training at the levels required or even have time for karate" (email to me on 04/27/22).

There are yet some more aspects to consider when we hear Western concerns that lethal *bunkai* of karate-jutsu is not taught during their Okinawan *honbu* dojo visits. One aspect may be even related to a karateka's character, since "the real applications were not revealed to all students but only to those who the headmaster considered worthy of receiving this knowledge" (Ballardini 2021a, p. 9). To accept the possible fact that a karateka's Okinawan master considers him/her of "not being worthy" to be taught the real thing is of course a very tough realization of reality and for some Western karateka almost impossible to accept. Assuming instead that their Okinawan masters do not have the relevant knowledge anymore is the easier way out to avoid such a hurtful cognition.

Another aspect of not sharing *Okuden* insight with Western students anymore may be a specific form of hidden and secret pushback against the stupendous impact of Western/US culture on the Ryukyu Islands, and to preserve, even to defend, the Okinawan culture and self-identity this way.[8] There are and there were other comparable examples of hidden Okinawan opposition against Western/US dominance, all based on the strategy of a specific *indirect* form of action to resist, which Okinawans, according to George H. Kerr, developed over 1,000 years. During all those years "courtesy and accommodation, hesitancy, delay, and passive resistance were the weapons . . . which they had perforce to adopt" (Kerr 2000, p. 167). Centuries of avoiding conflicts and pursuing their own intentions secretly in order to survive in close proximity to powerful neighboring imperial regimes, and

---

8. Over the last two decades a new form of not so much hidden conflicts and protests developed on Okinawa as well, shown as increased poll numbers and mass protests demanding to set limits to the spread of US military bases and to better prevent and prosecute criminal acts perpetrated by US soldiers. This kind of open confrontation is pretty remarkable and quite uncommon in Okinawa's culture of conformity and conciliation.

additional centuries of occupation by Japan, perfected this culturally specific form of indirect doings. In this sense, and back to the argument, silently uplifting karate-jutsu's *Okuden bunkai* into a revived status of secrecy may as well be a relevant possibility, as appropriate as any other speculation on this matter.

As mentioned, we touch an extremely sensible socio-cultural point with this topic, and it is my opinion that only the members of the culture in question are in the position to rightfully deal with aspects of their cultural heritage; this opinion was already introduced in Volume 1 (pp. 82f). Since karate is a part of Okinawan (sub-) cultural heritage, no foreigner is legitimized to decide on matters important to it, though there may be as outstanding karate experts outside of Okinawa in the West as on Okinawa itself. This is comparable to the fact that no foreigner is in the position to decide on the status of a monument in Italy as a part of Italian cultural heritage, though there may be many outstanding experts on Italian culture to be found outside of Italy. This decision should solely be in the hands of the Italians, whereas foreign experts on Italian culture may comment on that decision. The same line of argument applies to Okinawan karate-jutsu—even if non-Okinawans should claim to come up with a better insight, a better decision or a more adequate procedure than Okinawans themselves.

This is one of my philosophical, value-based axioms, comparable to the basis of international law, or, in politics, to the doctrine of nonintervention into foreign internal affairs. My position may not be shared by everyone. However, based on this maxim, all disputes about genuine Okinawan karate-jutsu are to be resolved by Okinawans alone, who are the only legitimate curators of their subcultural heritage.

* * * * *

To illustrate one core difference between karate-jutsu and karatedo and thus to allow a more specified comparison, let us look at the karateka's body when performing *Naihanchi kata*, "the heart and soul" of *Shorin Ryu*, the oldest Okinawan, and thus world-wide, karate-jutsu system. Characteristics of the (mostly lethal) moves in *Naihanchi kata* (Image 2) are a specific anchored stance/position with toes gripping the ground, knees bent inwards to lower the karateka's center of gravity (for explanations how many modern variations to this stance/position increase a karateka's vulnerability and damage knee-joints, see Volume 1, pp. 138ff), combined with short, hard, direct moves which are all prone to inflict severe damage to an opponent.

The position/stance displayed in Image 2 expresses one of the basic principles to create maximal damage to an opponent in the most effective way through optimized body-weight-power transfer into a technique, and this is vertically *aligning foot-knee-shoulder*. Let us compare this later to the according position/stance when performing the same *kata* in old-style Japanese karatedo.

Image 2: Naihanchi Ichidan as Practiced in Okinawan Shorin Ryu

This kata performance by *Shorin Ryu Shorinkan* practitioners at the 2019 Day of Karate in Naha City, Okinawa, shows some core characteristics of genuine karate-jutsu, for instance anchored stances with low center of gravity and the vertical alignment of feet and shoulders.

I want to point out that comparing karate-jutsu and karatedo does not mean that I think one system is superior to the other. It rather means that these versions follow unalike prevalent purposes which lead to some unalike prevalent outcomes. They are, however, two sides of the same coin.

Old-Style Japanese Karatedo

We use the term *old-style karatedo* for the Japanized self-perfection version with its emphasis on the *Do* [path] to improve the health of body and mind. As already mentioned in footnote 4, one may argue that there is no "traditional" Japanese karate, only a traditional Okinawan one. Yet, there is a need to distinguish the even more recent Japanese sports-karate variations from this earlier kind of non-sports Japanese karatedo, i.e., from the Japanized pure and non-competitive *Do*-systems or "*budo*-karate-systems" (Wittwer 2014, p. 193). These old-style Japanized systems represent their own category of karatedo versions which incorporated many of the characteristics of other traditional Japanese martial arts, and need to be pointed out in contrast to later created competitive sports-karate systems.

While we agree with Professor Paul Bowman's[9] statement that "the most familiar of 'ancient' East Asian martial arts emerged in their present form during the twentieth century" (Bowman n.d., p. 1) we have to disagree for karate-jutsu with his following general assertion that "virtually all styles of karate, aikido, taekwondo and Brazilian jujitsu, for instance, are twentieth-century inventions" (ibid.). The genuine Okinawan karate-jutsu styles were, in Sensei McCarthy's term, a "plebeian[10] fighting system of percussive impact" centuries before Karate's Japanization, they were not a "twentieth-century invention" as they are labeled in the quote. Only their pilfered derivatives are, which then, later, produced some Japanized variations.

The suitability of our suggested terminology for Japanized karatedo is supported by the communication at the 1936 meeting of Okinawan karate masters. When the art was called "karatedo" there during the discussion, the question was asked whether this would mean "that the cultivation of one's spirit, like that of judo and kendo, will be emphasized? Is that why the '*do*' was added?" which led to the answer "yes." "Its purpose seems to be the cultivation of the spirit" (meeting

---

9. Dr. Paul Bowman is Professor of Cultural Studies and Deputy School Head at Cardiff University in the UK, and Director of the Martial Arts Studies Research Network, a scholarly organization in this field. Together with Dr. Benjamin Judkins he edits and publishes *Martial Arts Studies*, the leading academic martial arts journal.

10. As we know today, the Okinawan fighting system was mostly practiced by the Ryukyu's nobility and less by commons, but the idea of striking someone with a clenched fist was not considered a refined form of combat by Japanese *budo* circles.

transcript in McCarthy 2018a, p. 187). Thus, the purpose of karatedo separated itself completely from the one of genuine Okinawan karate-jutsu. Individual efforts to optimize health and to develop one's character became the main focus and reduced self-defense skills to a by-product. This change is explicitly pointed out by Funakoshi Gichin Sensei when he suggests that the Zen-Buddhism concept of "emptiness" is as important for karatedo as it is for Zen (Bittmann 2005, p. 28). Karate-jutsu's initial purpose of self-protection, where effective combat skills were the main focus and character development were byproducts, is replaced by the new concept of the way, the *Do*, where self-development is the main focus and combat skills become a byproduct.

"Everywhere in Japan there is a *DO*. There is no spiritual process, no cultural performance without its relevant *DO*. It is the leading concept for the island country's manifold arts . . . the *DO* embodies the very tradition of an art; without it the art is non-viable"[11] (Hammitzsch 1957, p. 5; author's translation). Hence, "Karate [jutsu] refers to a martial art developed for the purpose of defending one's self . . . karatedo however, means a way of life . . . its significance lies in in fighting down the inner enemies, which are greater than the external enemies . . . karatedo aims at building up the whole man by karate training" (Nagamine 1976, p. 253).

* * * * *

To illustrate some of karatedo's differences from karate-jutsu, let us now look at a karateka's lower body in the above introduced essential *Shorin Ryu Naihanchi Ichidan kata* (called "*Shodan*" in other systems and "*Ichidan*" in *Kobayashi Ryu*).

> I want to point out again that comparing karate-jutsu and karatedo does not mean that I suppose one system to be superior to the other. It means instead that these versions have different purposes which lead to differing outcomes. Thus they are different, but they represent the two sides of the same coin.

---

11. „Überall gibt es in Japan einen WEG. Keine geistige Regung, kein kulturelles Schaffen findet ohne den jeweiligen WEG Gestalt. Er ist der maßgebende Begriff für eine jede der mannigfachen Künste des Insellandes ... der WEG bedeutet für eine Kunst jeweils ihre Tradition, ohne welche sie nicht lebensfähig ist."

The moves of the original Okinawan *Shorin Ryu* form are here used in an exaggerated way to attain maximal stretch of muscles and tendons for athletic-gymnastic optimization. Image 3 shows how in this sense karateka twist their torso backward to allow a double punch to the backside, and thus creating a move that is not to be found in Okinawan karate-jutsu.

Image 3: Derived Move in Naifanchi Shodan as Practiced in Some Japanese Karatedo

This photo illustrates, with a specific move not found in Okinawan karate-jutsu how some Japanese karatedo interprets *Naifanchi* (or *Naihanchi*) *Shodan*. A double punch is thrown to the backside by twisting the torso for maximal stretching of torso and leg muscles and tendons.

It was mentioned earlier that one of the basic principles for creating maximal damage in the most effective way is to optimize body-weight power transfer into a technique, whether defensive or offensive, by vertically aligning the foot knee, and shoulder at the moment of impact. The position/stance in Image 3 does not show this basic principle, as the karateka's shoulders are turned away from the vertical foot-knee line by almost 90 degrees. Hence, in my understanding of applying logic and physiological facts about the human body in combat, such a movement involving turning of the trunk has no obvious combat application, as the static, forward oriented stance/position, without moving a leg into a turn, creates a frail foundation for the hand technique since the shoulders are not vertically in line with foot and knee. Just imagine an opponent grabbing the karateka's right arm from behind and pulling it backward. Its purpose rather seems to be to improve physical flexibility by maximally stretching the torso, shoulder, and leg muscles.

But perhaps this attack to the back symbolizes another hidden *bunkai* concept and not a strike with the hand at all. However, assuming a hidden takedown-related concept underneath this move leaves us with an equally delicate foundation for a throw instead of a sturdy stance/position. Without moving the left leg, and thus turning the entire body into the rotating motion of a throw, it is doubtful that the necessary momentum can be created at all to break an opponent's balance and move a body. The same thought applies to the reverse motion of grabbing a rear opponent's top in preparation for a throw to the front.

In summation, whereas the function of the move as shown in Image 3 does make a lot of sense in terms of improving flexibility and athleticism, it is difficult to find the appropriate *bunkai*—again, based on my current level of understanding. This level of understanding could of course limit my insight into an underlying hidden combat application.

Be that as it may, the result of the artificial stretch to the backside is quite the opposite of the corresponding short, hard, and damaging move (a double punch, or an arm bar, or a throw, or . . .) in the genuine Okinawan *Naihanchi Ichidan kata* as shown in Image 4 and thus illustrates an obvious difference between karate-jutsu and karatedo (see Volume 1, pp. 138ff for further analysis of traditional versus modern stances/positions used in this *kata* today).

Image 4: Genuine Move in Naihanchi Ichidan
as Practiced in Okinawan Shorin Ryu Karate-jutsu

This image shows the original move in *Naihanchi* (*Naifanchi*) *Ichidan* (*Shodan*), i.e., for instance, a punch, an elbow- or knee-breaking armbar, or a throw (among other options) from the left hip to the right side (the preparation for the move is shown in the smaller picture on the left). This original move presents the blueprint for the derived punch version used in Japanese karatedo as shown in Image 3 above.

Modern Sports-Karate

Sports-karate created fascinating new competitive disciplines, completely new versions of karate, and there is no reason to question its value at all. It just needs to be distinguished from the other two versions of the art. Hence, we use the term modern sports-karate for these newest (about fifty years old) group of competitive styles.

On the other hand, it needs to be stressed again that *the sports-karate types created after World War II are neither classical karate-jutsu nor old-style karatedo, nor martial arts at all*, as explained in Volume 1 in great detail (p. 84ff). It is rather the development of a new sport with its own purpose and reason to exist, as was the case with other sport derivatives of combat arts, like javelin, fencing, archery, and biathlon. Sports-karate is as far removed from its combat version as fencing or javelin are from their martial use on the battlefield some centuries ago. There is no need at all to create a special philosophical superstructure for fencing or javelin, and there is no need at all for paltry efforts to reconnect them with their initial combat applications—likewise, there is no need to do that for sports-karate.

> I by no means want to create the impression that I have anything to say against sports-karate. To the contrary, I personally love and support it by competing in tournaments in their "gray hairs division."

The role of the newly created type of sports-karate is an extremely important and positive one; it channels aggression into healthy competition, and its training practices, which work the entire body, are perfect for working out, for physical education, and for holistic health and fitness. Under a responsible coach, students strengthen physically, grow mentally, and young people are guided toward positive values—reflected in learning outcomes in modern physical education and their corresponding instructional strategies.[12]

---

12. The trend away from eclectic teaching, where an instructor shows a few random techniques during class, often without any unifying theme or relation to previously taught material, and toward a more thoughtful curriculum is well underway. This is not only happening in courses at schools and universities, where the creation of sophisticated teaching strategies is part of the basic requirements for an instructor to facilitate classes. Relevant information about this topic are as well included in training camp programs for classic and old-style karate, as the example of Sensei Tom Ward, 6th Dan *Shorin Ryu, Shorinkan*, shows, who taught "Applying Modern Educational Concepts to Teaching Traditional Karate" at the 2018 Okinawan Karate and Kobudo Winter Camp on 03/10/2018.

14 ANALYSIS OF GENUINE KARATE 2

Watching the 2021 Olympic Games or other sports-karate events, one can witness outstanding athletic performances of sports-karateka who all deserve respect and admiration. Due to specific rules and regulations, sports-karate developed its own moves and techniques independent from—and even contrasting with—its ancient antecedents, thus paralleling a development other combat sports underwent too when for instance fencing moved away from its initial lethal martial purpose and became a kind of highly regulated game. Similar to the development of sport fencing, sports-karate's movement away from its ancient roots is initiated and guided by the logic of applied disarming rules and regulations.

Image 5: No Solid Stance/Position in Sports-Karate
But Bouncing Back and Forth When Fighting

Wikimedia Commons

When the speed needed to tag an opponent is of utmost importance, as is the case in sports-karate, anchored solid stances that would allow delivery of devastating strikes, blocks, and throws become obsolete. As the photo shows, to defend themselves, sports-karateka are bouncing, dancing, and tip-toeing back, forth, and around; they move constantly to avoid to become a stationary target for a tagging contact

In *kumite* competition, it is forbidden to damage an opponent, so speedy fencing moves with tagging contact are needed to replace lethal impact. When certain target areas are outlawed, new and modified techniques need to be developed to attack the permitted target areas that earn the highest scores when hit. When speed to tag an opponent is of utmost importance, anchored solid stances become obsolete, and when continuous flimsy attacks provide the highest probability for a victory, speedy evasion of an attack beats the kind of bone-breaking defense taught in karate-jutsu. And when the best defensive option is to move constantly to avoid being a stationary target for a tagging contact, bouncing, dancing, and tip-toeing back, forth and around (see Image 5) beats calmness of the mind and body, and it beats settling into anchored solid positions/stances, which would allow for the delivery of devastating blocks and blows.

Equivalently, when in *kata* competition the beauty of a move needs to be pointed out to spectators and jurors, its combat effectiveness becomes unimportant (Image 6 shows one of many examples).

In addition to the new interpretation and the new modeling of ancient moves, artificial gaps during *kata* performance become necessary to explicitly point out a certain position—while implementing such a break would be counterproductive, perhaps even deadly, in terms of *bunkai*.

When athletic extremes need to be expressively demonstrated to spectators and jurors, optimal stretched techniques need to be presented (e.g., head-high kicks, or jumps in order to turn, instead of turns by maintaining anchored positions and low center of gravity), which would be damaging to oneself in combat because of their inherent lack of body-weight-power transfer and lack of protection of sensitive body parts. When lethality and dedication need to be demonstrated orally rather than through efficiency of techniques, a *kiai*, the one-syllable breath/shout used in many martial arts when applying a technique, turns into a technique in itself, into a "battle-cry" or "spirit-cry" to be persuasively executed after the completion of a move instead of being an breathing technique empowering a move—and so on and so forth. All this makes sense for a sport; it creates a new approach and new disciplines and it has its own reason to exist in the sports arena—it just should not be confused with martial arts; all these (just) tagging contacts, which are the only ones allowed to be used in competition *kumite*, would not bother any karate-jutsu practitioner.

Sports-karateka, who are only familiar with their sports-karate approach, may be vulnerable in any realistic combat setting. In a real combat situation, blood pressure and adrenaline levels are off the charts; fighters are under pressure, most certainly in pain, and their perception can be narrowed down to tunnel vision. As a result, fighters use habitually ingrained training routines: "you do what you trained to do." Hence, sports-karateka most likely will unconsciously use the sport moves they trained and now have stored in their muscle memory, and thus could be an easy target for MMA practitioners and street fighters, let alone karate-jutsu practitioners (see Volume 1, pp. 86ff for more details).

Image 6: No Clear Bunkai Detectable in Some Sport-Karate's Kata

When in kata competition the beauty of a move needs to be explicitly demonstrated to spectators and jurors, its combat effectiveness is not a priority. In this sense, and contrary to the position shown in the photo, a karate-jutsu practitioner would (a) keep fingers closed, which when separated as shown could be more easily grappled and bent/broken by an opponent; (b) would bend slightly forward at the waist to bring the left shoulder over the left knee to optimize body-weight-power transfer into the arm move, and (c) would perhaps aim at an opponent's throat or eyes rather than at the chest.

This interpretation does not change the fact that the pictured athlete demonstrates extraordinary concentration, physical performance, and self-control.

Map: Wikimedia Commons, graph author

Chapter 2
Did Karate-jutsu Originate in Okinawa or in China? A Contribution to Historic Reasoning in Martial Arts History

Twenty years ago, when the average Western "person in the street" was asked where karate originated, the answer was "Japan," and karate was seen as one specific martial art among the group of (mainland) Japanese martial arts and their sports derivatives like judo, aikido, and kendo. It is only recently and in large part because of an extensive public relations effort by the Okinawan prefectural government and Okinawan karate officials over the last decade (Volume 1, pp. 50ff) that one may now hear the answer, "It comes from Okinawa."

Okinawan efforts to have karate registered as an intangible Okinawan cultural asset with the United Nations Education, Scientific, and Cultural Organization (UNESCO) have been underway for several years (Fuente/Niehaus 2020). The catchphrase government and karate officials use is "Okinawa Is the Birthplace of Karate," which targets the center of an ongoing dispute about karate's "true" origin.

Interestingly enough, today we find a strong movement back to origins and genuine forms of karate-jutsu, not just in Okinawa but in the West as well, a movement some call "the reality drive" (Bowman 2014,

p. 1).¹ Groups on social media discuss authentic karate-jutsu, interpretations of moves, and historic findings; important research is conducted by specialized research societies and published on the internet as well as in print format (see "'Back to the Roots' Karate-jutsu Movement as Countercultural Response" in Chapter 4 for examples). For more than two decades the renowned *Classic Fighting Arts* magazine has covered traditional martial arts topics, technical, and historical material at a high level. In 2020, *Bugeisha* magazine, the self-acclaimed "first magazine of traditional martial arts," which was founded 1996 and ceased to exist 1998, was reissued by one of its initial editors in the form of a collector's edition for all its previous issues and resumed production of new issues. Even the release of my books may be listed as examples in this context, which seem to bring more jutsu training practices back into today's training.² All these tendencies concentrate on efforts "to bring basics and foundation back into the limelight of martial arts" (*Bugeisha* Issue #1, p. 1).

Many martial arts historians agree that karate-jutsu is indeed an indigenous Okinawan martial art form, initially called *Te* (this is the term used here), *Ti* or *Di*, *Ti'gwa*, Okinawa-*Te* or *Uchinadi* (e.g., among others, Funakoshi 1973, p. 7f; Hokama 2000, p. 15; Nagamine 1976, p. 21; McCarthy 2016, p. 138; Chambers et. al. 2020, p. xiii). "It was an art that depended principally upon the use of clenched fists to strike an opponent in contrast to the open-hand method preferred by Chinese arts, according to both Kyan Chotoku and Miyagi Chojun, although the head, feet, shins, elbows, and knees were also favored" (IRKRS, n.d., n.p.). Okinawan *Te*, initially a "form of percussive impact" (ibid.) was completed by *tegumi,* an ancient system of grappling/wrestling, and by *tuite*, a system aimed at restraining opponents (see "The Loss of Essential Knowledge" in Chapter 4).

Other authors claim that karate was developed out of Chinese *ch'üan fa*; for instance, Mark Bishop (Bishop 1991), Heiko Bittmann (2005),

---

1. The author, Dr. Paul Bowman, professor at Cardiff University, UK, however, sees the invention of new "realistic styles" as a drive toward reality in martial arts instead a return to the origins within existing Okinawan karate systems, which we describe here.

2. For example, one sensei wrote in a review on Amazon.com that the first volume of *Analysis of Genuine Karate* "certainly has caused me to reflect on my teaching so I am passing down his ['his' refers to me] teaching to my students. It is a necessity for all sensei and karateka to understand the perspective of jutsu that makes karate more than just a sport or performance."

Werner Lind (Lind 1991), and, more recently, Jesse Encamp, who mostly uses the World Wide Web as his publishing platform (Enkamp n.d.). Beyond that, legend has it that sometime in the 6th century AD the Indian monk Bodhidharma came to China (e.g., Clarke, C.M. 2012a, pp. 49f; Funakoshi 1973, p. 7; Haines 1970, pp. 23ff; Herbert 2019) to teach and establish the Zen branch of Mahayana Buddhism. Legend also credits him with having trained monks of the Shaolin monasteries in meditation and in martial arts, which were then passed on to Okinawa through the island's long-standing trade relations with China, and that this would embody the real and initial birth of karate.

Allowing all those speculations to be what they are, the issue martial arts historians are confronted with is that no written records about the origin of *Te* exist due to centuries-long secrecy, natural disasters, and war. When historic facts and documents are not available, gathering "oral history" as interpretations of witnesses' statements results in a collection of historic possibilities, and these possibilities allow authors to put forth their personal views. As Henri Poincaré put it, "Science is built upon facts as a house is with stones; however, the mere collection of facts is no more a science than a heap of stones is a house." But, is it actually possible to organize this heap of stones, to advance beyond mere speculation, on the basis of an eclectic approach that says that "everything may be possible and everything is equally important?" And, if yes, what yardstick could help us to understand the logic and the "why" of karate's historical development?

As so often in historic research, plausible answers lie in a "heuristic-hermeneutic" perspective, which is the combination of a descriptive socio-cultural analysis with good old logic and with reference to comparable occurrences in history or in other socio-cultural fields to identify known developments as possible patterns (Gilje 2020). Such a heuristic-hermeneutic approach in historic research allows us to *understand* a development instead of only describing it and as such is comparable to heuristics in psychology.[3]

---

3. Heuristics in psychology and other social sciences are strategies or systematic mental processes that individuals, organizations, and machines use to form judgments, make decisions, and find solutions to complex problems. Evaluating those processes became a valuable method in forensic psychology and criminology, usually called "profiling," where the reconstruction of heuristic processes are used to find answers and solutions most likely to be correct when analyzing the behavior of an offender. Profiling is used internationally and was further developed as "behavioral case analysis," for instance in Germany, where "within the German police behavioral case analysis is considered to be a further development of profiling as established in the 1980s by the American FBI" (Dern 2010, p. 1).

So, let us begin with a historic example that shows a similar development and thus may allow us to find a possible pattern. It concerns an event that took place in a completely different area: space technology.

Throughout History Foreign Knowledge Has Been Integrated into Existing Knowledge

Do you believe that the US space program is solely an American project, created by NASA, and its predecessor NACA, the National Advisory Committee for Aeronautics? Yes, of course, you would agree, and you would be correct, since for more than one hundred years these US agencies developed and launched their missions. One of these missions in the 1950s was led by the engineer and rocket scientist Wernher von Braun and his team, who developed the first transportation rocket able to accommodate a satellite payload. Using that rocket, the West's first satellite was successfully launched in January 1958 and kicked off America's new space program in response to the Russian's "Sputnik" satellite launch one year earlier.

However, are you aware that Wernher von Braun as well as his team, who embodied US expertise in rocket science and space technology, were actually German rocket technology pioneers who carried out major research in their homeland before and during WWII? As Nazi-Germany's rocket scientists,[4] Wernher von Braun and his team developed in the 1930s and 1940s self-flying bombs and rockets.[5] After the war the United States and the Soviet Union captured large numbers of V-2 rockets and used them in research that led to the development of their missile and space exploration programs. Wernher von Braun himself was secretly moved to the US and naturalized, along with about 1,600 other German scientists, engineers, and technicians.

---

4. Wernher von Braun even held the rank of *Hauptsturmführer* (Captain) in the "Schutzstaffel" (abbreviated "SS" and meaning "protection squadron"), the foremost agency of security, surveillance, and terror within Nazi-Germany and German-occupied Europe. This fact is conveniently not mentioned in his NASA biography.

5. Those were the V-1, the world's first self-flying bomb and thereafter the V-2 rocket, the world's first guided, forty-five foot tall, long-range ballistic missile. More than 8,000 V-1 bombs and more than 3,000 V-2 rockets were launched at London and other European cities (https://www.britannica.com/technology/V-1-missile; https://www.britannica.com/technology/V-2-rocket).

Image 8: The US Explorer 1 Launch Team 1958 Is an Example of Integrating Foreign Skills into an American Idea

Right to left: Dr. Wernher von Braun was born and raised in Germany; he led the team that built the rocket able to carry a satellite payload and launched the West's first satellite "Explorer 1." Dr. James A. van Allen was an American; he designed and built the core instruments on Explorer 1. Dr. William H. Pickering was born and raised in New Zealand and held dual citizenship in the USA; he led the team that built and operated the satellite.

In other words, the entire transportation technology for the US-American space program in the 1950s was masterminded by Germans, by German-born, German-raised, and German-educated experts; and even the leadership of NASA's "launch and operations center" (later called "mission control center") was headed by Germans.

But, why do we—correctly—call the US-space program "American" and not "German"? It is because *the program's intellectual framework, its intentions, purpose, philosophy, and leading idea,*[6] *as well as its missions and projects were, from its very beginnings, created by Americans.*

These Americans in charge in relevant political and military institutions, as well as in related administrative organizations, carefully

---

6. "The effort to explore space was at its heart an effort to remain free, to ensure that the exploration of space would not become the launch pad of tyranny. The people who were in their twenties during World War II were then in their forties and running things; they remembered what tyranny looked like" (Standley 2008, p. 5).

integrated foreign knowledge and skills as useful improvements into an existing idea, into an existing intellectual framework and concept.

Now, let us apply this historic reasoning to the ongoing discussion about the origin of genuine Okinawan karate.

China Is the Birthplace of Ch'üan fa, Japan Is the Birthplace of Bu-jutsu, and Okinawa Is the Birthplace of Karate-jutsu

Through this lens, *an existing Okinawan martial art with its clear intention and purpose of self-protection integrated foreign (Chinese) knowledge and skills into its existing system, into its existing idea, and into its existing concept and intellectual framework.*

Te [karate-jutsu] itself seems "peculiar to Okinawa in its origins," (Funakoshi 1973 p. 7f), and as genuine as it can be. Okinawan *Te* integrated Chinese *ch'üan-fa* knowledge and skills as well as other foreign and domestic martial elements into its existing system, into its existing idea, and into its existing concept and intellectual framework—as mentioned above, *tegumi/shima*, the ancient Okinawan form of grappling/wrestling, or *torite*, "the Chinese Shaolin-based method of seizing and restraining an opponent" (IRKRS, n. d, n. p.).

So, in summation, Chinese martial arts were undoubtedly included in *Te*, perhaps after the famous "36 Chinese Families" took up residence in Okinawa in the late 14th century to spread crafts and arts (Kerr 2000, p. 75f), or perhaps because Okinawan nobility as well as Okinawan karate masters used to study in China too. It could also have been because Chinese sailors (*Chinto*), guards (*Ason*), royals, or military envoys (*Kusanku, Wanshu*), all known by the *kata* named after them (see Volume 1, p. 5 for more details), taught the art to Okinawans. However, these *Chinese martial arts were integrated into* Te (karate-jutsu) *and did not create* Te.

This "existing system, existing idea, and intellectual framework" of Okinawan karate-jutsu is the concept of unconditional empty-hand self-protection and lethality. Kane and Wilder describe the fundamental strategy for achieving this purpose for their system of *Goju Ryu*—in my opinion this explanation holds true for the other two Okinawan karate-jutsu systems of *Shorin Ryu* and *Uechi Ryu* as well: "The fundamental strategy is to (1) close distance, (2) imbalance, and (3) use physiological damage to incapacitate an opponent" (Kane/Wilder 2005, pp. 45ff). Every skill or piece of knowledge supporting this concept was integrated—whether of foreign or domestic origin—and shaped Okinawan karate-jutsu in its final sophisticated form as a chain of assimilated improvements.

Compared to more than a thousand years of *Te* (karate-jutsu), Japanese karatedo with less than one hundred years of existence is a relatively new development. It was only after the Ryukyu Islands became Japan's prefecture Okinawa that many of Okinawa's non-Japanese cultural elements were eliminated to integrate the province politically and culturally (Kerr 2018, p. 440ff), and in this process, in the decade before WWII, karate opened up its tradition as a secretly practiced combat art and became part of (mainland) Japan's martial history.

Before that time, (mainland) Japan had its own different, more than a millennium-old, martial arts, and *bushido* tradition. The specific role and purpose of a lethal empty-hand martial art that served as part of a warrior's education in ancient mainland Japan was *bu-jutsu*, known today as *jujutsu*. Karate was essentially unknown in mainland Japan until the early 1920s, though some Chinese military *ch'üan fa* representatives may have visited before that, and some Okinawan karate instructors may have travelled there sporadically.

Therefore, it is here assumed that Okinawa is the birthplace of karate-jutsu, whereas, drawing on a comparable historic argument, Japan is the birthplace of *bu-jutsu*, with its own unique genesis. Sensei H. E. Davey, 8th Dan *jujutsu* SMAA, explains that within a samurai's education in martial systems (*Ryu*), the study of weaponry (especially of the sword) was of primary importance, just as the study of weaponry and its use is the priority for modern-day soldiers. However, a number of *Ryu* included empty-handed grappling techniques as well, which were taught in unison and were never totally unconnected to the *Ryu's* weapons techniques. Simultaneously, these grappling arts were, and in certain cases still are, separate methods too, with their own differentia. The generic term "*jujutsu*" developed to give the average civilian an easy way to talk about a whole variety of related but still distinct grappling systems that were taught in Japan within the various classical *Ryu* (Davey 2021, p. 4f). Those traditional grappling *Ryu* have mainland Japan as their birthplace. However, what we see today in the Western world is a truncated form of *jujutsu* where it has been concluded erroneously that this grappling art is some sort of mixture of judo, karatedo, and aikido. Such a *jujutsu* derivative is found in overwhelming numbers outside of Japan (and in Japan in certain cases), and far outnumbers forms of authentic *jujutsu* (ibid.).

Isn't it fascinating to find such a parallel between misconceptions about today's *jujutsu* and misconceptions about today's karate-jutsu?

Is the Proposed Reasoning Plausible?

Because of the lack of verified historic facts, all statements on karate history should be generally taken with a pinch of salt and carefully double-checked. The heuristic-hermeneutic historic reasoning just presented is no exception and is, as a start, as good or as bad as any other historic analysis on this subject. Its line of reasoning seems highly plausible though, as many Asian countries or kingdoms developed their own genuine ancient martial art. This was a simple necessity to survive, because as long as tradition goes, records, memories, myths, and legends describe fights, battles, wars, crime, and combat as violent constants throughout history. During a centuries-long process of evolving, honing, and perfecting local martial practices, warriors learned from each other and the superiority of one concept over the other was established on the battlefield, on the streets, or via the tradition in which high-ranking masters challenged each other to fight.

In this way, martial elements from all over Asia amalgamated into local variations. They were integrated into a pre-existing local martial art, and ultimately resulted in what can be characterized as a specific local fighting system. *Te* was one of these genuine ancient martial arts. Orginating on the Ryukyu Islands, it was created 500 to 1,000 years ago independently of mainland Japan's bushido, martial arts, and samurai traditions. The art is as genuine as it can be. With a peak impact supposedly in the late 1700s and 1800s, Chinese martial arts were integrated as improvements to *Te*, but as noted earlier they did not create *Te* (karate-jutsu). They were integrated without sacrificing karate's essence but rather supporting it, that is, its true purpose and intention of self-defense.

That is why we dare to state that karate-jutsu is an Okinawan martial arts system (in line with karate masters like Funakoshi 1973, Motobu 2018, Shimabukuro/Smith 2020) and not a Chinese one, though Chinese martial arts were integrated into *Te*. That is why we call *ch'üan-fa* a Chinese martial art and not an Indian one—though, as mentioned above, an Indian monk may have introduced some fundamental concepts.

The logic here is the same that backs calling the US Constitution "American," though that political vision is exclusively based on European, not American, philosophical notions like Montesquieu's theory of separation of powers, Hobbes's considerations on social and political order, and Locke's postulate of people's natural rights to life and liberty. The bottom line is here again that foreign knowledge, thoughts, and skills were integrated into an existing idea and intellectual framework of its own.

Toyotas are referred to as Japanese cars, Fords as American, and Volkswagens as German, though more than 50 percent of all the parts in these vehicles were not produced by the company that created the brand but were integrated as "foreign knowledge and skills," including entire engines. Many of those parts are even identical across all brands, like air bags, gear boxes, brake systems, differentials, tires, seats, electrical equipment, and sunroofs, just to name a few. This does not mean these attributions of national origin are wrong, just as integrating Chinese moves and concepts into *Te* does not change karate-jutsu's identity as Okinawan. Car manufacturers learned from each other and *integrated foreign knowledge to make useful improvements in existing ideas, integrating that knowledge into an existing intellectual framework and concept.* Integration of foreign knowledge and skills do not bring about a whole new brand.

Summary of Chapter 2

This text supports the perspective that *Te*, the predecessor of Kara-*Te*-Jutsu, is an indigenous Okinawan martial art for self-protection, as genuine as it can be, that was created and developed on the Ryukyu Islands some 500 to 1,000 years ago. Unknown on mainland Japan during all these centuries, the art was honed to perfection on Okinawa independently of Japan's samurai and *budo* tradition.

The argument is illustrated by the metaphor of the hundred-year-old US space program, which was and is an American and not a German project, although it was masterminded by German experts after WWII. It is American because it had its genesis in an American idea into which the expertise and skills of German rocket scientists were integrated; this foreign expertise did not cause the US space program.

Applying this historic reasoning analogously, Chinese martial arts were integrated to improve the existing system, idea, and intellectual framework of Okinawan *Te* but were not the cause of *Te*. It is the same line of argument one can use to call the US Constitution "American" even though it is exclusively based on European philosophical ideas. It is the same line of argument according to which one can depict a Toyota as Japanese, a Ford as American, and a Volkswagen German even though more than 50 percent of the parts in these vehicles were not produced by the company that created the brand[7] and are even identical across all brands.

All these examples show the same pattern of foreign knowledge and skills being integrated into a brand, into an existing idea, philosophy, and intellectual framework; this foreign knowledge and skills were integrated but did not cause the brand, craft, or art.

Correspondingly, integrating Chinese moves and concepts into *Te* does not change karate-jutsu's originality as Okinawan; hence, Okinawa is the birthplace of karate-jutsu, China is the birthplace of *ch'üan-fa*, and Japan is the birthplace of *bujutsu*.

---

7. Fifty-five percent of the total value of a car's parts is enough to qualify an American car as made in the US. But, because the data come from reports mandated by the American Automobile Labeling Act of 1992, the legislation lumps together parts and content from the US and Canada, so the strictly US portion is less than 55 percent (https://fortune.com/2019/06/26/american-foreign-car-manufacturing/; retrieved 11/23/2021). Secondly, the statistics refer to the *value* of parts, a monetary figure, not to the *number* of parts. Because there are many relatively inexpensive foreign parts included (inexpensive due to large-scale production by specialized suppliers) the number of foreign parts in an American car is even more than 75 percent—but it is still called an American car, not a foreign one.

Chapter 3
Japan's Assertion of Okinawan Karate—How a Subcultural Intangible Heritage Is Used as a National Cultural Symbol

Today, "karate, together with judo, is commonly regarded as a Japanese national sport symbol" (Swennen 2006, p. 1). Mainland Japan claiming karate as a Japanese martial art—though correct in terms of the governmental sphere, is incorrect in terms of subcultural heritage—denies proper credit to the region that invented and cultivated the art, to Okinawa; it challenges subcultural identity (Chen/Lin 2016) and lacks acknowledgement of cultural traditions.

It was mentioned earlier that, compared to more than a thousand years of *Te*, Okinawan "*Kara-Te's*" predecessor, Japanese karatedo—with less than a hundred years of existence—is a relatively new development. Its incorporation into mainland Japan's cultural and martial tradition started in 1920 after the former feudal *province* "Ryukyu" had become Japan's *prefecture* "Okinawa." At that time the following evolution of Japanese karatedo became a part of Japan's general integration policies and efforts toward socio-cultural amalgamation when many of Okinawa's non-Japanese cultural elements were eliminated in order to politically and culturally integrate the region (Kerr 2018, p. 440ff). But interestingly enough, the dominant cultural element of karate was not eliminated. Quite the opposite: in this amalgamation process karate was required to open up its tradition as a secretly practiced combat art and became culturally integrated as a part of (mainland) Japan's martial history. In other words, though many Ryukyuan cultural artifacts were chosen to be eradicated, karate was taken over by Japan "according to the motto 'eliminate everything Ryukyuan but assimilate *todi*' [karate-jutsu]" (Feldmann 2021, p. 196).

Japan, the "karate-*reproducing*" country is—and used to be—the superior political power governing the "karate-*inventing*" and culturally autonomous region of Okinawa, beginning in the 1600s as the occupying force of the Ryukyu kingdoms and thereafter in the mid-1800s as the central government overseeing Okinawa prefecture. The sociological/social borders of cultures and subcultures and their unique symbols, cultural assets, and heritage do not necessarily match the political borders of governments, and even today the Okinawans have not totally assimilated into Japanese society (Hein/Selden 2003). A boundary remains, a dichotomy of culture and citizenship endures, and nothing indicates that it will disappear in the future (Meyer 2007). This means that an *Okinawan subcultural heritage and symbol does not necessarily represent the overarching culture of the nation*—or, in other words, the subcultural symbol that is karate may from the outside be incorrectly interpreted as a national Japanese cultural symbol, which it is not.

Okinawa's History Creates Unique Socio-Cultural Conditions

However, the picture is multifarious, and the Okinawan socio-cultural situation is more complex as one may assume after reading the last paragraph. A large group of Okinawan people then and today want to be both Japanese and Okinawan. In many aspects of daily life this cannot be consolidated and results in an overwhelming impression of Okinawa representing a basically Japanese culture. This is expressed in symbols like the language spoken, the food eaten, the educational and governmental systems implemented, the money used, the visible presence of Shintoism and Buddhism, the politics that determine society, and the policies to administer it.[1]

As such, Okinawans are subject to the same state canon and mindset that originated on the mainland. This mindset represents, beyond all dichotomy of culture and citizenship, an overlying culture of conformity. The impact of the Confucianism that ruled Okinawa for several hundred years is undeniable and created the prevalent, all-embracing culture of group conformity, including its components of not questioning authority, adhering to longstanding protocol, and using an imitative social mechanism, the *senpai/kohai* system (see Footnote 1), which will be explained in a moment.

This means that outright opposition between Okinawan subculture and mainland Japanese culture is unimaginable for all parties involved. Instead, Okinawans became used to combining different cultures during the hundreds of years when they maintained tributary relations in a dual subordination to Japan as well as to the Chinese court. Consequently, while carefully avoiding any confrontation with the mainland, Okinawans adapted and integrated relevant aspects of the Japanese culture into their own. For example, Shintoism as well as Buddhism were both installed and made mandatory belief systems in Okinawa by the Japanese government at different times in history. Shintoism and Buddhism mingled with Okinawa's traditional ancestor worship and, depending on the specific spiritual purpose and the demand for divine support, Okinawans still turn to both Shinto *kami* and shrines and to Buddhist priests and temples as well as to their home-based shrines where their ancestors symbolically rest.

The ability to integrate and synthetize such contrasting cultural demands, and to make them cooperate without giving offense, was a question of mere survival for an island people who lacked economic, political, and military power at the same time they were in close proximity to the powerful imperial neighbors of China, Korea, and Japan, any one of which could have swallowed up Okinawa had it not offered something unique, something everyone around it needed, appreciated, and therefore desired to protect.

---

1. The criteria stated here were suggested to me as cultural indicators by Sensei Patrick McCarthy in an email on November 17, 2021, where he also explains that the local language Uchinaguchi, which would be another cultural symbol, is almost non-existent today and became more a question of academic interest.

To illustrate this historic condition with another socio-cultural example, let us briefly look at Switzerland, a tiny but wealthy state and thus an alluring and supposedly easy prey for its neighbors. Since its foundation in the Middle Ages (1300s), this mountainous nation has been surrounded by sable-rattling large and powerful countries. But Switzerland was never occupied by any of them (with the exception of the two-month-long French invasion of 1798), not even by neighboring Nazi Germany during the latter's aggressive expansion all across Europe. One reason for this is that Switzerland exclusively offered, and still offers, something unique that all other nations and many powerful individuals all around the world want, need, appreciate, and therefore protect: a reliable and completely secret banking system.[2]

For Okinawa, the Ryukyus also seemed to offer something unique that all the surrounding nations as well as many powerful individuals in Asia wanted, needed, appreciated, and therefore protected: a reliable and secure trading post and hub, comfortably located halfway on the trade routes connecting these nations and allowing the controlled and reliable flow of goods. Okinawa functioned in this way for several hundred years. This status demanded that Okinawans integrate and synthetize contrasting cultural demands and cooperate with these cultures without offending them. Then the Satsuma invasion followed in the 1600s, and for another two-hundred-plus years Okinawans had to constantly combine their subcultural identity with the Japanese culture while maintaining positive relations with the Chinese empire as

---

2. Less known is the fact that Switzerland can only be occupied if invaders pay the price of the complete destruction of all important infrastructure and of a long, arduous guerilla battle: Firstly, Swiss citizens are armed to the teeth. The country has mandatory military service, and the soldiers take their weapons home after their service and store them privately. In addition, regulations surrounding the purchase of firearms in Switzerland were and are among the most liberal in the world; the law allows citizens to acquire semi-automatic and, with a permit, fully automatic weapons. Secondly, the country used the past century to carve out its mountains and to create shelters for its civilians as well as bunkers for its military. After the possibility of nuclear war arose in the 1960s, Switzerland would eventually construct bunkers to shelter the country's entire population with enough surplus space for foreign fugitives too. Thirdly, "Switzerland's military defense involves blowing up all roads into the country... To interrupt the utility of bridges, tunnels, highways, railroads, Switzerland has established three thousand points of demolition. That is the number officially printed" (Hickey 2012, n. p.). This strategy of self-sabotage and bringing the entire defense force underground was already developed in the 1800s, continuously perfected, and has since then threatened every potential invader with the prospect of an endless guerilla war in a completely inaccessible mountain area with all infrastructure blown to pieces.

well. "Every day the governing gentry had to weigh words and actions carefully in every decision of importance lest they come into conflict with Satsuma or with China; the arts of compromise and evasion were essential to survival" (Kerr 2000, p. 167).

Assertion of a Subcultural Symbol as a National Cultural Symbol

Because of these centuries-long socio-cultural conditions, "acceptance of alien controls became a habit of mind, but the characteristics of initiative, individualism, and self-assertion, which had secured independence and prosperity, began to fade," whereas "the arts of compromise and evasion were essential to survival" (Kerr 2000, p. 167). Bearing this in mind and combining it with the impact of the prevalent Japanese culture of conformity, it becomes understandable why it was relatively easy for mainland Japan to adopt karate without visible resistance, leave aside open conflict, and to turn it into a part of its own martial tradition.

When we look through this lens at the track-switching 1936 meeting of government officials and other interested parties with Okinawan karate masters,[3] it turns out to be understandable—though regrettable—that these living karate monuments formulated no opposing opinion against the change of their beloved combat art. They made no demand to keep *tode-jutsu* (karate-jutsu) as-is. Nakasone Genwa, a politician, writer, and renowned karate historian who studied karate at Toyama Sensei's *Shudokan* in Tokyo, was the primary force behind this meeting. He introduced the change from the term *tode-jutsu* to karatedo[4] (meeting transcript in McCarthy 2018, p. 186), and from that moment on, we only find clarifying questions and answers in the transcript, but not one single objection or protest. Everyone in the meeting was, however, well aware that this change was not only a name change

---

3. In attendance were the Okinawan Sensei Hanashiro Chomo, Kyan Chotoku, Motobu Choki, Chibana Choshin, Kyoda Juhatsu, Miyagi Chojun, Orotu Chokei, Gusukuma Shinpan (meeting transcript in McCarthy 2018, p. 182).

4. The term *karatedo* was already in use on the mainland before that meeting; definitely since 1929, when the karate workgroup at the private school of Keio, with Funakoshi Gichin Sensei present, announced that "empty hand" is not just an art/craft (jutsu), but that a spiritual development is desirable as well (Wittwer 2014, p. 70f).

but a complete and radical change of the art itself because, as mentioned in Chapter 1, the question was asked (by special guest Shimabukuro Zenpatchi, the chief librarian for Okinawa Prefecture) whether this would mean "that the cultivation of one's spirit, like that of judo and kendo, will be emphasized. Is that why the '*do*' was added?" which led to Nakasone Genwa's answer: "Yes. Its purpose seems to be the cultivation of the spirit" (ibid. p. 187).

The attending influential karate masters either kept quiet, like Kyan Chotoku Sensei, or only brusquely and gruffly answered some rather unimportant questions, like Chibana Choshin Sensei. When asking karate historian and professor Sensei Bruno Ballardini whether one may see Chibana Sensei's reaction as a kind of protest, his comment was that "the reason for his silence could be surely the disagreement with what was proposed by the organizer of the meeting, that was to adhere supinely to the government diktat abandoning the original name of the native Okinawan discipline (it would be like having to change the name of your own child by order of others), or he remained silent because he was simply outraged . . . We could link Chibana's supposed silence to the much more significant silence of Kyan Chotoku, who we know that both before and afterwards he opposed modernization with all his might. If, hypothetically, their attitude during the meeting was the same, it is then possible to explain Chibana's silence as a concordant attitude with Kyan's: two masters proudly defending the Okinawan tradition."[5]

This silent protest can be seen as the strongest possible form of opposition within the Japanese culture where questioning authority was unimaginable—and the meeting attendants from the mainland and from the prefectural administration, including Nakasone Genwa, most definitely embodied governmental authority. So, realistically, there was no conceivable alternative form of opposition in this culture of all-encompassing conformity.

However, this silent protest, as understandable as it is in socio-cultural terms, was not successful in defending the Okinawan tradition, and it did not change or achieve anything in this sense. Instead, Okinawan karate's Japanization was well and unavoidably underway, and the Okinawan subcultural symbol and cultural heritage of self-protection was, quasi-unopposed, turned into a form of recreational

---

5. Sensei Bruno Ballardini in a personal message to me on April 5, 2021.

self-perfection, was overtaken as a national cultural symbol of Japan, and soon evolved further, together with judo, into a symbol of Japan's national cultural identity. There are opinions suggesting that this Japanization, supported by Itosu Anko Sensei's work to create the foundation of modern training methods for physical education in the school system, was the only way to save and maintain an art that otherwise would have faded into historic oblivion (Swift 2019; Feldmann 2021; Enkamp, n.d.). More on this assumption later in this chapter.

A view "from the outside" on cultures rarely distinguishes between national cultural identities and local subcultural heritage. There are many examples to be found all over the world for comparable misconceptions of collective identities in this sense. As one example, it was explained in Volume 1 (pp. 78ff) that the folk festival "Oktoberfest" is almost everywhere in the world believed to be a German cultural symbol but is actually a Bavarian subcultural symbol and represents this region's cultural heritage.[6] Hence, despite being German in terms of today's governmental sphere, the over-two-centuries-old *Oktoberfest is an intangible part of Bavaria's subcultural heritage*, including all its genuine Bavarian—often imprecisely called "German"—components of "Lederhosen" and "Dirndl" costumes, brass and folk music, and traditional Bavarian beer and food.

Image 9: A Bavarian Subcultural Heritage Is Misinterpreted as a German Cultural Symbol

Two Hundred Years of Oktoberfest Celebration in Munich, Germany, 2010

---

6. Bavaria is a state in the German south, which in social-cultural symptoms like language and dialect, traditional attire and costumes, Catholicism, architecture, folk music, and other symbols of cultural heritage is much closer to the country of Austria to its south than to the rest of Germany to its north.

Image 10: An Okinawan Subcultural Heritage Is Misinterpreted as a Japanese Cultural Symbol

This well-known and often-used photograph shows kata performance at Shuri Castle in Okinawa 1938, under the leadership of Gusukuma Shinpan Sensei (one of the legendary Okinawan masters) who are today "virtually unknown outside of this small circle [of] old-time traditionalist Okinawan karateka" (Sells 1997 in *Bugeisha* Issue#3, p. 62). The photograph displays drills conducted in orderly rows within a large training group, as well as students' matching uniforms and head bands, which all suggests the adaption of Japanese militaristic karatedo's impact on Okinawa at that time. And indeed, in 1938 Japan's second war with China was well underway and the Japanization of Okinawan karate was in full swing.

Applying this thought to our topic, we find Okinawan intangible subcultural heritage within the governmental sphere of the Japanese nation as Ryukyu-specific rituals, in the performing arts, as oral traditions, and as other symbols of indigenous subcultural origin, *including karate*. Some of these subcultural symbols were left untouched by Japan, for instance the famous local drum dance *Eisa*. However, the situation with karate is different as it was not left untouched; instead, karate faced a serious Japanese takeover, which was later called the Japanization of Okinawan karate (Volume 1, pp. 14ff; Johnson 2012).

As Japan has its own, sophisticated, more than a millennium-old martial arts and *bushido* tradition, it seems difficult to understand why the mainland undertook such considerable efforts to absorb a local fighting system from the nation's farthest and poorest region—a fighting system even considered crude and rural compared to the mainland's noble arts of *koryu bujutsu*.

As so often in history, the resolution to this puzzle is rooted in sociocultural conditions which help to explain how *karate became part of Japan's effort to support its prewar nationalistic aggressiveness* and how karate was used to create a warrior spirit in younger generations, to establish the concept of militaristic superiority, and to prepare the entire nation for the upcoming decades of total war.

The First Reason for Japanization of Okinawan Karate: Japan's Preparations for War

This spiritual mobilization is one side of the coin. On the other side, Japan, as an island state, faced crucial limitations of space for its growing population as well as a dangerous scarcity of natural resources for its ongoing industrialization. Both placed critical pressure on the empire, pressure which intensified even more during the economic depression of the 1920s and 1930s. The empire developed an urgent need for oil, coal, rubber, and minerals like tin, bauxite, and iron ore, which are all to be found in other Southeast Asian countries. Thus, expanding by way of conquering Taiwan, Manchuria, Korea, the Philippines, and some Pacific islands was Japan's way of gaining access to those natural resources and simultaneously win space for Japanese settlements in new territories.

The official ideology justifying the invasion and occupation of Southeast Asia was that it was Japan's calling to some kind of a crusade to (a) free this region from the influence of the Western imperialists, the barbarians who took advantage of Asia only to enrich themselves, and (b) to uplift Southeast Asia's oppressed civilizations up to a modern Japanese standard through temporarily occupying and governing them, thereby reforming their systems, educating their populations, and releasing them with a new elevated, self-regulated independence thereafter (Park 2020)—as client/puppet states of Japan, of course. The Sino-Japanese War (1894–1895), the Russo-Japanese War (1904–1905), the country's participation in WWI, the preparation for the second war with China, its initiation in 1937, and Japan entering WWII by attacking Pearl Harbor in 1941, all represent facets thereof; "great efforts were made to convince the people that Japan was a 'have not' nation engaged upon a righteous crusade" (Kerr 2018, p. 462).

Widely practiced martial arts with their combined end products of physical strength and mental focus came in handy as major means to the end of undergirding Japan's militaristic intentions spiritually.

Budo and Karate as Means to Create an All-Embracing Warrior Spirit
At the time Funakoshi Gichin Sensei introduced karate to the mainland in 1922 (Funakoshi 1983 p. 85f), Japan's preparation for its second war with China had already started. It was a time in which the military, in the name of the emperor, wielded the actual power and a strong and rigid system of oppression and extreme discrimination was established. This period was later called "the dark valley" in Japanese history (Finney 2011 p. 264ff). The emperor himself was built up as a strong symbolic figure, and no criticism of militarism or of the apotheosis of the emperor was tolerated. Japan was preparing itself for extensive military campaigns based on an all-embracing nationalistic warrior spirit. "For every lack in physical equipment and manpower the military leaders attempted to compensate by developing fanatic spirit" (Kerr 2018, p. 461). The main factors feeding this spirit, and those most closely related to our topic, were:

- The emphasis on the warrior spirit in martial arts, on *budo*, and the integration of all martial arts taught into one organization to be in charge of cultivating *budo*: the ultra-conservative Dai Nippon Butoku-Kai (McCarthy 2018b, pp. 258ff), at that time an essentially nationalistic organization with close links to the emperor and to the military.
- The reform of the entire educational system, including the adoption of *budo*, "which took the lead in the Japanization program" (Kerr 2018, p. 447) under the leadership of the Dai Nippon Butoku-Kai. This was not just for purposes of physical education in schools and universities but was to mold the warrior spirit of younger generations by means of all propaganda and indoctrination available in order to promote Japan's nationalistic-militaristic enthusiasm.[7] "Children at

---

7. This strategy of combining *budo* training with militaristic purposes is convincingly described by historians, as well as empirically illustrated, e.g., by interpreting a pre-WWII postcard/photograph of judoka training in their educational institution in front of a rack of bayoneted rifles (Judkins/Bowman 2018, pp 2ff).

school were subjected to an intensive propaganda campaign and stirred to admiration for heroic deeds reported from the China warfront after the continental invasion began in 1931" (ibid., p. 462).

Budo itself, the martial (*bu* 武) way or path (*do* 道), is a philosophical synthesis of (1) *bu-jutsu*, the martial craft or skills (*jutsu* 術), which describes the various Japanese martial disciplines in their original function as arts of war, with (2) *bushido*, with the code of conduct and chivalry that guides warriors' demeanor underneath their military skills (Benesch 2011). Instead of solely focusing on the art of fighting, on the craft of combat and war, as *bu-jutsu* does, *budo* widens this system of thought into a philosophy of a comprehensive development of body, mind, spirit, and character and as such denotes the process by which the study of *bu-jutsu* becomes a means to self-development and self-realization. In the order of its inherent priority, *budo* emphasizes principles first whereas *bu-jutsu* emphasizes combat first (Wittwer 2018, p. 177).

Budo is thus broader in scope than *bu-jutsu* and is simultaneously rooted in warrior skills and in a warrior's mentality rather than representing solely the practical arts of the warrior class. In this way, some parts of the traditional value system of *bushido* and physical martial arts training were pragmatically synthesized to allow the cultivation of a warrior spirit for the entire nation.

"Perhaps the most significant continuous theme leading to the ... *budo* martial arts is the emphasis on the study of death ... As a point of practicality on the battlefield it was felt that by accepting the inevitability of death the preoccupation with dying could be superseded with simply the need to perform, making the warrior more effective" (Dodd/Brown 2016, p. 35). Thus, the traditional comprehensive *bushido* values were transformed into a cold-hearted philosophy of mercilessness and unwavering dedication. It was to be a utilitarian synthesis of values around "honor," "courage," and "loyalty," which the imperial nationalistic-military complex favored and needed.

Consequently, the spread of *budo* may be characterized as the indoctrination of a modified warrior spirit for everyone and as implementing a set of values for all Japanese, be it in the military, in the business world, in governmental and private administrations, in organizations and associations, in education, in sports—in short: everywhere in everyday life. *The way of the warrior was taught as the core attitude and commitment to everyone everywhere in a militaristic nation.*

For this effort the role of martial arts became paramount, and the process shows the importance the national government, the military, and the Dai Nippon Butoku-Kai placed upon martial arts for their spiritual mobilization program. "Supported by government bureaus, Dai Nippon Butokukai propaganda from the prewar era maintained that *budo* (of which karatedo became a part in December 1933) was 'the Way' through which common men built uncommon bravery" (McCarthy 1998a, p. 40).

Successfully creating such a fanatic warrior spirit, which found expression in the imperial army's "no-surrender-doctrine,"[8] introduced the entire world to Japanese terms connoting honorable death, like "*kamikaze*" or "*hara-kiri*." Moreover, it "paved the way for extraordinary sacrifices exacted from the common people in World War II" (Kerr 2018, p. 461) which, with reference to Okinawa, led to the death of roughly half of the island's prewar population.

Though Japan's defeat was obvious at the eve of the Battle of Okinawa, and though a group of Japanese officials strongly pushed for surrender, the assumed humiliation with possible abdication of the emperor and the abolition of imperial reign still appeared impossible to accept for influential Japanese commanders. They decided to fight on—causing the deaths of 150,000 Okinawans, of at least 50,000 Allied soldiers, and of more than 100,000 Japanese service members.[9] "Warrior spirit" led to the devastating demolition of Okinawa, to deplorable violence by the Imperial Army against Okinawan civilians, to thousands of forced suicides of Okinawans—not to mention other

---

8. In January 1941 the Tokyo *Gazette* published the Imperial War Department's newly adopted Japanese Field Service Code. It advised soldiers in part, "Do not give up under any circumstances, keeping in mind your responsibility not to tarnish the glorious history of the Imperial Army with its tradition of invincibility" (Haskett 2016, 01/08/1941 record).

9. Some US commanders, as well as the new (1945) US President Harry Truman, believed that these deaths and sacrifices, as the direct consequence of fanatic warrior spirit, portended further unimaginable losses for the Western Allies as well as for the Japanese population if they would invade the mainland. Examples like the Japanese General Nakai Ryotaro demanding in his nationwide radio broadcast after the Battle of Okinawa the "suicide of 100 million" Japanese, meaning that every man between the age of twelve and sixty is expected to give their life in the last "ultimate battle" to defend the main islands, may have resulted in the decision to use atomic bombs to end the fighting rather than to invade the mainland, as initially planned by the US-military. There are of course other reasons as well for this controversial decision, e.g., demonstrating America's new weapons technology to Russia (Hein/Selden 1997). The ethical and legal justification for the bombings is still debated.

unspeakable atrocities all over occupied Southeast Asia, like massacres of civilians, severe mistreatment of prisoners of war, and forcing men into slave labor and women to become pleasure slaves (Park 2020).

Image 11: Japan's "No-Surrender" Doctrine Made Budo into the Spiritual Shield of Soldiers Who Were to Fight to the Death

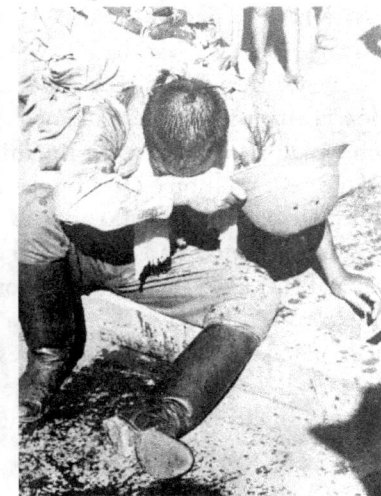

The unit of giretsu (heroic) paratroopers (left photo) was formed in November 1944 as an airborne special forces unit of the Imperial Japanese Army. It represents another desperate attempt to delay or to limit the Allied advance on the Japanese islands. Thousands of fanatic young soldiers like these paratroopers ended up committing suicide after their defeat in the Battle of Okinawa (right photograph). Driven by a steadfast warrior spirit, they were on a supposedly righteous crusade for the emperor and an underdog nation, as it was characterized by their military leaders and by the Dai Nippon Butoku-Kai; to them war was purifying and their unavoidable death was their duty.

A warrior spirit that leads to these kind of actions seems like a caricature of *bushido*, the Japanese warrior ethic, which is based on the seven principles of (1) rectitude or justice; (2) courage, bravery, heroism; (3) benevolence to all; (4) politeness; (5) veracity or truthfulness; (6) honor; and (7) devotion and loyalty (Nitobe 2014). Though Nitobe's explanation of *bushido*, which was written shortly before 1900, may contain some romanticized facets when he compares the Japanese warrior ideal to the European concepts of chivalry and to the art of the gentleman—and well aware of a possible cultural misunderstanding, from a Western viewpoint—I dare to suggest that the well-documented inhumanity of the imperial armed forces in the 1930s and 1940s all over Southeast Asia (Park 2020) were guided neither by rectitude or justice, nor by benevolence or compassion, nor by courtesy or politeness. Whereas "benevolence to the weak, the downtrodden, or the vanquished was ever extolled as peculiarity becoming to a samurai" (Nitobe 2014, p. 44), this kind of ethics was apparently lacking in the imperial army's interpretation of the warrior spirit at that time. It rather seems that the warrior spirit the military and the Dai Nippon Butoku-Kai created, promoted, and implemented via martial arts training, was a solely utilitarian reduction of the above seven principles into the three of courage, honor, and loyalty. "The ability to inflict violence (*jutsu*) is itself taken to be laudatory and not the tendency also to be courteous or peaceable" (Lloyd p. 20). Such a truncated *bushido-* and *budo-*influenced martial arts education, corresponding with militaristic-nationalistic ideals, was pressed into use for bellicosity and provided the spiritual shield to let soldiers fight to the end as it presented war as purifying and death as duty.[10]

In its militaristic-nationalistic adoption of *bushido* principles, the propagated warrior spirit "did not take interest in the morality of an action itself, or in the consequences of the action, but rather maintained its focus on pure-mindedness. This was done for highly pragmatic reasons. 'Warrior Zen' . . . rather underpinned the *bushido* mentality in the sense that it encouraged the warrior to move resolutely ahead once he had made up his mind to act, whether that decision was rational or moral" (Lloyd 2014, p. 20)—which represents a *bushido* interpretation called "utilitarian" earlier in this text.

Karate as One Way to Secure the Human Raw Material for Pre-War Japan's Armed Forces and to Demonstrate Socio-Cultural Superiority
Researchers and contemporaries find in all totalitarian regimes a close relationship among sport, nationalism, and militarism. The reason for the emphasis on sport in these regimes is multifold. On the one hand,

---

10. In this context "Japan had refused to ratify the 1929 Geneva Convention on the treatment of prisoners of war partly, as the country's vice minister of the navy explained, because the Japanese had no concept of being captured" (Haskett 2016, 01/08/1941 record).

promoting grassroots sport through physical education curricula starting in preschool and through party/government-related youth organizations[11] builds up the human resources needed for the regime's military forces. Stimulating physical education in pre-schools, schools, and colleges as was the case in prewar Japan through karatedo, judo, and other *budo*-arts, aims not just at creating warrior spirit but also a pipeline of physically strong human raw material for its armed forces as well.

The use of sport to build up widespread physical and mental strength within a populace is also important for totalitarian regimes because this strength can be (and was) used in political propaganda to demonstrate the superiority of a people. Superiority in this sense was propagated in different nomenclatures in recent history, either in the form of a so-called "fully developed socialistic personality" in East Germany, or to prove overall racial superiority as in Nazi-Germany, or to establish a nation's cultural and mental superiority as it was the case in Japan, where the *budo* martial arts fulfilled this function from the late Meiji period up to the Second World War (Swennen 2006, p. 9).

In summation, it is no surprise at all that physical and mental education in schools and preschools becomes a priority for totalitarian regimes and hence is found in Japan too to undergird the nation's militarism. "The professional military men believed that the civil population existed only to feed and service the war machine. They looked upon every activity not directly geared to military preparation as a waste of time if not indeed an act of sabotage" (Kerr 2018, p. 462).

In terms of karate, oral tradition states that this local Okinawan martial art first drew the military's attention during a draft (McCarthy 2018, p. 269), when Okinawan youths displayed exemplary physique and strength. It was, thereafter, noticed by the Dai Nippon Butoku-Kai when it was incorporated into the physical education program at Okinawan public schools (ibid. p. 271). That this broad educational approach included elementary schools as well is to be credited to Okinawan karate master Itosu Anko, who suggested in his famous letter to the prefectural education board in 1908 that student-teachers at the prefectural teachers college should practice karate, in that "they could, after graduation, introduce karate at the local levels; namely

---

11. Examples for this strategy of totalitarian regimes in Europe are the national-socialist "Hitler Youth" in Nazi Germany (1933–1945) and the socialist "Young Pioneers" in East Germany (1945–1990).

elementary schools. In this way karate could be disseminated throughout the entire nation and not only benefit people in general but also serve as an enormous asset to our military forces" (Itosu 1908, in McCarty 2018, p. 26). From then on, there were efforts underway to Japanize karate, to make it part of the *budo* under the supervision of the Dai Nippon Butoku-Kai, and to spread it nationwide.

It is unclear why Itosu Sensei highlighted karate's military aspects since he did not show any other militaristic attitude and promoted the art's ability to prevent fighting "as a means of avoiding the use of one's hands and feet in the event of a potentially dangerous encounter" (ibid. p. 23)—in other words, as a non-aggressive, fight-preventing art, reserved for rare just-cause applications. A recent study of Itosu Sensei's letter suggests that "maybe for Itosu it was kind of dance with the devil cooperating with the Japanese authorities [*sic*]. His intention was undoubtedly to emphasize the positive aspects of *todi* [i.e., karate-jutsu] and to make it useful for the community. And thus at the same time to ensure that Ryukyu's cultural heritage is not lost through the ongoing process of Japanization" (Feldmann 2021, p. 275).

And indeed the most successful way to extend karate's importance seemed to be through supporting Japan's militaristic intentions. On the flipside of the same coin, the best way for militaristic-nationalistic Japan to make use of karate's utilitarian benefits on a wide scale—i.e., building up physical strengths and creating warrior spirit through reinvented *budo*—was by turning the martial art into grassroots sport. That way the art could be easily incorporated into the physical education programs of schools and colleges, and thereby reach youth of all ages. So it seems a win-win-arrangement for all parties involved was reached, with the exception of karate-jutsu itself, which was transformed into a near caricature of its real nature.

Consequently, specific *kata* were created to allow the safe teaching of kids and college students and, from this perspective, the reasons for all those well-documented succeeding changes to karate become clear as components of karate's Japanization into *budo*-sports, such as redesigning the method of teaching it so that instruction was more like judo. At that time, judo was seen as the prototype of all *budo*. One way this redesign was carried out was by creating equivalent curricula, rank-systems, etiquette, and attire (Herbert 2021, p. 18). Another aspect was the transformation from karate-jutsu into karatedo, into recreational athletics combined with spiritual development.

Karate adapted itself to the desired reforms and became—together with the other Japanese *budo* arts—closely associated with Japan's national identity. "Karate is a sport that has spread over the entire world and yet its image has remained linked with the country of the 'rising sun.' Karate, together with judo, is commonly regarded as a Japanese national sport symbol" (Swennen 2006, p. 1).

After the prewar Japanization process, the Okinawan roots of the art seem to be lost for the public for several decades.

> ### My Experience with Remnants of a Totalitarian Regime's Physical Education Program in Preparation for Military Service
>
> Two totalitarian regimes are well-known to this author who was born in early 1949 in West-Germany and raised there. Both regimes were socialist ones; namely right-wing national-socialist (today often called Nazi) Germany (1933–45) and left-wing socialist East Germany (1949–90).
>
> Twice in elementary school, at the age of six and at the age of seven, I encountered relics of Nazi-Germany's physical education program, which was designed to prepare kids from an early age for military service. This was in the mid-1950s during my participation at the Federal Youth Games (Bundesjugendspiele), which was (and still is) a nationwide sports event at all German schools on the same day and which is obligatory for all students age six and older. This sports event is the successor of similar prewar competitive games that had been conducted in Germany since 1920. Individual results for each student were then (and still are today) recorded and reported for nationwide and state-specific comparison, competition, and recognition.
>
> The surprising encounter with relics of Nazi-Germany's militaristic physical education happened in a throwing discipline (Weitwurf) in elementary school 1956 and 1957. The object to be thrown was a dummy stick hand grenade (Stielhandgranate; see photos), a famous German hand grenade with a wooden handle, which was widely used during both world wars.
>
> The dummy version my classmates and I threw was a solid wooden model of the grenade with a thick iron band wrapped around its bulky head to add weight to the top and thus to match the weight and physical conditions of an original grenade and to realistically simulate throwing the real thing.

> Apparently, a careful check of physical education curricula and its related equipment in elementary schools slipped through the cracks of Germany's postwar demilitarization.
>
> At that time, the six-year-old students did not know what they were throwing, they just enjoyed the competition of the games and tried to give their best to score high for their final grades in sports; only a few years later I became aware of the fact that I had practiced throwing a grenade while attending elementary school. I competed several times in that discipline before it was turned into a baseball-throwing competition.

Image 12: Original WWII German Stick Hand Grenade (left) used in WWII (right)

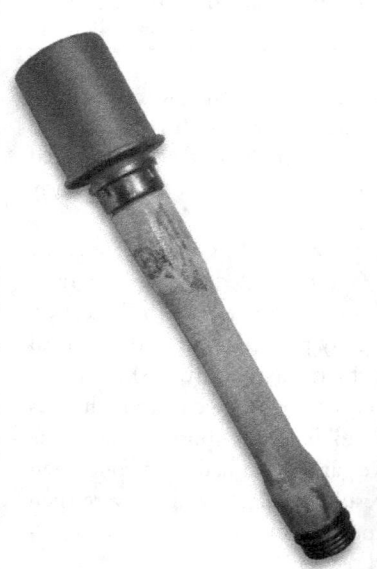

The Second Reason for the Japanization of Okinawan Karate: Japan's Cultural Integration Efforts

Japan's culture, imbued with the virtues, values, and philosophies of a millennium-old Confucian thought system, explains from a socio-cultural standpoint the necessity of eliminating many Ryukyuan-specific subcultural peculiarities and to flatten major differences between the culture of the mainland and that of its province. The socialization of Okinawans, in its sociological-psychological sense, and their formal education involving the Confucian values of conformity and collectivism, inherited from centuries of Chinese influence and Japanese occupation, as well as the unavoidable adoption of the inherent all-embracing *senpai-kohai* system (see below) as part of this philosophy by the Okinawan people, left little to no room for opposition from a subcultural tradition.

Conformity and Group Orientation in Japanese Culture
Therefore, in socio-cultural terms, it seems unimaginable that the governing Japanese mainland would allow an independent and different sub-culture like the Okinawan to remain untouched. To further clarify this statement, we need to shed light on some defining aspects of the Japanese culture, starting with "Groupism."[12] This social orientation and philosophical concept clearly sets itself apart from Western individualism, and it represented—and still represents—an aspect of Japanese culture of utmost importance, namely the aspect which was earlier called a culture of conformity. It represents an alternative form of togetherness where the reference group, the community or the nation, is valued above the individual, and an individual's role in the social, political, and economic life of the community is largely determined by its membership in a specific class or caste.

It has to be noted, however, that "the group model pays attention only to public expressions involving social and interpersonal relations" (Hasegawa/Hirose 2005, p. 219). There is another side, pointed out by scientific research, a private side standing in contrast to public appearance, and the private side of the Japanese, at least today, "is contrary to the group model depiction: they are individualistic beings with strong inner self-consciousness" (ibid.). So it looks like there is a public version of culture and that there is a parallel private one too; however, the public version of Groupism still anchors the visible norm of everyday togetherness for the Japanese people, including Okinawans.

This still-predominant culture of conformity perpetuates a Confucian-based mindset with its emphasis upon the community, with belief in unquestionable authority, with its obligations to adhere to

---

12. Sociologists use the term "Groupism" to depict an individual's tendency to conform to the cultural pattern of a group at the expense of individualism and cultural diversity. On a side note: some Japanese scientists claim that such a social pattern may actually create some difficulties for Japan being a no longer a closed system today, but a competitor in a worldwide open-market economy (Haitani 1990).

longstanding protocol, and with its use of the imitative social mechanism of the *senpai/kohai* (senior/junior) system (see the following section).

Further contrasting with Western philosophical individualism in which the interests of different groups or individuals may be dissimilar and even opposed, with Confucianism possible differences morph into reciprocal obligations when it comes to the official state norms and core codes of Ryukyuan education, right up until modern times.[13] Possible differences between governing and governed, between children and parents, husband and wife, older and younger siblings, supervisor and subordinate, colleague and colleague, friend and friend melt into a moral relation and dissolve into one single mutually shared interest. Hence, diverse interests become united in a reciprocal relationship of giving and taking.

Senpai Seniority as Social Mechanism to Integrate Karate into Japan's Martial Arts Tradition

The means of implementing and preserving long-standing traditions, practices, and routines in the social system of Japan is the *senpai-kohai* mechanism. It represents an often informal (though sometimes a formal) hierarchical interpersonal relationship of seniority in administrations, associations, clubs, businesses, schools, and many other social institutions and organizations, including families, neighborhoods, and social gatherings. The status of *senpai* seniority is often, but not necessarily, based on age, though it is based most often on time of membership in an organization and thus on the length of time it takes to become familiar with specific internal social conditions and specific knowledge and experience. The concept has its roots in Confucian teaching, but it has developed a distinct Japanese style over the centuries and ultimately became a defining part of Japanese culture,

---

13. Another example of how the Japanese understand conflict differently than Westerners, for whom conflict involves a clash between competing interests, is that Eastern philosophy sees the meeting (not "clashing") of opposing individuals, groups, and forces that do not exist without each other and define each other by contrast, often forming a new whole together. Their initial opposition dissolves itself and morphs into a new overarching unity, like yin and yang together as a whole constitute the well-known symbol, or like night and day together as a whole form the unity of time, which in the West is the twenty-four-hour day.

impacting public and private social life, and even some legislative norms (Davis/Osamu 2002).

The *senpai's* obligation is to care for the *kohai*, to give directions, to set the tone, to personify an ethical, professional, and behavioral standard. A *senpai's* authority is not questioned and he (traditionally "he," today "he or she") provides comprehensive guidance and advice benefitting the organization as well as the *kohai*. The *kohai's* reciprocal obligation is to follow the *senpai*, to learn and to imitate, and to develop matching skills and abilities. This interpersonal social process leads to the assumed identity of individual goals among all parties involved, *senpai*, *kohai*, and group. It is easy to understand how such a social mechanism on the one hand perpetuates the status quo, and on the other hand *uplifts seniority to a status of unquestioned authority*.

Let us apply this concept to the history of martial arts, viewed through the Japanese lens. Japan has from antiquity seen its martial traditions uniquely, elevating warrior skills to the level of art, and undergirding these skills with meditative-philosophical systems. The resulting cultural mindset of mainland Japan's martial arts and political officials seems to be that, because of the nation's sophisticated and distinguished *koryu bu-jutsu* (traditional fighting arts), because of its noble samurai tradition, and because of its elaborate *bushido, this very tradition establishes the mainland's senpai-seniority, perhaps even pure superiority, in all martial arts per se*, eventually leading to the claim that only the mainland's *budo* arts best embody or represent the core of all Japanese martial arts—including the Japanized (and thus "cultivated") versions from occupied territories. In this perspective, Okinawan karate in its original version "embodied backwardness" (Feldmann 2021, p. 196) to the Japanese eye and was considered socially acceptable only after its conversion into its Japanized form based on *budo*. Because martial arts are such an important and essential socio-cultural pillar of Japan, holding the status of socio-cultural self-definition, and because karate came "only" from the Okinawan subculture, it becomes comprehensible how thinking formed by the *senpai/kohai* relationship and its values leads to the assumed seniority of the mainland's martial art tradition over the one from Okinawa.

On the other hand, because karate was such an important symbol of Okinawan subculture, Japanizing this local fighting art became a priority not just for militaristic purposes but also for the purpose of creating some kind of cultural homogeneity across all of Japan. By integrating a subcultural form of art specific to a certain people and region into the Japanese culture, the identity-defining role of karate is changed from an Okinawan subcultural symbol into a cultural symbol for the entire nation of Japan. Hence, integrating the Ryukyu Islands culturally by amalgamating a local fighting art into the mainland's martial arts traditions seems a promising tactic for Japan's overall cultural integration efforts.

As a result, the initial Okinawan karate-jutsu concept of self-protection underwent the well-known and aptly described revisions that distinguish Japanese karatedo considerably from its Okinawan karate-jutsu origin; it matched karatedo to the way judo was structured and taught and drove the change of purpose from self-defense and protection of one's life into self-perfection. The loss of ancient knowledge in this Japanization process—knowledge about *bunkai* in general and about nerve strikes and pressure points in particular—is considerable and will be looked at more closely in Chapter 4 in the section "Loss of Essential Knowledge."

Karatedo became a recreational and meditative activity prioritizing health, spirituality, and character development, and most of the lethal combat applications were eliminated. Today's statement of the (mainland) Japanese Karate Association convincingly illustrate this transformation: "True karate is based on *bushido*. In true karate, the body, mind, and spirit—the whole person—must be developed simultaneously... Our aims through karate training are the mental and physical well-being of our members and improving one's character ... The result of true karate is natural, effortless action, and the confidence, humility, openness, and peace only possible through perfect unity of mind and body. This is the core teaching of *Zen*, the basis of *bushido*, and the basis of the JKA's karate philosophy" (JKA tab "Philosophy," n.d., n.p.).

As explicitly stated in the above quote, this kind of meditative karatedo is linked to Zen Buddhism. However, classic karate-jutsu developed independently from religious or philosophical belief systems, as already pointed out by Itosu Anko Sensei, who in his introductory words to his famous "Ten Articles" on karate training, unequivocally states that "karate did not descend from Buddhism or Confucianism" (Itosu 1908, in McCarthy 2018, p. 23). Instead, "Zen in karate ... was 'imported' through 'Zen-inspired' swordsmanship. This happened in the process of 'budozation' of karate in the 1930s after its introduction on mainland Japan" (Herbert 2021, p. 18; my translation).

In addition to what was already laid out in Volume 1 (pp. 31ff), karate-jutsu's *independence from philosophically based religions or belief paradigms* is supported by the fact that—in spite of all Japanese efforts to force Okinawans into their belief systems of Shintoism and Buddhism—the traditional Okinawan belief system of ancestor worship remained intact as an essentially psychologically based paradigm of human relationships and not as a philosophically based religion (Matayoshi/Trafton 2000). Ancestor worship sets itself apart from all other belief systems that represent philosophically based religions: in the tradition of Okinawan ancestor worship, all life comes from the "ultimate ancestors" at the beginning of time, which are Heaven, Earth, and Sea. In other words, all life comes from Mother Nature, and individual fate and well-being is based on healthy and positive relationships to these ultimate ancestors as well as to all the generations that came after them. Buddha, Allah, Christ, and other major figures of philosophically based religions are integrated into the Okinawan belief system as ancestors who lived in the "middle ages," which came after the ultimate ancestors and before a specific family's own ancestors' generations (ibid. pp. 40ff).

Summarizing the philosophical underpinnings of Japanese martial arts and contrasting classic Okinawan karate-jutsu, *budo*-specific philosophical Zen- and health-related super-structures became more important in today's Japanese karatedo than the art's original purpose. This Japanized approach, though old-style in the sense that it does not contain modern sports applications, does not sufficiently represent the "jutsu" aspect of karate, its original and true purpose at its birthplace of Okinawa.[14] The genuine art and its true purpose developed without

---

14. For the example of *Doshinkan* karatedo, the importance and assumed sole focus on an all-embracing spiritual development in this style by some members was recently described in detail by one of the organization's higher-ranking practitioners, without mentioning any martial aspect as a fighting art and without quoting any literature related to that subject of combat (Meissl 2021). Based on that writer's background in philosophy, Buddhism, and fine arts, his text focuses exclusively on the "*Do*" in karatedo, on an adept's individual path and related experiences while pursuing a way of meditative athletics. The issue here is that the view presented creates a reduced image of *Doshinkan* karatedo in the public's eye and weakens all efforts to maintain the style's martial roots as it is clearly enforced today under the organization's new leadership of Masako Fujimoto-Stock, 10th Dan *Doshinkan*.

connection to mainland Japan's *budo* or Samurai tradition and without an initial connection to Buddhism or Confucianism. All references and links in this sense were later added on mainland Japan and represent a completely new approach.

However, when considering the *senpai/kohai* relationship in connection with karate's cultural integration into the Japanese martial arts tradition, a few important facets of karate's development become clear. The claimed superiority of *koryu* Japanese martial arts over rural Okinawan karate explains the metamorphosis of the latter into its new Japanized styles. It accounts for the new and utmost importance of a Zen-related *Do* towards character development. And, finally, it helps us understand the loss of traditional karate-jutsu knowledge that followed this development.

Summary of Chapter 3

Though claiming Okinawan karate as a traditional Japanese martial art is correct in terms of the governmental sphere, it is incorrect in terms of its actual subcultural heritage, and it denies proper credit to the region that invented and cultivated the art.

Mainland Japan has a different martial tradition: Japan is the birthplace of *bu-jutsu*, while Okinawa is the Birthplace of *(kara-) te-jutsu*. It was only after a millennium of Okinawan *Te* that Japan discovered the fighting art of its province and started cultural integration efforts to make karate a part of Japan's history.

The example of the subcultural symbol "Oktoberfest," which is a Bavarian tradition but internationally mislabeled as a German one, illustrates how cultural borders may not match national borders, and how a dichotomy of culture and citizenship within a nation remains. Consequently, as a subcultural symbol, Okinawan karate may be misinterpreted "from the outside" as a national Japanese cultural symbol.

It seems difficult to understand why Japan took over a local fighting system from its farthest and poorest region, a fighting system even considered crude and rural compared to the mainland's noble arts of *koryu bu-jutsu*. But realizing that "Japanization" as an effort to integrate a sub-culture and the use of karate to develop Japan's prewar nationalistic warrior spirit provides the answers.

Referring to the use of martial arts as preparation for war, the warrior spirit as the core attitude and commitment in a militaristic nation was taught to everyone in a joint educational effort by government, military, and Dai Nippon Butoku-Kai. This educational campaign was aimed especially at youths in schools, pre-schools, and colleges, thus preparing the nation's population for war. A reinvented ethical system, *budo*, which is the combination of a truncated version of the traditional Japanese warrior code (*bushido*) with martial skills training, served as the principal resource for this purpose.

In terms of integrating the Okinawan subculture, a Japan-specific, Confucian-based practice of social imitation that defines seniority as the guiding authority, the *senpai* (senior)-*kohai* (junior) system, was used to amalgamate martial arts traditions under the guidance of the assumed more sophisticated ancient one of the mainland and thus contributed to integrate the Ryukyu Islands into Japanese culture.

In this process the transformation of karate-jutsu from a combat art into karatedo, into a recreational, health-related, and spiritual way intensified. Zen- and health-related super-structures became more important for karatedo than the art's original self-protection purpose.

In summation, the Japanization of Okinawan karate was in political terms a two-fold process before WWII; (a) it became part of Japan's preparation for the nation's planned imperial conquests and its second war with China; and (b) it was a means to an end in Japan's cultural amalgamation efforts.

Chapter 4:
The Metamorphosis of an Ancient Fighting Art into Athletic Showmanship

After WWII, things changed dramatically in Japan. A collective attitudinal shift away from hegemonic prewar militarism (Hashimoto 2015) impacted the way in which war, violence, the warrior spirit, *bushido,* and *budo* were viewed and what role they would play in the society. "Even to this day it has been reported that Japanese society has lost its interest in both modern and ancient martial ways . . . as a post-World War II Japan came to terms with its nationalistic and militaristic heritage" (Dodd/Brown 2016, p. 37). Interestingly enough, the US's cruel act of dropping atomic bombs on Japan also allowed the birth of a postwar narrative of a victimized Japan[1] which overshadows, if not quasi-erases, the imperial army's own atrocities all over Southeast Asia.[2] These Japanese war crimes were for a long time neglected by the

---

1. An illustrative example of how commonplace such victimization narratives were are the Japanese *Godzilla* motion pictures, launched in 1954 and 1955, where an unstoppable monster, coming from the general direction of the USA, is awakened by a nuclear explosion (!) and creates havoc while there is nothing the population can do.

2. The most prominent examples of this kind of mayhem are the Nanjing Massacre in China as well as other mass killings in Southeast Asia; the rape, mistreatment, and forcing of women into sexual slavery as "comfort women" for the imperial army; enslavement of men as forced labor; mistreating prisoners of war who, because they had surrendered, were viewed as having forfeited all honor and merited nothing but contempt. Estimates of the number of deaths that resulted from Japanese war crimes range from 3 to 14 million (Park 2020).

country's postwar historic research and did not appear in the history curriculum in Japanese schools for some decades.

On the other hand, karate was already included in educational programs as karatedo before WWII, which allowed a smooth official redefinition of the socio-cultural role of martial arts. Japan's attitude shift led to a redefinition of karate as a recreational, health-related, and spiritual way rather than the way of the warrior. The art's lethal combat skills had already been softened for educational purposes before WWII, and beginning in the 1950s were strongly redirected toward sport applications and consequently and systematically moved further away from their martial origin. New public attitudes and sport-political objectives accelerated not only the transformation of karate-jutsu from a combat art into karatedo but developed and altered the art even further by creating sports-karate as a new derivative of karatedo with its own *kata* and purpose.

Change is usually called progress. We no longer use manual typewriters, power brakes have replaced non-power brakes, television sets don't have tubes, and thousands of other devices in common use at the end of World War II are now forgotten. The common denominator here is that something becomes obsolete when something better comes along to serve the same purpose. Things are different, however, with respect to the development of the art and craft of karate. Here we do not find an improvement in the way we achieve a certain purpose; we see instead a *change* of purpose (from self-defense and combat to recreation and spirituality) and the creation of a new approach to achieve this new purpose.

When the art's inherent lethal combat skills were strongly redirected into athletics, health-improvement, and meditation, Zen-related superstructures became more important for karate than the art's original self-protection purpose (see above and also Volume 1, pp. 29ff). But whereas culturally integrated Japanized karatedo was still grounded in the powerful execution of martial *kata* moves, though hitting air instead of opponents in applied *bunkai* or combat training, the new version of sports-karate required an additional change of techniques from creating the most possible damage in the most effective way toward speedy fencing-type moves with tagging contact with limited target areas.

Consequently, even more Okinawan karate techniques were eliminated in sports karate after WWII, especially bone-breaking block-strikes, throws, back-leg sweeps and groundwork; as well as grappling, nerve suppression, joint locks, limb-, head-, or neck-manipulations. Other techniques were radically altered by outlawing the traditional targets of Okinawan karate-jutsu, which were organs, eyes, throat, groin, wrists, ankles, knees, elbows and points of nerve concentration—all prone to immediately end a fight when severely hit and damaged—and the essence of the original fighting system was eventually completely lost in its transition from Okinawa into mainland Japan's karate versions.

Sports-Karate: The Commercialization of Karatedo and Its Consequences

After WWII, Japan's national efforts to prove the country's significance and importance shifted from an emphasis on martial success to economic success—however, not with the Western concept of a free-market economy centered on individual self-interest, but with a Japanese version of "common interest first" (Drucker 1981) in a governmentally regulated market. Large and successful Japanese corporations optimized their strategic advantage by basing their corporate culture on traditional socio-cultural philosophical concepts, e.g., on "harmony," thus matching the cultural norms of the Japanese society (Feldmann 2007, pp. 61ff). Thus, a dedicated workforce and strong enterprises were created in a corporate economic structure that strongly barred entry of foreign businesses. In this corporate economy the Japanese government heavily supported its own domestic companies with subsidies and created legal barriers for foreigners to enter a market. Japan became a powerful exporting country and succeeded in heavily penetrating Western markets, sometimes even taking over entire markets, e.g., cameras, consumer electronics, and, later, large sections of the automobile market. Postwar Japan changed the orientation of the country's trade relations, which for many centuries were concentrated toward Southeast Asia and on China. Now the US and European markets replaced the (still-communist) Chinese market as Japan's major international trading partner.

In this economic context, *karate developed into a government-supported sports-oriented business of considerable size.*

In economics and business terms, we may say that karate, especially in its *Shotokan* version, was turned into a commodity and followed the typical path of industrialization by successfully mimicking the manufacturing process of other goods and services (see "Postwar Industrialization and Commercialization of Japanese Karatedo" in Chapter 6). It is the path of standardization (standardizing techniques and curricula), multiplication (educating dozens of instructors to teach based on these standardized curricula), and large-scale-production (sending accredited instructors all over the world to educate local students who then in turn open accredited dojo overseas) that created nothing less than a worldwide karate inflation after 1950^3 (Volume 1, p. 28ff). The resulting sports-karate represents one more example of how "traditional martial arts have been uprooted from their historical locations, new hybrid forms have emerged, and in the process, the places, roles, and functions of martial arts have changed considerably" (Bowman 2010, p. 2).

Sport-business opportunities reached a crescendo in the Olympic Games, the self-acclaimed "greatest show on earth" where its economic aspect became at least as important as the initial Olympic idea.[4] Recognition of a sport in the Olympic program creates a booming business opportunity by stimulating and increasing worldwide participation in this sport; it leads to television exposure, to more sponsors, and to amplified income for the parties involved. In addition, "Victory at the Olympics very much symbolizes the strength of a nation. Thus, because of its political importance, governments want to do whatever it takes to win. Sports used effectively to strengthen the unity of a nation is the wish of any government" (Swennen 2006, p. 4).

So, understandably, after WWII Japanese governmental officials and mainland karate associations worked hand in hand to initiate and aggressively pursue the installation of a new Olympic karate

---

3. In this Volume, we do not look at the modifications karate underwent in the course of its "Americanization" in the Western world, which created another branch of commercialized sports by selecting specific approaches from Asian martial arts and combining those for competition purposes, e.g., as mixed martial arts, or as kickboxing (Volume 1, pp. 33ff). These new hybrid forms in the West are usually not called "karate" like the Japanese sports-karate version are.

4. The initial Olympic idea was to build a peaceful and better world based on mutual understanding with a spirit of friendship, solidarity, and fair play (https://olympics.com/ioc/beyond-the-games; retrieved 09/30/2021). The phrase "greatest show on earth" is quoted from https://olympics.com/en/news/the-greatest-show-on-earth ; retrieved 09/30/2021.

discipline—an effort that went on for decades and finally, though preliminary, succeeded with karate's inclusion as a new sport in the 2020/21 Tokyo Olympics.

In order to be accepted at the Olympic Games, a sport must be widely practiced[5] and be represented by one national umbrella organization. For karate to meet both of these criteria after WWII, (a) Japanese instructors were sent all across the world to boost its popularity as a form of recreation and rule-bound competitive sport (Kotek 2016). These efforts were highly successful indeed—and (b) the Japanese government and sports officials made efforts to place karate in Japan under one umbrella organization. However, these latter efforts were not as successful, and the integration of traditional Okinawan karate-jutsu into one overarching (mainland) Japanese organization has failed until today.

Volume 1 explained (pp. 21ff) how Toyama Kanken Sensei—who, like Funakoshi Gichin Sensei, initially studied in Okinawa under Itosu Anko Sensei and taught on the mainland since the early 1930s—was tasked by the Japanese government with unifying all Japanese and Okinawan karate into the Federation of All Japan Karate (FAJKO), established in 1959. As mentioned earlier, this endeavor was supposedly based on the attitude that the sophisticated tradition of mainland Japanese martial arts establishes (*sempai*) seniority and thereby the authority to make rules and define the art. Many Okinawan masters, however, ignored Toyama Sensei's invitation, refused to attend the conference, and rejected any effort to integrate Okinawan karate-jutsu into Japanese karatedo.[6]

In 1969, FAJKO and some other style-specific organizations coalesced into the Japan Karate Federation (JKF), which today represents the four officially recognized Japanese karate styles of *Shotokan*,

---

5. Regulations require widespread practice of a sport by men in at least seventy-five countries and on four continents, and by women in no fewer than forty countries and on three continents (https://www.britannica.com/story/how-are-sports-chosen-for-the-olympics; retrieved 10/04/2021).

6. This initiative by FAJKO with its inherent patronizing of Okinawan karate sensei is described in Volume 1 (p. 21ff) and was shared with the author in detail by David Chambers, author and publisher of *Classical Fighting Arts* magazine and OPG Okinawa Goodwill Ambassador, who backs up his view by pointing to the fact that "I was working for FAJKO in Minato-ku, Tokyo, at that time (1975–1980) as an assistant to the General Secretary, General Eichi Eriguchi, and therefore know exactly what was going on" (email to the author on June 27, 2019).

Wado Ryu, *Shito Ryu*, and a Japanese Form of *Goju Ryu*, and continues its sports-specific undertakings. To counter the Japanese initiatives, the Okinawans formed their own umbrella organization shortly after the foundation of FAJKO, leading to the formation of Okinawa Dento Karate-Do Shinkokai in 2008, which integrated all previously separate groups into one federation for all genuine Okinawan karate. This limits karate's preliminary Olympic recognition to just the Tokyo Games 2020/21 because regulations today state categorically that only one national governing body of a sport can apply for Olympic status, and this is clearly not the case with karate in Japan.

Sports-karate evolved as a new and fascinating modern sport with its own purpose and reason for existing, as was the case with other sport derivatives of combat arts, like javelin, fencing, archery, biathlon, and many others. All these sports rightfully lost their initial martial purpose and became new sports; *there is no need to create a special philosophical superstructure* for them. Nobody would claim that today's sport of foil fencing, where only straight moves back and forth are allowed, where target areas are restricted, and where tags are sufficient to score a point, represents the ancient martial art of French or Italian musketeers, who moved in all directions and pierced all parts of the body. Even without being familiar with the ancient art of swordsmanship, it is obvious to everyone that today's fencing is a new creation and not anything like a perpetuation of its ancient predecessor.

The situation with karate, however, is different. The Japan karate federations JKF and JKA still associate the sport with ancient roots, twisting karate's history when they claim it is part of the mainland's samurai and *bushido* traditions, which it is not, while also transforming prewar Japan's militaristic-nationalistic distortion of *bushido* into a tradition of positive humane values: "Martial spirit and courage were, of course, essential aspects of *bushido*. But for the samurai, *bushido*'s highest goal was complete virtue in thought and action. Each samurai followed a carefully designed regimen of polite ceremony and etiquette intended to promote such virtue. With its emphasis on prescribed form, *bushido* helped the samurai harmonize mind with body, enabling them to maintain a certain calmness, or *heijoshin* (literally, 'ordinary everyday mind'), even in the face of hardship. Sincerity, kindness, honesty, filial piety, and honor all formed part of the core of *bushido*. And they were the seed from which the karate tradition grew. These attributes, and the wisdom, understanding, and peaceful strength they promote are some of karate's greatest benefits. They are also among Japan's greatest gifts to the world" (JKA tab "Philosophy," n.d., n.p.).

The "seed from which the karate tradition grew," however, is not Japan's samurai tradition; it is a local fighting system from the country's poor and outermost island, Okinawa; it is a local fighting system that developed for more than five centuries independently of the mainland's samurai and *budo* traditions. And secondly, "kindness" was definitely not a part of the imperial army's prewar warrior spirit, and neither was "filial piety."

Sports-karate experienced its most recent high point in 2020/21, when, after more than sixty years, efforts to have karate included into the Olympic Games bore fruit. This triumph concludes a difficult historical process beset with special interests, politics, socio-cultural frustrations, and hubris. Its success, however, cannot be overestimated as an important example for the recognition of East Asia's socio-cultural impact on the world: whereas the vast majority of new sports and new disciplines in the Olympic Games since their beginnings was of Western origin, remarkable non-Western games are the three Asian martial arts derivatives of judo, taekwondo, and now sports-karate. Before 1964, when judo was included for the first time in the Tokyo Olympics, all Asian martial arts were relegated to "demonstration sport" status. Judo was excluded again in 1968, returned in 1972, and has been a fixture since. Taekwondo became a full-medal sport from 2000 on continuously after its first appearance and following exclusion. Sport-karate shows up as a newly recognized sport in the 2020/21 Tokyo Olympics but will be excluded again thereafter. After the Tokyo games, some felt strongly that sports-karate in its existing form has no place as a regular Olympic sport in addition to taekwondo because of its rules that disarm the art and its specifically required technique applications make it less interesting for spectators than boxing (Imbrišević 2021). The further development remains to be seen; it is quite possible as well that rules and regulations will be changed to allow sports-karate's repeated presence at the Olympic Games.

The role of sports-karate for public health and for competition is an extremely important one. It created a captivating new discipline and there is no reason to question its desirability at all. Sports-karate not only canalizes aggressions into fun and competitive activities, training techniques are also perfect for physical education, health, and fitness. Under a responsible coach the training has near-therapeutic impacts on both kids and adults facing challenges (Volume 1, p. 63f); students grow mentally and are guided towards positive social values—reflected in modern physical education learning objectives and their corresponding training designs.

In summation, sports karate evolved as a new and attractive modern sport with its own purpose and reason for existing.

> Hence, again and in all earnest, I want to point out that there is no reason to say anything against sports-karate and that I by no means intend to do that. I simply intend to point out the differing origins and developments of karate-jutsu, karatedo, and sports-karate, their alterations, and their most common misconceptions, as well as to clarify the consequences of these changes.

Consequence One:
The Loss of Essential Knowledge

According to research,[7] karate-jutsu evolved as the synthesis of several martial arts components, especially as the synthesis of the following.

- *Tegumi/shima,* a form of grappling dating back in Okinawa to the 11th century, which is the predecessor of Okinawan sumo (McCarthy 1998a, p. 38). *Shima* apparently has a longer recorded history than *tegumi* (Quast 2022), but the term *tegumi* became popular in the 1990s when it was seen as karate-jutsu's most prevalent two-person training method and perhaps became some kind of a buzzword thereafter.[8] Be that as it may, grappling, throwing, and technique application in partner exercises are one ancient ingredient of classic karate-jutsu.

- *Torite* (*tuite* in Okinawan dialect), which is the method of seizing and restraining an opponent through limb manipulation and joint locks. It was mainly used by law enforcement officials, security

---

7. https://irkrs.blogspot.com/2013/04/siamese-boxing-original-source-of.html?view=magazine.

8. The uses of the term *tegumi* are further explained by Andreas Quast in his Ryukyu Bugei website in the archive Category *"tegumi"* (https://ryukyu-bugei.com/?cat=1894) and suggest a range of definitions such as (1) Okinawan folk-style wrestling performed as a pastime until the late 19th century and predecessor of Okinawa sumo; (2) a set of practices developed by Patrick McCarthy in the 1990s to provide practical karate-related practices; (3) free fight in some Japanese karate schools; (4) a term variously used by Western karate teachers to refer to grappling.

agencies, and correctional officers in the Ryukyu kingdoms and in Japan. Today, police practice a form of this martial art, *taiho jutsu,* to assist with arresting criminals (Quast 2021b, n.p.).
- *Kata,* which is the pattern of ancient solo fighting routines. It is the one training component supposedly familiar to all karate practitioners. *Kata* was developed to effectively teach an encyclopedia of combat movements to more than one person (and in relatively narrow dojo spaces). In other words, the moves were initially taught individually before being compiled into *kata* by the ancient masters. It is a patterned system of offensive and defensive moves.
- *Te,* which is Okinawa's original form of percussive impact. This art depended principally upon the use of clenched fists to strike an opponent.

Drawing on classic karate-jutsu training modules, other valuable research states that "karate (then called *tode*) consisted of several disciplines: *kata* (the practice of applications hidden in the movements of forms), *tuite* (hold, leverage, and disarticulations), *kyusho jutsu* (the use of vital points), *hojo undo* (conditioning and strengthening techniques), *kiko* (techniques for the development of internal energy)" (Ballardini, *Bugeisha* 2021, Issue #8, p. 10).

The discipline of *kata* is undisputed between the two sources, and so is *torite/tuite* (hold, leverage, and disarticulations); the latter being the term *torite* in Okinawan dialect, and *"tuite* lives on its own within ancient karate as a complementary art to karate and it is studied only at the highest levels" as Sensei Ballardini points out (personal email communication, August 23rd, 2022). Hence, through the second quote the ancient curriculum of karate-jutsu is completed with the addition of (a) knowledge about striking vital points and nerve suppression as well as the addition of (b) conditioning/strengthening exercises; i.e., *hojo undo,* to strengthen muscles, tendons, ligaments, and bones (joints and forearms) through partner exercises and the use of traditional training equipment (Clarke, M. 2009).

Combat training itself in classic karate-jutsu was mainly done in the form of *tegumi,* as two-person "training methods that linked basic techniques to defensive applications" (McCarthy 1998a, p. 36). In support of this statement, "Karate practice was based exclusively on *kata* but this did not consist simply in the repetitions of forms (which held fairly limited space in the economy of training), but instead consisted of the study with a partner of the applications contained in each movement" (Ballardini, *Bugeisha* 2021 Issue #10, p. 8).

Sensei Dan Smith (see footnote 7 in chapter 1) pointed out in a conversation with me in April 2022 that in his opinion *kata* is not a scenario-based method of passing on its understanding, but a technique/concept-based general way of how to carry out a task where "form follows function." Hence, in Kyan Chotoku Sensei's words, to understand *kata*, one needs to understand which techniques are general concepts and which ones are specific applications, and one needs to define the task to be carried out. There were no specific terms for specific stances, foot or hand techniques in the Okinawan language *Uchinaguchi*. As Sensei Dan Smith explained, teaching occurred by demonstrations using the corresponding *Uchinaguchi* expressions of *tichiki* (hands show what I do) or *tichikun* (move your hands like this). All the terms for techniques, positions, and so on, that we use today are Japanese terms, inventions, and standardizations that often lead to misconceptions. The term "block" (*uke*) may serve as an example: there is no block in karate-jutsu; there is "the art of receiving and giving." Karate-jutsu (through *ippon kumite*) teaches "*uke* = to receive" and "*kogeki* = to attack/give." Receiving and giving is the first goal of Okinawan karate, manifesting itself as "receive and counter," "receive and seize/hold" (and then "give"), or "receive and immobilize."

The art was practiced for centuries in complete secrecy, and knowledge was handed down only orally and only internally within the schools themselves. As mentioned earlier, a headmaster chose who to share the secret art with, and since no system-specific written records exist (with the exception of the more general *Bubishi*), the knowledge was inaccessible to those who do not belong to the dojo and neither to those within the school who were not considered of worthy character. "This is exactly what also happened to the Japanese who learned only the most superficial part of Okinawan karate and thus gave birth to a different karate, disconnected from the original roots of the art" (Ballardini, *Bugeisha* 2021 Issue #9, p. 8).

As long as karate in its new form is used as recreation or as a sport in tournaments, "Why learn to traumatize a limb, gouge an eye, twist a joint, or even squeeze the air out of someone if the sole purpose of your efforts is to win by a full point or to get into better physical shape?" (McCarthy 1998b, p. 16). This new and different karate is characterized by essential changes of techniques from offensive moves into defensive ones and by the loss of systematic knowledge about nerve strikes and grappling. No longer teaching the systematic knowledge about hitting vital points and how to utilize that knowledge in combat (*kyusho jutsu*) is not the only regrettable loss of knowledge in today's karatedo versions; another loss is caused by the transformation of many offensive open-hand techniques into closed-fist moves, thereby suggesting their defensive use instead of their initial offensive one.

Sensei Angel Lemus summed it up nicely in a Facebook discussion within the "Okinawan Karate" group: "People don't know what they don't know. They are indoctrinated from what someone else teaches them, and they also don't know what they don't know. It is the blind leading the blind. This has been one of the biggest problems (in general) with karate as taught in the modern age (post-1900), where fighting applications were lost as the Japanese sports *kumite* craze took root and that became the main focus as opposed to fighting."

A good example for this development is a general postwar misconception created by simplification of the art while categorizing karate methods and techniques. As mentioned earlier, initially there were no specific Okinawan terms in use for karate-jutsu methods or techniques in the Okinawan language. As Sensei Dan Smith explained to the author, an Okinawan sensei would demonstrate moves while his students closely watched and then imitate his benchmark. Terms for moves were only introduced later, during the Japanization of karate-jutsu into karatedo, which did quite a disservice to the art by "crystallizing" everything and "causing immense cultural damage" (Ballardini in *Bugeisha* #12, 2022, p. 9). Within the Japan Karate Association (JKA), "Karate techniques were developed into a complete system. For the first time there emerged a clear, scientific, and practical 'best' form for each *kumite* stance, posture, and movement. There also emerged a clear delineation between the 'correct' and 'incorrect' way to execute each stance, punch, kick or technique" (JKA "History" tab, n.d., n.p.). However, what happened while categorizing moves and techniques that way was that the fluidity of the art was lost and turned into a chain of stagnant "techniques." Thus, fluid positions as preparations for technique application turned into stances; concepts with multiple application options turned into constricted techniques; and, as the following section explains, concepts of receiving and giving, called "block-strike" in Volume 1, turned into simple blocks.

Offensive Moves Were Changed into Defensive Ones
In the early 1900s, when Itosu Anko Sensei opened up the art to the public, especially to kids in elementary schools, the process of losing knowledge about crucial components of karate-jutsu was initiated. Understandably, it was not permissible to share lethal, paralyzing, crippling, and joint-breaking moves with children. So, by creating new *kata* adequate for physical education, many of those techniques were changed into some disarmed versions that completely changed the purpose and meaning—hence *bunkai*—of these moves.

A prominent example of this change is the alteration of open-hand offensive moves to clenched-fist moves, where the latter suggest defensive instead of offensive applications. *Nukite* (spear-hand) thrusts to the eyes were initially a technique to end a fight quickly which, however, cannot be taught to children. In a combat *kata* like *Passai*, where spear-hand moves were extensively used (Nagamine 1976, p. 195), Itosu Sensei replaced many of those open-hand *nukite* with closed fists, and *Passai* "was changed from a combat *kata* to a physical education *kata* based on defensive movements" (Ballardini, *Bugeisha* 2021 Issue #11, p. 8f).

In this process, "*Passai* underwent the most drastic modifications with the aim of spreading karate in the public schools. Itosu changed many attacking *nukite* moves to closed fist which were by the immediately following generation definitely interpreted as blocks" (ibid.). One example Sensei Ballardini uses to describe this change is characterized below to further illustrate this alteration.

As one representative of the "immediately following sensei generation" after Itosu Sensei, Funakoshi Gichin Sensei's interpretation of *Passai kata bunkai* in the *Shotokan* karatedo system, where the *kata* is called *Bassai*, is used for comparison to combat *Passai bunkai* in *Shorin Ryu* karate-jutsu. Itosu Sensei's changes may explain an utter misunderstanding of the first move in *Passai Sho*, when it is suggested, during stepping/lunging forward into a crossed-leg stance/position, to "execute a middle level forearm block (uchi-uke) with the right fist, placing the left palm against the inside of the elbow" (Funakoshi 1973, p, 88). The *bunkai* for this move is, in another *Shotokan* publication, explained as blocking a front kick to the defending karateka's head or chest with a *morote-uchi-uke* (supported middle block) as a "very strong block using the entire body" ("sehr starker Block unter Einsatz des ganzen Körpers") (Wichmann 1998, p. 130; translated by author), in spite of it being supposedly wiser to step 45 degrees out of the way of such a strong attack when defending, instead of lunging forward.

Image 13: Passai/Bassai Bunkai as a Hidden Nukite in Shorin Ryu Karate-jutsu versus Morote Uke in Shotokan Karatedo

Karate-jutsu Example Shorin Ryu

Karatedo Example Shotokan

In spite of his drastic alterations to the ancient combat *kata Passai*, Itosu Sensei seems to have continued to teach the initial kata applications to his senior students. Evidence for this assumption is the hand position for the first move in Chibana Choshin Sensei's *Kobayashi Ryu Passai*, where stretched left fingers rest on a clenched right fist (upper photo) indicating an imminent left *nukite* while blocking with the right arm (lower photo).

Funakoshi Gichin Sensei's interpretation of *Bassai* in the *Shotokan* karatedo system changed the *kata's* combat intention from offense into defense. As the first move in the *kata*, an augmented middle block (*morote-uchi-uke*) with the supporting left hand pushing against the inside of the right arm close to the elbow (upper photo) is supposed to allow a strong block against a substantial kicking attack (Wichmann 1998, p. 130) to a defender's chest or head (lower photo).

The basic idea for this example is taken from Sensei Ballardini's explanation in *Bugeisha* 2021, Issue 10; pp. 8–10.

The suspicion that this is a misconception in Japanized karatedo is bolstered by the fact that for the suggested "very strong middle block" (Image 13 Example *Shotokan*) the cross-legged stance/position renders a relative flimsy base of support. With the following 180-degree turn in the *kata*, and based on the fact that many turns in a *kata* are actually hidden indicators for throws, it looks like the cross-legged stance/position is instead an effective preparation for a throw (after having taken out the opponent's eye with a *nukite* thrust; see below). Such a throw-interpretation is not mentioned in *Shotokan* publications at all, but it is an interpretation Sensei Ballardini suggests and which I learned as well from *Shorin Ryu* instructors, who, even if they did not mention a hidden *nukite* move, interpreted the step/jump forward with the supported fist as a strong slap or push to the upper body in order to destabilize the opponent followed by immediately grabbing the opponent's top lapels of the *gi* and turning 180 degrees into a hip throw.

Contrasting the hand positions and its related *bunkai* explanation in karatedo, as quoted above, in *Shorin Ryu* karate-jutsu, where stretched left fingers rest on the clenched right fist instead of inside the elbow, this first *Passai* move indicates an imminent left *nukite* to the opponent's eye(s) while blocking a possible counter with the right arm (Image 13 Example *Shorin Ryu*). This version of the position of the hands was passed on by Itosu Anko Sensei to his students, but it was obviously not incorporated by Funakoshi Gichin Sensei into *Shotokan* karatedo. However, another student of Itosu Sensei's, Chibana Choshin Sensei, uses Itosu Sensei's instruction for his *Kobayashi Ryu* system and preserves the heritage of a genuine offensive first move in *Passai*.

I want to add, amidst all these proposals in favor of preserving genuine open-hand techniques, that my US sensei, Noel Smith, categorically requests closed fists for all moves when fighting/sparring for all his *Kyu*- and lower *Dan*-ranks, though more than a few karateka use open hands while parrying in a fight. The request to clench fists in a fight is not because of changing the intention of a move from an offensive into a defensive one but because of the higher probability of breaking a finger when open handedly connecting with an opponent's limb and because of the opportunity a less-experienced karateka gives to an adversary to grab one or two fingers and to manipulate the karateka by bending them.

Systematic Knowledge about Nerve Strikes and Grappling Came to Be Patchy

The history, mission, vision, and policies of the Japanese Karate Association (JKA) show that Japanese karate is heavily based on Funakoshi Gichin Sensei's interpretation of karatedo. "He dedicated his whole life to promoting the values of the art, and introduced the way of karate-jutsu to Japan, where it spread across the country. By 1949, his followers had established an association for the promotion of karate; they called it . . . Japan Karate Association. It was the beginning of the JKA" (JKA "History" tab, n.d., n.p.). One consequence thereof is the further disarmament of Okinawan karate-jutsu in Japanized karatedo, way beyond Itosu Sensei's initial alteration, which is exemplified in the loss of entire modules of the initial karate-jutsu syllabus, namely the almost complete loss of knowledge about *kyosho* and *torite* in Japanese karatedo systems. "De facto, Funakoshi represents the broken link in the chain of transmission of ancient karate" (Ballardini, *Bugeisha* 2021, Issue #10, p. 9).

Whereas in Funakoshi Sensei's *Master Text of Karatedo Kyohan* an entire chapter is devoted to vital points of the human body and the advantage and challenge of striking those (Funakoshi 1973, p. 237ff), it seems that he himself did not teach this application in a systematic way and neither did the succeeding sensei generations. Thus, it is evident "that this immense martial heritage totally disappeared in the styles which have been codified in the modern era (i.e., after Itosu) because starting from the following generation—that of Funakoshi—those techniques were no longer handed down" (Ballardini, *Bugeisha* 2021, Issue #8, p. 12). Pressure-point- and nerve-strike techniques were considered too difficult to learn and, most importantly, were suitable neither for teaching kids nor necessary for modern disarmed karatedo and its sports derivatives.

The question whether Itosu Sensei himself knew the art of pressure-point and nerve-strike techniques, later termed *kyusho jutsu*, cannot be answered with certainty, albeit there are strong indicators that he did and some that he did not. Convincing speculations about this topic are presented by Sensei Bruno Ballardini under the rubric "Karate Archeology" in some 2021 issues of *Bugeisha* magazine (*Bugeisha* 2021, Issues #8, 9, 11), which are summed up here as follows.

Matsumura Sokon Sensei, the teacher of Itosu Sensei and of Asato Sensei (who both were Funakoshi Gichin Sensei's teachers) did teach the art of *kyusho*. Whereas there is no evidence that Itosu Sensei did transmit any knowledge of *kyusho*, there is evidence that Asato Sensei knew, taught, and applied it in street fights. Thus, Funakoshi Sensei could have learned *kyusho* from his teacher Asato Sensei, but he devoted his whole life to another purpose, not to preserve the art in its initial form, shape, and intentions, but to bring karatedo to the Japanese mainland and to spread it there by way of transforming it into a recreational form of a physical and spiritual path for everyone. This process eliminated the arts of *kyusho* and of *torite* from much of Japanized karatedo, where it is not taught, neither in many old-style karatedo systems,[9] nor, and definitely not, in modern sports-karate derivations.

Kyusho and *torite*, however, are not completely lost in today's Okinawan karate-jutsu systems. They are preserved as hidden knowledge and are only shared with a limited number of practitioners. "Many of the last heirs of karate-jutsu have passed on, but many are still alive and have already left their legacy to older Okinawan and Western students—curiously, no Japanese students are among them" (Ballardini, *Bugeisha* 2021, Issue #10, p. 9). Hence, worthy senior students of the art who personify *shoshin*, i.e., the eagerness to learn like a novice despite having studied for years at an advanced level, can still become a part of the "thread of traditional transmission" (ibid.) and possibly learn the entire system of karate-jutsu.

As pointed out several times in this text, whether a student is considered worthy to receive complete *Okuden*-level teaching depends not just heavily but solely on the pure mind and character of the student and on his or her trustworthiness (as judged by a headmaster, not as seen by the student) to preserve the knowledge and to perpetuate it secretly the way it was intended to be maintained. "The elderly guardians of these secrets" (ibid.), the Okinawan headmasters of traditional karate-jutsu, have no problem if they cannot find this kind of student; they simply do not share all of their knowledge. Attending seminars or trainings at *honbu* dojos in Okinawa is no guarantee that karateka have learned the real thing. If students are considered unworthy to receive *Okuden*-level training, "the master welcomes them anyway into his dojo, sometimes asking them to pay large sums of money and handing

---

9. However, I personally experienced that *Doshinkan* karatedo teaches grappling, as well as joint and limb manipulation, though occasionally and not in a systematic manner.

out pompous diplomas even after only one week of practice. Many Westerners and Orientals still fall into this trap and return from Okinawa believing to have learned everything, to have grabbed the secrets of ancient karate, but do not realize that they have brought home only the skin of the fruit. The pulp is left in Okinawa, carefully preserved, awaiting the arrival of a real student" (ibid., p. 10).

Though the arts of *kyusho* and of *torite* may no longer *systematically* be taught in the majority of today's karate-jutsu systems, I can confirm by my own experience that they are, at least partly, still taught in some traditional dojo as well as during specialized training seminars, for I had the privilege of being introduced to (at least some of) these concepts over the last couple of years. The fact that *tuite* techniques were not freely shared by Okinawan masters is supported by my US-sensei's assertion that in the 1960s and 1970s, "They did not tell us everything; they kept some techniques a secret; they especially did not teach grappling to the Americans."[10] Only decades later, during a training visit at the Shorin Ryu Shorinkan Honbu Dojo in the early 2000s, Sensei Nakazato Shugoro demonstrated *tuite* applications in *Passai* and other *kata* to Sensei Smith and another high-ranking black belt who accompanied him during that training trip.

Referring to *kyusho*, the benefit of solely using nerve strikes in serious combat is disputed, because they do not always work on everyone. "Most people (more than 80 percent) will react strongly to pressure point techniques. Some, perhaps 15 percent, will react to some, but not all pressure points. There are also a small number of individuals who do not respond to most points at all" (Kane/Wilder 2005, p. 75). Most importantly, as verified by incident reports issued by the police force, nerve strikes become much less effective for individuals in an altered state of consciousness, whether because of drugs, alcohol, or mental conditions. Therefore it seems advisable not to solely rely on nerve strikes, especially in grim combat situations where blood pressure and adrenaline levels are off the charts and perception is dangerously narrowed by stress and pain. The best way to succeed here is to use the strongest possible version of the most direct move that may work

---

10. Sensei Noel Smith shared this insight and his Okinawan training experience several times in the last couple of years during training sessions with me and other students at his dojo.

without trying out any fancy application, and to stop an opponent as effectively and quickly as possible.

Based on this consideration, it is suggested that nerve strikes in combat be understood as "extra credit" (Kane/Wilder, 2005, p. 74). For instance, to stop an attack it may be a better idea to severely damage/break an attacker's forearm with a devastating "block-strike"[11] instead of trying to hit exactly the pressure point mid forearm on the lung meridian. In Sensei Kane and Wilder's terms, hitting the point while damaging/break the forearm would be "extra credit."[12]

* * * *

Excurse: A Psychological Perspective on Itosu Anko Sensei's Motivation to Teach Karate to Kids[13]

It is undisputed that the change of combat karate-jutsu into recreational karatedo was pioneered by Itosu Anko Sensei's changes to the art in the early 1900s, i.e., shortly before its all-encompassing Japanization. Because of his success in implementing his disarmed version of karate in the physical education program of public elementary schools, and because of the following, first nationwide then worldwide, spread of this new karatedo version, Itosu Anko Sensei is called "the father of modern karate" (e.g., by Enkamp n.d., n.p.) and even the "savior of a cultural heritage" (Swift 2019).

Such a laureateship, however, contains some speculation as Itosu Sensei's endeavors were not in line with the intentions of other Okinawan karate-jutsu masters who wanted to keep the art as a privately practiced craft of lethal fighting, and we actually do not know what

---

11. The term "block-strike" is used here as it was in Volume 1 (p. 19) to recognize the fact that there is no block as such in Okinawan karate-jutsu; every defensive move can be an offensive one at the same time. In this case, the karateka would, for instance, hit the side of the attacker's neck simultaneously with this move. Whereas a simple block would allow an attacker to continue the attack, a block-strike creates damage and can thus stop an attack.

12. This paragraph is of course based on my limited insight as result of my personal learning opportunities, which perhaps does not allow me to grasp the full extent of *kyusho* in classic karate-jutsu.

13. Since we look at Itosu Sensei's psychological motivation, we will not refer to speculations that his intention of creating his disarmed karate versions for kids may have been to protect karate-jutsu from being pilfered by Japan by hiding its essence. A previous, shorter version of this was published on 4/4/2022 at the YMAA website https://ymaa.com/articles/2022/04/itosu-anko-senseis-motivation-to-teach-karate-to-kids.

would have happened if karate-jutsu had been kept a secret and taught privately as it was for centuries before. Interestingly enough, during all these centuries before the 1900s karate-jutsu did not just survive on Okinawa but flourished and produced all those legendary masters who we still use as benchmarks and points of reference today. So, the art did not vanish at all though it was practiced secretly by a large circle of devotees.

Times changed, however; the broad need for hand-to-hand combat and for guardianship of noblemen, warehouses, trade vessels, and caravans decreased considerably. So it may be that in modern times widespread demand for genuine karate-jutsu has vanished too. It has at least decreased substantially in its role as a professional skill-set, though it is still preserved by a dedicated group who maintain the genuine karate-jutsu systems. The worldwide Japanized karatedo inflation before and after WWII, on the other hand, was initiated and rendered possible by Itosu Sensei's alterations to the art and craft of karate-jutsu.

Although, as described earlier, Itosu Sensei pointed out the importance of karatedo for preparing youths at an early age to later serve in the nation's military forces, it remains unclear why exactly he pursued his path, perhaps even dream, "to bring karate out of secrecy and to make it a new form of physical education, suitable for all people—in stark contrast to the views of other headmasters" (Ballardini, *Bugeisha* 2021, Issue #8, p. 10). It seems unlikely that the militaristic perspective represented the gist of his character. Though in his younger years Itosu Sensei definitely knew how to have a good time, though he had to defend himself from serious attacks, and though he did not shy away from brawls (Feldmann 2021, pp. 123ff), there is no indication that in his later years he would propagate militarism. Quite the contrary, in his "sunset years" he stressed the benefits of karate as a successful means to avoid a fight.

Hence, it was suggested, which seems rather plausible, that emphasizing karate's possible use for supporting Japan's armed forces was his pragmatic strategy to secure sufficient funds for his educational campaign (ibid., 2021, p. 276) through tapping into Japan's budgets for its ongoing militarization, *whereas the final and underlying goal of this educational campaign may not have been to create the raw material for the nation's military forces, but something different, something nobler.* Thus, jumping on the bandwagon of Japan's militarization could have been the means to another underlying end, while it seems to be the most promising strategy to secure the necessary budgets for teachers' education, for training facilities, and for teaching materials.

Be that as it may, to my knowledge nobody ever really tried to explain the WHY of Itosu Sensei's personal motivation to go public with his beloved art, especially the WHY for sharing it with young kids. This personal WHY seems to imply an individual psychological explanation as well and should not only be seen as the application of a political strategy. The political viewpoint, as plausible as it may be, does not unveil the nature of any other underlying end beyond militaristic benefits for the nation; it does not answer the basic question of WHY Itosu Sensei wanted to make karate suitable especially for young kids.

Although there are quite a few psychological considerations to be found explaining the actions of other famous public persons and of politicians, there is not one out there shedding light on this very topic of Itosu Sensei's motivation, on a subject of utmost importance for the entire karate-world. Such a psychological explanation is not too hard to sketch, as it can be sufficiently based on the available sources about his childhood, his social background, and his upbringing. These subjacent social-cultural conditions are in the meantime satisfactorily researched and document how one of the strongest human motivations came into play, the *motivation of trying to support others by sharing and spreading one's own positive experience.*

As laid out in the following paragraphs, Itosu Sensei's path of practicing martial arts shows signs of a deeply liberating, self-esteem-improving, and life-changing experience. If that is the case, a psychological explanation is possible based on the theories of motivation, i.e., referring to the theories explaining an individual's desire to act in service of his or her goals. Such behavior is rooted in several "intrinsic" factors, in factors of inspiration "within" an individual as desires and as strong tendencies to achieve conscious or subconscious personal goals (Ryan/ Deci 2018, pp. 123ff). Accomplishments based on such intrinsic motivation are usually more powerful, more fulfilling, and longer lasting than those based on "extrinsic" factors, e.g., based on forces outside an individual (Rogner/Titze 1985), material and emotional rewards, or expectations by other people. Intrinsic factors are used in this text to shed some light on Itosu Sensei's possible psychological motivation.

A life-changing experience is usually based on a combination of a person's *compensation*, which is the effort to overcome feelings of inadequacy (Dreikurs 1981, pp. 31ff; Rogner 1985, pp. 230–232), with *self-actualization*, which is the internal drive of a person to fully realize one's creative, intellectual, and social potential—a concept that became broadly known over the last couple of years as a strong form of motivation (Maslow 2013; Kretch et.al. 1958, pp. 483ff). Especially in our Western culture with its philosophical focus on the individual, self-actualization may be seen as the end result of a fully developed personality. However, there is one more aspect to be looked at. If self-actualization as such would be the only component of a fully developed personality, there would be nothing preventing serial killers or rapists going about their business. The additional psychological component that distinguishes the "social directions" of compensation are the options for an individual to either destructively move away from other people toward social isolation and aggression, or to constructively relate to others when overcoming feelings of inadequacy while developing one's own personality. Hence, there is, in terms of social interactions, a constructive as well as a destructive way of compensation to be found; a way where one's compensation constructively leads to benefits for others, versus a way where others pay the price or even suffer as a result of an individual's compensation (Andriessens 1985, pp. 300–304). Constructive compensation is driven by *social interest*, the third intrinsic motivational factor applied here—which is the wish and the felt responsibility to support others (Dreikurs 1981, pp. 15ff; Ryan/Deci 2017, pp. 561ff; Seidenfuß 1985). Such social interest and felt social responsibility is a motivation that very often grows stronger in a person's golden years (Blumenthal 1984).

The combination of these three psychological purposes of (a) compensation, (b) self-actualization, and (c) social interest constitutes a powerful motivational driving force, a core motivation of human behavior.

To support this psychological explanation with specific historic facts in Itosu Sensei's life, a recent historic study helps. By means of re-evaluating available Okinawan sources, it is convincingly documented that Itosu Sensei at a young age used to be a child of poor health, who "suffered from stomach digestion problems . . . and was often teased by his friends . . . [as] a weakling. Thus he is described as introverted and comparatively small for his age" (Feldmann 2021, p. 61), as well as being "extremely shy" (ibid.), "without passion and unwilling to refine himself" (ibid., p. 64). All these criteria are strong indicators for the boy's inherent feeling of inadequacy and damaged self-esteem, which constitutes the baseline for compensation. Such self-definitions of inadequacy often go hand in hand with hidden anxiety stemming from anything that causes insecurity in a child (Horney 1937). According to oral tradition, the boy's feeling in this sense may have been perhaps deepened through the challenging experience of harsh physical training by his father, who hoped for his son to become physically and mentally stronger. This oral tradition, reported by Shimabukuro Enzo Sensei (Wittwer 2007, p. 31), cannot be verified, but it can be stated without a doubt that "it certainly was not an easy time for the young Anko growing up" (Feldmann 2021, p. 61).

The boy's weak and valetudinarian constitution obviously changed entirely, expressed in Funakoshi Sensei's comment that "my teacher, Master Itosu, had a body that could be likened to a cast-iron torso . . . The human body can be developed with training into such a powerful body as that of Master Itosu" (Funakoshi 1973, p. 240). The weak, feeble and fragile child transformed completely through the training of karate-jutsu.

Born into a family of the Ryukyu gentry, and thus introduced at an early age to the martial arts by his father, "he thought [karate-jutsu] would be good training for improving his health and strengthening his body" (Itosu Buyuden 1915, in McCarthy 2018, p. 43). Consequently, at the age of fourteen or fifteen young Itosu Sensei asked the-then famous and cherished Matsumura Sokon Sensei for training, was accepted by the latter, commuted regularly to Matsumura Sensei's residence to train karate-jutsu, and "within his first year of training he was transformed beyond all recognition" (ibid.).

The lasting impact such a transformation from weak and sick to healthy and strong has on a young person's self-esteem, self-definition, and general attitude toward life cannot be overestimated. It is enormous, and it is the result of the psychological drive of compensation. "Rising from a permanently more or less felt inferiority towards perfection is the driving force, the essential root per se of human motivation" (Bayer 2000, p. 73; author's translation).[14]

---

14. "Das allen seelischen Handlungen inhärente ‚nach-oben-wollen' aus der permanent mehr oder weniger stark erlebten Minderwertigkeit hin zur Vollkommenheit ist die treibende Kraft, die wirkliche Wurzel der Motivation des Menschen schlechthin" (Bayer 2000, p. 73).

Itosu Anko Sensei's personal experience matches the core reason for attending martial arts training pinpointed in a most recent empirical study, where "the aspiring practitioner found themselves lacking something and looked towards the martial arts to fill that void . . . interestingly this moment often came in youth" (Kane/Wilder 2022, p. 292).

One can easily understand how Itosu Sensei's transformation from a weak and shy boy into a strong, masculine, and cherished leader with broad public admiration, which is the outcome of psychological self-actualization, not only led to Itosu Sensei's new positive self-definition at a young age, but also forcefully stimulated his calling in his later years. This calling was to support everyone, but especially young children, who were challenged with a comparable inferior starting position in life (psychologically speaking, not necessarily in terms of social status), like the one he faced, to help them surmount their disadvantages and gain the strength and self-confidence he had achieved for himself. It is interesting that Itosu Sensei wrote in his 1908 letter that karate-jutsu "practice strengthens muscle and bone, *improves the digestive organs*, and regulates blood circulation" (Itosu in McCarthy 2018, p. 26; italics are mine). Why explicitly point out the strengthening of *digestive* organs instead of organs in general? Why not mention lungs, heart, reflexes, or brain? An implicit conscious, or perhaps even subconscious, reference to his own stomach and digestion issues may not be implausible.

Felt social responsibility to make his own positive, life-changing experience accessible to others and thereby allow them to experience the same positive self-actualization is the "means to another underlying end beyond militarism" of Itosu Sensei's intentions suggested above. Social responsibility very often becomes a priority for successful people toward the end of their careers and in the later years of their life, expressing itself as volunteering in honorary offices, as taking active social roles in organizations and associations, as founding or promoting charities, and as giving back to communities by contributing in many ways to the common welfare. The desire to compensate, self-actualize, and further social interests are the strongest psychological motivations known to man and thus offer an additional perspective on Itosu Sensei's magnificent gift to the public. His calling provided nothing less than a path to a positive, life-changing experience to everyone.

* * * * *

Image 14: Correct (left) and Incorrect (right) Photographs of Itosu Anko Sensei and Portrait Created by Sensei and Artist Lara Chamberlain

This photo was discovered at the Okinawan Kochi Prefectural library and is considered to show Itosu Anko. The discovery was introduced in 2019.

From its discovery, published in Okinawa Times in 2006, until 2019 this photo was assumed to show Itosu Anko Sensei but it actually shows the fencing instructor Miyake Sango instead.

http://okic.okinawa/en/archives/news/p2666

Consequence Two:
The Initial Unity of Kata and Kumite Separated into Unconnected Sport Disciplines

Each and every one of the legendary Okinawan masters teach that karate-jutsu training has to be an *inextricable unit consisting of kata practice* (individual training of offensive and defensive moves arranged in a specific pattern) *and kumite practice* (two-person training to apply *kata* moves in combat). In Volume 1 it was shown that a large part of today's karatedo training, in opposition to this advice, broke up this unity and almost exclusively focuses on practicing *kata* (p. 111f) as a new physical-meditative path of individual improvement. Karate-jutsu, however, "must be practiced without forgetting the existence of the opponent or opponents seeking the opportunity to attack from every angle and in every possible way. The preparation for this attack cannot be achieved through the mastery of *kata* alone. So, practice of *kumite* (sparring) is needed . . . to develop the ability to read an opponent's mind" (Nagamine 1976, p. 246).

Losing the unity of *kata* concepts and their application in *kumite* by practicing *kata* exclusively implies that the latter is an independent and isolated discipline of its own. And indeed, due to specific rules and regulations, sports-karate went this way and separated the two approaches. Sports-karate developed its own moves and techniques independent from—and sometimes even contrasting with—its ancient antecedents, thus paralleling the development that other combat sports underwent too, when for instance fencing moved away from its initial lethal martial purpose to become a highly regulated game. Consequently, in sports-karate, *kata* moves changed from "creating the most possible damage to an opponent in the most effective way" to spectacularly exaggerated moves to emphasize athletic performance and even to using moves not connected to any realistic fighting concept and that would be therefore harmful to oneself in any form of combat, as illustrated in Image 15.

The other side of the coin is that *kumite*, the two-person fight training, separated itself completely from *kata* concepts by excluding target areas, by creating another narrow rule-set, and by introducing the one-point-scoring system for competition. This *kumite* development produced the need for new techniques to hit permitted target areas, and competitors needed to focus on speed to tag an opponent rather than

Image 15: Spectacularly Exaggerated Sports-Karate Moves Are Not Realistic Fighting Concepts

By comparing the two photographs it is easy to understand what a beautiful target the high-kicking sports karateka on the left would offer to his karate-jutsu opponent for a quick snap kick-counter with the front leg (left photo). The preferred target area is clearly demonstrated in the right photograph by Miyagi Chojun (right photo on the left) who counters Kyoda Juhatsu Sensei's attack with this kind of very effective, and supposedly fight-ending, snap kick.

to damage vulnerable target areas: "karate competition is a sport, and for that reason some of the most dangerous techniques are banned and all techniques must be controlled. Trained adult competitors can absorb relatively powerful blows on muscled areas such as the abdomen, but the fact remains that the head, face, neck, groin, and joints are particularly susceptible to injury. Therefore any technique which results in injury may be penalized unless caused by the recipient" (WKF 2020, p. 16).

On the other hand, an independent scoring system for *kata*, separated from scoring *kumite*, was developed, where "the judges will evaluate the performance based on the two major criteria of 'technical performance' and 'athletic performance'" (ibid., p. 39).

Understandably, the entire purpose of combat karate-jutsu had to be abandoned in sports-karate to avoid injuries while playing games; this refers to *kata* competition as well as to *kumite* competition. More details will be offered below, but at this point a valid summation seems to be that *in sports-karate there is no* kumite *included anymore in* kata—*and there is no* kata *included anymore in* kumite.

Playing games, on the other hand, has its own merit and reason to exist, as has been pointed out several times in this text. It just should not be confused with practicing a martial art and there is absolutely no need to philosophically reconnect modern sports-karate with its ancient combat form.

Kumite's Changed Role and Purpose in Sports Karate
The earlier-mentioned traditional training method of *tegumi* and the one mentioned in this chapter, *kumite*, are closely related: "*kumi-te*" is actually the term "*te-gumi*" backwards where the syllable "*gu*" turned into "*ku*."

From the 1920s until today, basically all Okinawan karate-jutsu masters developed their *kumite* exercises, i.e., a set of "receive and give" moves, to help students developing the basic technical skills needed to fight an attacking adversary. Since fighting is based on a group of fundamental principles and on the parameters of the human body, these concepts created by different masters show similarities, which can easily be spotted when comparing some classic sets, e.g., Motobu Choki Sensei's twenty drills (Motobu 2020, p. 112-149) and the ones in *Shorin Ryu*, for instance, in Kyan Sensei's *Seibukan* (Shimabukuro/Smith 2020, p. 351ff), or in Nagamine Sensei's *Matsubayashi Ryu* (Nagamine 1976, p. 246ff), or in Nakazato Sensei's *Kobayashi Ryu*, which I practice.

Kumite is trained in its three forms of:
(a) *Ippon kumite* in karate-jutsu teaches concepts to successfully interrupt attacks, create damage, and thus prevent opponents from continuing their attack. Hence, *ippon kumite* is not just a drill to learn techniques, which, as Sensei Dan Smith, 9th Dan *Shorin Ryu Seibukan* (see footnote 7 in Chapter 1), pointed out to me, is a wide-spread misconception about *ippon kumite* in modern karate practice; it rather is a way to end a fight.
(b) *Renzoku* or *yakusoku kumite* are pre-arranged, scenario-based partner drills. This training approach did not exist until the 1970s. Solely using this form of training to prepare oneself for self-defense carries the risk of developing a mindset of impractical attack scenarios, of rules and of compliant training partners. Such practices alone do not achieve their goal of self-defense.

(c) *Jiyu kumite* is often called free fighting; today the fighters may wear more or less protective gear as introduced in Japanese karatedo; in the old days Okinawans did not, but there were and there are guidelines for not injuring the partner.

After gaining familiarity with the basic techniques of fighting and after having reached a reasonably good understanding of timing and distance, students may move toward training sets and exercises beyond *yakusoku kumite* that more closely resemble real combat, where moves are executed with full or with reduced speed and power; with full contact, controlled contact, or without contact, but with less or no restriction of target areas or of techniques used. In these combat versions of classic training techniques, which are no longer common in most of today's karatedo practice, *tegumi* and *kumite* are executed as "free fighting"—albeit with specific rules to avoid injuries, but without all the limiting restrictions of sports-karate (see Volume 1, p. 86ff).

Hence, Okinawans did test their combative skills before competitions in Japan were developed. They could participate on an individual basis in a real fight as a challenge match (*kakedameshi*). The aim of these matches was for students to find their own weakness so that they could improve their art. The better fighter paced himself to the other person's level, and neither of the fighters tried to deliberately injury the other one (Swennen 2009, p. 30). On the master level, however, challenge fights could be serious combat, in rare cases fought to the bitter end. In addition, many karateka tested their skills—or were forced to prove their skills—outside the dojo, e.g., in nightlife scenarios or in encounters with criminals. Stories of such fights involving Matsumura Sensei, Itosu Sensei, Asato Sensei, and Motobu Sensei were orally handed down.

As mentioned, *kata* and its application in *kumite* were once an inseparable unit. We find this unity today in traditional karate-jutsu, not just in traditional *tegumi/kumite*, but in other modern applications too; for example, in 10th Dan *Shorin Ryu Shorinkan* Yamashita Tadashi Sensei's fighting system *Suikendo*, one of today's most advanced karate-jutsu combat systems. Yamashita Tadashi Sensei used the old ways of *kata*—*Kihon, Naihanchi, Passai, Kusanku*—and modernized the teaching of their applications by creating an "endless" sequence of moves he calls "fists flowing like water." In training sessions I had the privilege to attend with Sensei Yamashita himself and with other sensei of Yamashita International Budo Association, the traditional training method of two-person *kumite* was exclusively used to practice the application of offensive and defensive *kata* moves in their most realistic combat simulation possible.

This training setting matches—in my understanding—some of the classic ways of *tegumi*, where the opponents faced each other with their forearms crossed (see Image 16) and where, after the "start" command was given, the adversaries challenged and fought each other by trying to find an opening and successfully apply a *kata* move while using hard-style, short movements. In this way, *tegumi/kumite*, the ancient two-person-training method, embodies the traditional way to use *kata* concepts in fighting and to hone their applications.

"The closer a competition format is to a real fight, the more dangerous it becomes. The safer the competition is, the further it distances itself from actual combat. There is always a trade-off between safety and realism" (Swennen 2009, p. 25). Karate was introduced from Okinawa to the mainland mostly to Japanese university students. These young men preferred to challenge each other instead of just training *kata* and *bunkai* and thus initiated karate's transformation from a martial art into a sport with light contact rules on the Japanese mainland. In contrast, the Okinawans continued training karate as a martial art.

The first national competition for students was held in November 1957, where twenty-nine universities participated (ibid. p. 32). Then, in 1964, the Japanese Karate Federation was established and confirmed karate's status as a sport with light contact (*sundome*) rules. The Okinawans saw this format of competition some years later for the first time, when they were allowed to travel freely to the Japanese mainland. Hence, most Okinawans were not exposed to the idea of organizing competitions in a sparring format before the 1970s. "The new *sundome* competitions differed substantially from the old *kakedameshi*, as the karateka were not allowed to really hit each other anymore and the referees decided who wins, often in a confusing matter. The Okinawans initially resisted and criticized the new competition format strongly, but succumbed after a while and applied the new rules" (ibid., p. 33).

When looking at the rules and regulations of sports-karate, one may assume that the traditional ways are preserved in its *kumite* discipline. Isn't a score awarded when a technique is performed to an allowed target area with a) good form, b) sporting attitude, c) vigorous application, d) awareness/*zanshin*, e) good timing, and f) correct distance (WKF 2020, p. 11)? This sounds like combat-adequate technique

Image 16: Genuine Okinawan Karate-jutsu Kumite:
Miyagi Chojun and Kyoda Juhatsu in the early 1900s

This famous historic photograph presents a time capsule of classic Okinawan Naha-Te Karate: practitioners trained and acquired fighting skills without showing any ranks or belts. No specific training attire was requested, students wore whatever came in handy to work out in the island's muggy-hot climate. Research suggests that *tegumi* was practiced using two-person training methods that linked basic techniques to defensive applications and from which the pre-arranged, formal *kumite* of today was derived. The stance Miyagi Chojun Sensei (left) uses was taught to me by my sensei, Noel Smith, as "sparring-stance," a position that allows immediate movement in any direction due to 50/50 weight spread between both legs. Kyoda Juhatsu Sensei (right) supposedly blocks and attacks and therefore has turned his sparring stance into a high forward stance with his right knee in line above his toes and stretched back leg. Both karateka have their feet flatfooted and anchored on the ground; there is no hopping or bouncing around like in today's sports-karate *kumite*.

"Juhatsu started training with Kanryo Higaonna one month before Chojun Miyagi entered Kanryo Higaonna's dojo. They were born within months of each other and were often paired together in training" (Izumikawa 2020).

application, although the allowed target areas, or scoring areas, are limited to a) head, b) face, c) neck, d) abdomen, e) chest, f) back, and g) side (ibid.).

A closer look, however, reveals that in sports-karate *the entire scoring system is based on creating illusions* instead of factual applications. It's based on the fact that athletes create an impression; hence the reality of fighting may be better approxmiated in other combat sports like boxing or mixed martial arts. For instance, whereas in karate-jutsu "good" or "correct" is easily validated as "most effective" through the impact a move creates, there is no option to validate "good form," "good timing," or "correct distance" in sports-karate *kumite* other than to compare it to an ideal picture of an athletic dance where correctness is defined by the Japanese karate associations as a specific position. The athletes have to create the impression of *zanshin* (relaxed alertness); they have to create the impression of vigorously hitting—as soon as they would actually hit more or less vigorously, they are disqualified. Hence, in competitions, the winner is not always the better fighter, but it is the one who makes the best impression.[15]

Creating impressions instead of actually fighting allows the flimsy stances/positions to be witnessed in sports-karate *kumite*, which are quite different to the solid, grounded, toe-grabbing basis necessary to deliver a fight-ending technique in karate-jutsu. But when it is outlawed to damage an opponent, speedy, fencing moves with tagging contact are needed to create the impression of hitting hard, instead of actually hitting hard. Hence, again, impressions replace impact.

Footwork in the form of moving on toes increases the speed of moves for both, for steps and for punches, and stepping quickly out of the way of an adversary's attack (often backward instead of angled) turns out to be the core sport-*kumite* defense rather than parrying or block-striking. In short, though moving on the balls of feet rather than flatfooted is the way to step in karate-jutsu as well, *footwork strategies taken from the sport of boxing replace stances/positions of karate-jutsu in sports-karate's* kumite. This, of course, makes sense under the sport's ruleset. When it is necessary to constantly move to avoid being a stationary target for a tagging contact, bouncing around, dancing, and

---

15. As shown by the example from the 2020 Olympics of Tareg Hamedi, a Saudi Arabian who delivered a head kick with good stance and timing, but knocked out his Iranian opponent Sajad Ganjzadeh during the +75kg men's *kumite* final. He was disqualified and received the silver medal, whereas his knocked-out opponent was awarded gold.

tip-toeing back and forth beats calmness of the body and mind. When continuous flimsy impressions of attacking moves provide the highest probability for a victory, speedy evasion of an attack beats the kind of bone-breaking defense taught in karate-jutsu. And last but not least, when certain target areas are outlawed, new and modified techniques, like high kicks and roundhouse kicks, need to be developed to create the impression of better attacking the allowed and high-scored target areas, which, however, ends up in combat-wise ridiculous moves, and which completely change the ancient art (example Image 15).

These new techniques, footwork, steps, mindsets, strategies, tactics, and positions used in today's sports-karate's *kumite* illustrate best the discipline's far-reaching separation from karate-jutsu's *kata*: *there is no* kata *anymore in sports-karate's* kumite.

Kata's Changed Role and Purpose in Sports-Karate

Taken the other way round, *there is no* kumite *anymore in sports-karate's* kata *practice* either, as will be explained below. "*Kata* should be taught as close as possible to its use in reality (i.e., actual combat) and not selectively to increase strength (i.e., for physical training purposes)" (Motobu 2020, p. 39). This way *kata* and *kumite* are interwoven, *kata* and its applications in *kumite* were initially the two sides of the same coin.

Traditional *kata* is furthermore a "time capsule for transmission of knowledge" which was kept secret and "passed down both orally and kinesthetically from one generation to the next" (McCarthy 1998a, p. 36). Since the true application of moves were hidden underneath obvious moves (Volume 1, pp. 68ff), only a few trusted adepts within a karate-jutsu system are able to correctly decipher these hidden concepts, which were camouflaged in various ways and by several methods, as illustrated by the following strategies to hide the real technique in *kata*. These five ways are based on Sensei Ballardini's explanations (*Bugeisha* 2021, Issue #10, pp. 8–9) with examples I have added:

1. *Showing only a partial movement and not the complete technique*, which may result in a *kata* move without any meaning (an example could be a large circular move with the left arm to the right hip while stepping to the right as in *Passai Dai*, when there may actually be an arm manipulation with the right arm, supported by the left hand/arm, taking place).

2. *Introducing a move closely paralleling another one* in a way that it would be regularly misinterpreted (an example could be various defensive closed-fist blocks as in *Passai*, which actually should be attacking spear-hand moves).
3. *Showing the reversed movements of the real application* (an example could be parries while stepping forward, as in *Kusanku*, whereas defensive moves would be done while stepping backward or out of the way).
4. *Teaching a* kata *separated from the principles* which define the application of its techniques and using only elementary applications (the entire *Naihanchi kata* series with its restricted moves to the side into a single stance/position and its carefully hidden real applications may be an example for this method).
5. *Teaching fake versions of katas* until a student was considered mature enough to be taught the real thing (an example may be all the *kata* created for physical education purposes in schools, like the *Pinan kata* series, which are heavily based on *Kusanku* and on *Chinto*).

So, in spite of the fact that it is not too difficult for a karateka to mechanically learn a classical *kata* of karate-jutsu, it is quite difficult to uncover the hidden and real techniques and their applications for everyone outside of a traditional system who does not know the code to decipher it. "It goes without saying that when the Japanese tried to steal Okinawan karate, what they brought home were only the *kata* without the real application, which they believed they could 'reconstruct' . . . fatally falling into the trap of a literal interpretation of the movement based on appearances" (ibid., p. 9).

Correspondingly, *in sports-karate, kata is taken at face value*, and often the true purpose of a move or a sequence is entirely misunderstood. Today's *kata* interpretations are in many cases no longer connected to the *bunkai* of their classic version. This separates sports-karate's *kata* from *kumite* and transforms *kata* into an athletic dance, into a separate discipline of its own, unconnected to the discipline of *kumite* and unconnected to combat.

Empirical evidence for this statement is amply available for every karate-jutsu practitioner who participates in or just observes a sports-karate tournament. One salient example for me is the use of the *kiai*, i.e., the method of focusing all energy into a move. In doing so, a karateka concentrates all of his or her internal energy into the application of an offensive technique by combining mental concentration with body movement and with exhaling. This kind of flexing while strongly breathing out may create a distinct tonal sound,[16] like a shout, but not exactly. The application, the "work" in its physics sense, i.e., the attack, happens during the move, shortly after the technique's explosion point, which is located at about one-third to two-thirds before the move's completion and it is underlain by flexing and breathing out as *kiai* from the explosion point of the move to its end. For *kata* demonstrations in tournaments, however, this *kiai* seems to have been turned into a Western misconception of a "spirit shout" or "battle cry" and is often added as a symbol of dedication after the completion of a move instead of using its enforcing power during the move. Again, the "physics work," the application of a technique, happens in karate-jutsu during the move, not at the endpoint of a move. In sports karate's kata demonstration, by contrast, the endpoint of a move, the final position, combined with a battle-cry is presented to be judged. This often leads to artificial breaks of a *kata*'s flow after a move is completed, leading in turn to interruptions which have nothing to do with combat and which would actually open up a karateka for damaging counters during a fight. The purpose of these interruptions is to point out correct positions, highlight athleticism, and exaggerate those positions to the judges; it has nothing to do with *bunkai*.

Other quite obvious examples for *bunkai* misconceptions in sports-karate's *kata* demonstrations can be found in modern interpretations of *Passai* and *Kusanku*. In terms of *Passai*, some of those simultaneously blocking, *nukite* eye-stabbing, and throw-preparing grappling moves with both arms are now presented as a beautiful dance-move while placing both open hands gracefully stomach-high to the side, instead of its initial eye-high powerful block-strike-grab combination. In terms of *Kusanku*, I witnessed how a turning move into squatting down with a backward stretched left leg is taken at face value and transformed into a flying side-kick to the backside. However, in its classic application this move may be actually camouflaging a multi-optional takedown applied

---

16. It has to be noted that there are martial arts that use *kiai* silently, for example some forms of the Japanese art of swordsmanship *ken-jutsu*.

forward,[17] not backward (see hiding technique #3 above), and so on and so forth; these are just two examples out of a very long list.

The rules and regulations for *kata* demonstrations state—with the best intentions—that *"kata* is not a dance or theatrical performance. It must adhere to the traditional values and principles. It must be realistic in fighting terms and display concentration, power, and potential impact in its techniques. It must demonstrate strength, power, and speed—as well as grace, rhythm, and balance" (WKF 2020, p. 41). However, whereas it may be quite possible to validly judge the obvious criteria of athletic performance like "strength, speed, and balance" (ibid. p. 39), how to judge the adequacy of a karateka's understanding of the *kata*'s combat application, when these applications itself are unknown or misunderstood? It only seems possible to me if it is indeed accepted that *kata* ought to be taken at their face value, i.e., to focus on their *bunkai* misinterpretation, on their *omote* (surface) purpose. Then it is possible to look at a sports-*kata* demonstration in terms of athletic performance and call it "technical performance," i.e., looking at *kata* performance not in terms of showing the real combat techniques but in terms of *assessing the* kata's *face value* of "a. Stances; b. Techniques; c. Transitional movements; d. Timing; e. Correct breathing; f. Focus; g. Conformance: Consistence [*sic*] in the performance of the KIHON of the style (Ryu-ha) in the *kata*" (ibid.). And this is how *kata* judging it is done today.

In the Japanese karatedo styles of sports-karate's *kata* competition, "the movements of the classical *kata*, which in the meantime had been modified and simplified, were interpreted in a completely different way by introducing applications and *bunkai* invented from scratch, very far from the real applications handed down by the school of origin" (Ballardini, *Bugeisha* 2021, Issue #10, p. 9). Okinawan karate-jutsu *kata* that were accepted to be used in competition under WKF/JKF rules were listed in the early 1970s as (Japanese) *Shito-Ryu kata* "and have since been technically and terminologically manipulated. In other words, there are many *kata* that were pilfered from other (Okinawan) schools, while at the same time these schools of origin could not participate under JKF/WKF rules except [if] they adjusted to the manipulated techniques" (Quast 2020b, n.p.). That led to a serious dispute in

---

17. Detailed and illustrating examples for this move's possible applications are to be found for instance on Sensei Jesse Enkamp's site
https://www.karatebyjesse.com/11-useful-bunkai-for-the-kusanku-ninja-move/.

the early 1980s between the Okinawan karate associations, spearheaded by Nagamine Shoshin Sensei, and the Japanese Karate Federation (Volume 1, pp. 25ff) which is still unresolved today and has perpetuated considerable animosity between Okinawan and Japanese karate ever since that time with no resolution in sight. As Japanese karatedo in the 1950s–1980s was "industrialized" into "large scale production" and developed—as planned and organized by JKF/WKF—into a huge, multibillion-dollar business (see the section "Postwar Industrialization and Commercialization of Japanese Karatedo" in Chapter 6), mainstream karate officials were neither interested in resolving this above-mentioned dispute, nor in rectifying the thievery of Okinawan *kata* and their transformation into sports forms.

Countless young people do love sports-karate and represent a never-ending wordwide supply of customers and prospects with many Japanese and Okinawan beneficiaries in this business (Quast 2020b, n.p.). So, the process was continued with more *kata* being pilfered from genuine Okinawan karate-jutsu, accepted for competition and labeled under the Japanese *Shito Ryu* system "from 60 in 2012 to 89 in 2013 and to 102 in 2020" (ibid.). This way, WKF/JKF actually created a new unified *kata* and *kumite* style of sports-karate; a new style with its own aesthetics and technical logic.

"It was the above described system of false labeling in combination with technical manipulation that bestowed on Japan (including Okinawa) tons of gold medals, international fame, money, careers ... Seen from the perspective of athletes and coaches, one can hardly blame any of them for not protesting, especially because they never knew better and also—why would they care? Naturally, the industry's successes made the Japanese and Okinawans proud, so the results are considered to be very good" (ibid.).

Consequence Three:
The Modern Misconception about Avoiding a Fight at All Costs

There is another consequence of Japan's general attitude shift from prewar militarism toward the rejection of violence in martial arts and toward stressing the nation's contributions to world peace—and this refers to karate's often so-called "sacred" principle of "*karate ni sente nashi*" (there is no first attack/move in karate). The not-to-attack-first principle, like so many other karate components mentioned in this text and in Volume 1, is a modern invention. As recently pointed out, fresh from the printing press (Shimabukuro/Pellman 2022), and in line with numerous publications before that, prior to 1900 karate-jutsu was exclusively an art of unarmed self-defense, representing "the art of killing" (ibid.). Its practice was designed for life-or-death situations—it was essentially a way to restore or to prevent peace without avoiding violent means. Hence, the *"karate ni sente nashi"* principle is not, as believed by many, a traditional and genuine moral code of Okinawan martial arts. Quite the opposite, and though aimed at "peacemaking," the traditional moral code took into account that combat may be unavoidable and focused on ending it ultimately and as fast as possible.

The *"karate ni sente nashi"* phrase was (perhaps) created, but most certainly made famous, by Funakoshi Gichin Sensei, who postulated it as his most important ethical guideline for his students. His guideline, however, was and is entwined by possible misunderstandings (see Volume 1, pp. 18ff), which were already brought up, e.g. by Motobu Choki Sensei, in the prewar period at the time of the principle's promotion (see below), but which were especially further divulged after WWII.

The philosophical legitimization of having the skills to use lethal combat karate-jutsu concepts while living in a society where violence remains an unfortunate reality was explained in Volume 1 (pp. 61–63) with the metaphor that being (or acting like) a sheep does not prevent predators from attacking as long as the latter are to be found roaming. So, as long as there are lethal threats to be fended off, the use of all means necessary can be justified. Otsuka Hironori Sensei, student of Funakoshi Sensei in mainland Japan and founder of the Japanese *Wado Ryu* karate system, clarifies this use of karate, in line with the classic moral code, as follows: "If indeed it has to be used, then peace must be restored by all means. In order to do this, we must gain victory decisively. For this reason there is the instruction: if your skin is cut, cut the opponent's flesh; if your flesh is cut, cut the opponent's bone; if your bone is cut, cut the opponent's marrow [clarification by the author: this is a metaphor for 'to kill']– one must win regardless of life or death" (Otsuka, in Bittmann 2005, p. 111).

In contrast, the reason for the new postwar emphasis on a presumed peaceful aspect of martial arts becomes transparent when viewed through the lens of modern anti-war and anti-violence movements and mindsets. As laid out in Chapter 3, karate was misused during Japan's prewar militarism to create a nation-wide ferocious warrior spirit by focusing on a cold-hearted utilitarian philosophy of a truncated *bushido*. Merciless combat attitudes and unwavering dedication was promoted, whereas other, nobler parts of the Japanese warrior's code were neglected. During the attitude shift in postwar Japan away from this prewar militarism, karate was newly positioned in philosophical terms as a peaceful art of meditative athletics and was undergirded by those *bushido* virtues that were undervalued in the decades before, for instance, the virtues of rectitude and justice, of benevolence and compassion, of courtesy and politeness.

The sacred principle of not attacking first is to be seen in this context. Karatedo's new emphasis on peace, inaugurated by Funakoshi Sensei, was not created solely out of the goodness of his heart though; it was also a simple necessity to gain governmental permission for spreading the art all across mainland Japan. Funakoshi Sensei describes that early concerns were shared with him by the Tokyo's police force, concerns that karate could be used as an offensive weapon. He furthermore quotes a high-ranking police officer who, some years later, requested that he ensure that young men will not use the art inappropriately or even illegally (Funakoshi 1983, p. 109). Referring to this request, he states that "out of the tens of thousands who learned and practiced the art of karate in my dojo, there is not a single one known to me who would have used his skills illegally" (ibid.; translated by author).

The fact, surprising perhaps to some readers, that "highly verified accomplished martial artists are in fact paradoxically peaceable people" (Lloyd p. 20) is closely examined in Volume 1 and it was scientifically explained there how karate-jutsu competency leads to higher levels of self-control and reduces over-compensatory aggression by reducing self-doubt and its related sense of individual inferiority. New self-definitions based on the attainment of individual capabilities and the substantial reduction of fear are initiated through karate-jutsu training (Volume 1, pp. 62ff). Thus the saying is verified that "only people capable of great violence can be peaceful," and if karateka are not capable of great violence, they are not peaceful but harmless.

Karate-jutsu's Initial Moral Code
When looking at the history of philosophical conceptions in martial arts through a scientific lens, it has to be noted that "moral systems are external to the martial arts, not intrinsic to them and, in fact, the philosophy of martial arts may have nothing to do with morality at all" (Lloyd p. 21f). In other words, martial arts were initially understood as a "value-neutral tool," like a weapon, and the specific code or moral guideline for how to use this tool, how to handle this weapon, was developed separately, in a scholarly fashion, and outside of the art, not within the art.

This initial understanding never questioned the use of martial arts as such; instead, it stressed its benefits and constructive social function as peacekeeping and as supporting the greater good of humans living together. For Okinawan karate-jutsu, this means, expressed as the guiding "seven virtues" by Matsumura Sokon Sensei in the late 1880s—based on Chinese articulations from 2,200 years earlier (Quast 2020a, p. 20)—that "true martial arts [1] prohibits violence, [2] makes warriors courageous, [3] supports the people, [4] renders meritorious services, [5] helps people to live in peace, [6] harmonizes the masses, and [7] allows assets to prosper" (Matsumura 2020, p. 14; numbering is mine).

Though unspecified violence is forbidden by these early ethical principles, they also do not question or offer reasons for tempering the use of martial arts as a combat art, which Matsumura Sensei calls the "true martial arts" (*bugei no bugei*), by any ethical restraint. He contrasts this real karate-jutsu to two other more debatable forms, namely to the "martial arts of scholars" (*bugei* of the scholars), which is the art of a theorist and a dreamer, one may say, where "the rules of fighting and self-protection against an enemy assault" are unknown, and "dedication to training weakens to become superficial, like a dance" (ibid., p. 13). This kind of practice is in Matsumura Sensei's eyes as inadequate as "the martial arts in name only," which is the one of a player and braggart, it could be said, where "there is no real ability to get things done"; "they debate" and "unsettled, they only talk about victory" (ibid.).

The "*bugei* of the scholars," in combination with the "martial arts in name only"—and both obviously do not just exist today but were already around in the early years of the Meiji Restoration—seem like a foretelling of the coming rise of non-martial karate versions. The

Japanized version of karatedo seems to fit the bill as martial arts of scholars since the "ways of scholarship," and thus the *bugei* of scholars, is characterized as the practice of individuals educated in 1) poem and prose, 2) in moral teachings, and 3) in Confucianism" (ibid., p. 11f), all of which characterize the path of postwar karatedo (Volume 1, pp. 29ff; Bittmann 2005, p. 24ff; Meissl 2021)—the path of emphasizing spiritual and mental developments over martial applications. Comparably, sports-karate seems to fit the bill as a derivation of martial arts "in name only," documented by its separation of *kata* and *kumite* and by its reinvention of new techniques and new interpretations independent from, and even contradicting, classic *bunkai*, as well as by its sole focus on winning and victory.

Both inadequate martial arts forms, the one of dreamers and the one of players, show the *common denominator of missing combat experience*, of exercising a certain version of the art without understanding its application in real life. Dreamers with their *bugei* of scholars theoretically know something and glorify philosophical conceptions without having the skill to act on them in a violent situation. Martial arts in name only seems comparable to the attitude and bragging of some wannabe warriors who only play tag in paintball games and thereafter believe they know how to fight—without ever having been exposed to the lethal challenges, terrifying sounds, disturbing smells, and overwhelming emotions of an actual battlefield.

With his elaborations, Matsumura Sensei strongly undergirds the considerations presented in Volume 1 about Japanized karate's misconceptions (pp. 28ff), and he even seems to prognosticate, early on, the development of the art's later variations as karate-jutsu, karatedo, and sports-karate.

Hence—in bringing it all together in terms of karate-jutsu's moral code—when violence is forbidden but true karate-jutsu is forged through real-life combat experience, the early moral code for karate-jutsu did not involve a principle of "not to attack first" but a "just cause" principle for attack. It was focused on a situation where a first attack is not just justified but actually needed. Hence, Eastern martial arts philosophy and Western ethics seem to share a comparable principle justifying the use of violence, which was formulated for Western culture by Saint Augustine some 1,600 years ago and further developed by Saint Thomas Aquinas 800 years later, as the "Just War Doctrine" (Regan 2013).

"The thing called martial spirit is never practiced to beat up other people without reason . . . you should not cause harm indiscriminately, and if you are forced to, that is, when it is unavoidable, and the enemy tries to harm you, . . . it is essential to dominate the enemy, and to dominate the enemy, you must move (attack) first" (Motobu 2020, p. 109). Motobu Sensei's statement refers to the fact that true combat does not have rules. There is no "sportsmanship" in lethal combat and the term "fairness" does not apply when it comes to surviving a life-threatening situation. As soon as any kind of rules are implemented, combat changes into some kind of game. Life-protecting fighting is no game. Life-protecting fighting is not pretty. Life-protecting fighting is pure violence and merciless full-power action.

Modern Alterations to Karate-jutsu's Initial Moral Code
But even for such a life-threatening situation, Funakoshi Sensei would not promote or allow a first attack, using the argument that "as soon as karate comes into play the situation turns into a matter of life and death . . . and how can we justify becoming involved in such kinds of confrontations?" (Funakoshi 1983, p. 110; my translation). That is all well and good, but how about a situation that has already turned into a matter of life and death? For instance, when a karateka is dealing with a lethal challenge while protecting others from an imminent lethal attack. With his interpretation, Funakoshi Sensei explicitly contradicts Motobu Sensei's advice when he states verbatim that even for such a just cause karate cannot be used. He rather suggests that the just-cause-argument resembles a "complete misunderstanding of true karate" (ibid., p. 110; my translation).

However, in spite of Funakoshi Sensei's position, Motobu Sensei's argument is definitely to be taken seriously; not only because he is a senior karate authority, but also because he was one of the few sensei in modern times with extensive grim street-fight experience and who faced life-threatening challenges to ultimate fights by other masters. These are combat experiences not reported in the same way of Funakoshi Sensei. Quite to the contrary, the examples Funakoshi Sensei gives for his "true karate" in terms of avoiding a fight are not situations leading to lethal combat but examples of situations of brawls in the making. These kinds of threats are easier to retreat from than situations where actual lethal threats evolve and where leaving the scene is no longer an option. Motobu Sensei went even so far as to characterize

Funakoshi Sensei's practice as "copying only the outer portion" of what his masters taught him and thus "misleading others into believing him to be an expert," which, in Motobu Sensei's view, he is not.

Motobu Sensei's perspective and interpretation of the not-to-attack-first principle is shared by other Okinawan masters before WWII and in the postwar period as well. *Seibukan* Headmaster Shimabukuro Zenryo Sensei explained half a century ago to Sensei Dan Smith that there is indeed a justified use of karate-jutsu, which is to save your family. Either by standing up to someone who attacks it or by defending yourself if attacked, which then refers back to protecting your family (phone conversation 04/26/22).

An Okinawan newspaper article from 1914 shows that not only Motobu Choki Sensei but Funakoshi Gichin's important and cherished sensei Asato Anko also promoted a different view than his famous student when he states that "if an opponent attacks, one absorbs the attack and counters simultaneously and equivalently. In questions of survival . . . however, or if parents, wife, or children are affronted, if the enemy comes close and compels, a first move is allowed" (Asato 1914, p. 20). Again we find the importance of protecting the family in Asato Anko Sensei's point, which contradicts his student and represents a more realistic approach to lethal combat, where "they don't hand out silver medals," as Sensei Doug Perry, 10th Dan *Shorin Ryu Kensankai*, retired US Marine Corps Major, and student of Shiroma Jiro Sensei, put it during a training camp I attended.

Hence, we cannot exclude the possibility that in this ongoing dispute about the "*karate ni sente nashi*" principle, Matsumuro Sensei's categories of true martial arts versus the one of theorists come into play.

In bringing everything together and to understand the no-first-attack-principle correctly, the principle should perhaps be rephrased into "karateka aim at not attacking first, but they may move first," in case a "not yet physical" attack is already underway as a clear intention. Hence, karateka will of course defend themselves by all means necessary if attacked, including being the target of an attack that has not yet taken on a physical form but which has already begun in intent. They will use pre-emptive strikes, which may be blocks or parries at the same time, and other offensive techniques.

In Volume 1 (p. 19f) it was pointed out that *the physical move of an attack is the end point in a series of preceding intents, gestures, and other announcements,* called "telegraphing" in combat karate. These occurrences constitute a timeline during a real-life attack, leaving an attacked karateka ample time and opportunities to act pre-emptively, *including the option of leaving the scene* to avoid a fight altogether. But if leaving the scene is not an option, and now karateka would wait until the opponent's assault in its physical form is finally launched, they would irresponsibly sacrifice all their advantages in a desperate situation.

Karateka do not start a fight, they always end a fight. They aim to not attack first, but they may move first when reacting to a nonphysical pre-fight tell. Only in this way is the "no first attack in karate" principle realistically related to combat. It is in this sense that the principle was understood by Okinawan karate masters like Asato Anko Sensei, Motobu Choki Sensei, Kyan Chotoku Sensei, Chibana Choshin Sensei, Shimabukuro Zenryo Sensei, Nakazato Shugoro Sensei, and others. Without this qualification, the "no first attack in karate" principle would be an unrealistic artificial construct and not a sound correlate of the goal of self-protection in the genuine Okinawan martial arts.

Though refraining from speculative exegesis, the possibility cannot be excluded that political reasons played an important role already in prewar Japan, which made it wise to emphasize the no-first-attack principle in support of karate's official recognition on the mainland and its approval by the police force. Such reasons, as well as socio-cultural attitude shifts, definitely played a huge role in postwar Japan when the image of karate as some kind of a "peaceful martial art" was created as a sports-related, character-building "gift to the world" (JKA "Philosophy" tab, n.d., n.p.). Only with this connotation was the practice permitted by the ruling US-military and only with this connotation was the creation of a sports-karate business realistically achievable. Karate then came to realize the business goal of accessing new consumer groups who were more interested in the art's recreational and athletic possibilities than in its martial roots (see the section "Postwar Industrialization and Commercialization of Japanese karatedo" in Chapter 6).

Not one single fellow karateka I asked about why they sought martial arts training answered that they intended to "develop their personality." The answers I received rather matched the responses listed in a recent study about why martial artists were motivated to start their training. "Common answers to this question included, 'I was bullied.' 'I got in a fight and I lost, so I needed to become better at fighting.' 'I was small.' 'I was weak.' 'I was raped.' 'I needed self-confidence'" (Kane/Wilder 2022, p. 292).

Violence is unfortunately still a part of modern life; it is not extinct. The average person who is not confronted regularly with violence may have a difficult time accepting that reality. Nevertheless, it takes the form of domestic violence, as violence against women and children, as criminal activity, as human trafficking, as home invasions, as gang violence including their initiation rituals, as bashing individuals of a specific race or religion, and randomly on the streets in various forms. "According to the US Bureau of Justice Statistics, less than half (41%) of violent victimizations are actually reported to law enforcement authorities. Nevertheless, based on the best data we can uncover from crime victimization surveys, somewhere between 1.1 and 1.4 million people a year are seriously physically assaulted (generally feloniously) and an additional 4.0 million people a year become the victim of simple assault (generally misdemeanors) in the United States" (Kane/Wilder 2022, p. 63). However, "statistics don't matter one iota if we find ourselves confronted by someone who thinks we would make a good victim" (ibid. p. 64), so one needs to be prepared in the sense that "it would be better to be a skilled fighter in a garden than a skilled gardener in a fight."

Almost always when innocent people suffer, violence comes as a surprise, unexpected and unannounced. When confronted that way, passivity or non-violence does not stop the predator. Examples show that there is absolutely no guarantee that anyone will be there to help the victim, even if there were bystanders. And since most of those potential attackers are not older, overweight individuals who avoid the gym, but rather slim and trim males (in the vast majority of cases), in the prime of their lives, violence needs to be reflected and countered with an immediate and sufficient, attack-ending, defense-counter.

Based on a pre-emptive block-strike concept, as well as on the concept that pre-physical indicators show that an attack is already underway, the two viewpoints of "there is no first attack in karate" and "an attack with a just cause is acceptable" coexist and are not mutually exclusive.

Though these arguments may be accepted by many readers, it is to be expected that sheltered individuals, who never faced actual combat or who never encountered ill-willed people in a violent situation, will have a hard time understanding the parallelism of both approaches.

The vast majority of innocent people, including many karateka, have never faced a violent situation, nor even witnessed one. This does not change the fact that more than a few ill-willed people exist today and may have to be dealt with. The already quoted empirical study about martial artists reports that "it is common to engage in 2 to 5 fights over a lifetime." This led the authors to their conclusion that "while it may be possible to go a lifetime without facing any type of physical violence, most folks have a reasonable chance of needing their expertise to defend themselves at some point" (Kane/Wilder 2022, p. 68).

This fact was unequivocally brought into the public eye over the last decade not just by political demonstrations that started peacefully but got violently out of hand, but also by the light that has been shed recently on the fact that women, girls, and boys were and are physically and sexually harassed, trafficked, and abused. The "Me Too" Movement uncovered a widespread reality in athletics, the performing arts, schools, camps, and the military, which shows a magnitude of disrespect and barbarism through emotional and physical violence that renders many speechless and angry (complemented by the fact of sexually

Image 17: Great Violence Still Exists in Modern Societies; It Is Not At All Extinct . . .

Photos Creative Commons

. . . either in its hidden form of violence, rape, and misuse of women (see text below by Dr. Joyce Trafton, 7th Dan *Goju Ryu Seibukai*), or in its public form of gang activities, crimes, brawls, and street fights that often have brutal, even deadly outcomes.

abused boys within allegedly honorable religious institutions). According to figures presented by the National Center for Injury Prevention and Control of the Centers for Disease Control and Prevention show that "nearly 1 in 5 women (18.3%) . . . in the United States have been raped at some time in their lives" (Black et. al. 2011, p. 1).), and these atrocities happened to them in their teens and twenties as "female victims of completed rape (79.6%) experienced their first rape before the age of 25; 42.2% experienced their first completed rape before the age of 18 years" (ibid., p. 2). When physical violence/stalking is included, "more than 1 in 3 women (35.6%) and more than 1 in 4 men (28.5%) in the United States have experienced rape, physical violence, and/or stalking by an intimate partner in their lifetime" (ibid., p. 2).

Teaching women and girls to defend themselves against domestic violence or against other predators needs a different approach than teaching men or boys. Besides differing physical capacities, there is a social definition of perceived gender roles in place, which supports a wide-spread assumption of universal differences between masculinity and femininity (Preddy n.d., n.p.). Such an attitude in turn unconsciously impacts behavior and training settings within a dojo. The traditional training approach cannot resolve this specific challenge; in particular, it cannot avoid flashbacks and their impact on practice and thus cannot successfully empower abused women and girls—although this very group urgently needs to learn how to defend themselves against (generally male) aggressors. There is another possible issue of mixed-sex training, because "whenever men and women were training together . . . a number of specifically gendered anxieties arose around touch. In particular, these tended to involve either an aversion to 'hurting' one's training partner, or a fear of sexual impropriety" (Channon/Jennings 2013, p. 5f), which would make training experience somewhat unrealistic for female karateka.

Dr. Joyce Trafton, 7th Dan *Goju Ryu Seibukai*, an experienced sensei, researcher, and educational expert who focuses on helping victimized women and girls, developed an appropriate self-defense approach for enabling her female students to successfully deal with those dangerous situations. She shares her insight in the following section.

> ### Learning to Bite: Karate-jutsu and Karatedo in Women's Self-Defense Training
> By Dr. Joyce Trafton,[*] 7th Dan Goju Ryu, Seibukai

Based on the experience of more than 80 years of joint martial arts training and teaching of two female instructors (Dr. Joyce Trafton, *Nanadan* [7th Dan] *Goju-Ryu Seibukai* and Denise Story, *Godan* [5th Dan] *Goju-Ryu Seibukai*), on discussions with male and female instructors and students, as well as on ideas expressed by non-participant females, we summarize major reasons and excuses that women have about training avoidance, some problems with current women's self-defense training, and suggestions for improvements. Furthermore, it is to help martial arts dojo investigate training discrepancies where males dominate all aspects of training and use negative and/or sexist language when addressing female participants. I know from personal experience, as do many other women, that a dojo is not always a safe training place for women. We remain silent about those unpleasant experiences so as not to shame anyone.

Our passion for teaching women and girls comes from our own experiences with attacks, those of family, and those of many friends. Such an experience is life changing. What has further driven our concern are news articles about the needless deaths of women and children and also women's life stories of sexual abuse and violence, some of which have taken decades to be shared. As we trained primarily women and children over the past several years, we became aware that women's defense is not like men's for many reasons and that some male instructors teach women unrealistically based on their male physique, engagement rules, and ego. We have also noted that rank does not guarantee the ability to teach.

Most girls learn early in life that they are to be timid, immobile, and giving. Therefore, as they grow older, they react to male aggression by freezing, fainting, or flailing their arms and legs uncontrollably. Seldom do they fight efficiently or flee deliberately. To overcome those unhelpful spontaneous reactions, women need to be in charge of their contexts (where, with whom, when, why, what) and they need to learn to adequately respond to intuitive urges, especially to fear. Thus, over time, women can be trained to develop strategies and the wisdom to cope with dangerous situations.

Most women were exposed to sexual harassment and perhaps sexual encounters as girls. When social media was not ubiquitous, most of the time the frightening encounters remained secret. I myself remember several occasions as a teen when men pulled up along the curb and exposed themselves, and an occasion when two high school boys lured my friend and me (then nine years of age) into a remote area where we were faced with an uncomfortable situation we did not understand, but our instincts told us to run. Nowadays, girls are even more exposed to danger because of the Internet, because of group activities that used to specialize in either male or female involvement but are now mixed, because of changes in public education that pushed sexual content even in elementary school, because of sexual content, violence, and perversion in the media. Female teens complain unsuccessfully about sexual advances and threats from boys and men in athletics, theater rehearsals, schools, camps, military environments, and other places. Ironically, the adult response even today is often an unhelpful "boys will be boys." There are two sexes, male and female, regardless of what gender people choose to be. Once either sex chooses to change to an opposite gender, they may increase their chances for abuse and attack. Some women who have been raped decide to become male in gender and do everything they can to avoid attention. Ironically, their choice oftentimes actually increases their danger for attack and abuse.

Research found that people embody their mindset and self-confidence with posture and may project vulnerability through body language as they walk down a street. So it is no surprise that psychopaths mention gait as a prevalent reason for target choice. Consequently, before any physical self-defenses are taught, basic awareness and safety are priorities; postural feedback encourages confident body language as directly impacting on how others perceive them. Applying the theme of posture to young women today, it is evident that poor posture, including while talking or texting on a cell phone, makes them look vulnerable, physically weak, and inadequately prepared for the realities of dating, dominance, and unexpected sexual encounters by male aggressors.

Women have many excuses for not participating in self-defense classes. Because of the media representation of karate as a challenging sport, many consider it outside their physical ability. They have doubtless watched martial arts movies where extreme physical fitness, speed, and high kicks are promoted. In fact, a recent comment from a group of women was that if self-defense were karate, they did not want to train. Consider also their plight as they walk into a dojo of mainly men. Then there are other excuses: no time, embarrassment because of size or weight, competition, the supposed advantage of concealed weapons, PTSD, and opinions that "my significant other will protect me." Adult education (andragogy) addressing these excuses is the best way to alter their perceptions of karate and encourage them to actively participate in their self-preservation.

Another experience that undermines women are challenges from related males (boyfriends, husbands, sons . . .) when demonstrating their newly acquired skills. In order to survive, females must attack male vulnerability; however, even males intimate with females felt such an approach "unreasonable." Techniques like throat punches, eye gouges, knee strikes, and other combat moves, were seen as not acceptable because "men don't fight that way." Unless in military combat, it looks like males have game-like rules of engagement that ultimately dictate dominance, but, in contrast, women fight male attackers not to dominate but to survive. Therefore, women's self-defense is closer to combat and no game at all. For a woman it requires an aggressive, unexpected response to defend herself using the aggressive techniques of karate-jutsu (grabbing, tearing, twisting, kicking, breaking, etc.) that disable the attacker. Women must attack male vulnerabilities in spite of male rules of engagement, but they need to be supported and encouraged by those men who matter in their lives.

Perhaps one of the most powerful deterrents for training is a woman's unresolved emotional baggage or emotional instability caused by negative experiences, such as childhood trauma, relational abuse, or other previous psychological or physical trauma. If such individuals participate in classes, everything may appear to be going well until they are faced with authentic practice or an actual attack. Then, past baggage may ascend from the unconscious causing fear and inadequate responses to the attack. Discussions on that matter may arise during class when a woman suffers flashbacks, which need to be addressed right away. Hence, women need "*kuchibushi*" [meaning here: time to talk and to comfort] to resolve deeply emotional issues that come up during training. Thus karatedo in its specific version of allowing personal healing and development complements the combat techniques of karate-jutsu.

Training to prevent violence is a long-term endeavor requiring education of both males and females about relationships, acceptable behaviors, moral conduct, and physical training in a respectful social environment. In many karate dojo, men far outnumber women, so women are usually trained like men, are trained as time permits, or are ignored. In any case, women can wisely take advantage of such a learning environment, if they can tolerate it, by studying male techniques and strategies, as well as their psychological and physiological vulnerabilities. Kudos to men who teach women in the dojo awareness, safety, and effective strategies and techniques that attack male vulnerability. The efficacy of training should be monitored and changes made to meet the needs of all participants so they emerge with the best-practical toolbox of personal self-defense skills. Furthermore, in martial arts schools males should learn about the ever-increasing nature of sexual violence against women as part of their training. It is unfortunate that women are sometimes seen as prey by male karate participants thus making the dojo yet another dangerous place. Most women who have experienced advances, bribes, or threats in a dojo remain silent or leave. My approach for staying was to set up clear boundaries. When I trained off-base in Okinawa over a twelve year period, I never felt uncomfortable nor was I treated differently than other participants in all-male dojo. I also enjoyed the comradery of the first Okinawan all-female *Uechi-Ryu* dojo with Machida Hatsuko Sensei.

Since many women we have trained have been harassed, abused, accosted, or raped, our role as sensei is not just combat training or jutsu but transformative discussions during training when flashbacks need to be addressed or past experiences emerge as participants set aside fear, shame, or unpleasant memories once buried in the unconscious. They will eventually share their stories of violence in an all-women's class or with a female instructor, but they will not usually do so in a mixed class. Recently, I met an obviously abused woman, who by just watching a demonstration of techniques, developed great anxiety. She was not ready for jutsu, for combat training, because she was a victim of "combat." She needed to address deeply emotional issues first because she herself was her worst enemy. Such oral communication is not really an aspect of *Do*; so, initially, I was perplexed by these kinds of interruptions because I thought physical training more important than discussion. However, class and individual progress diminished unless these issues were discussed immediately and openly. Additionally, victims' descriptions of harassment and attacks generated more effective strategies with the realization that each woman had different strengths and needs. Consequently, *Do* aspects of training in its specificity of soul seeking and story revelation are restorative, investigative, and enlightening.

A "not me, not today" attitude starts with awareness training, which includes situational awareness, postural awareness, perpetrator awareness, breathing for power and calmness, *kiai* (spirit shout), stress-reduction techniques, fitness, the laws of the state regarding self-defense, and a willingness to practice. The efficacy of training should be monitored and changes made to meet the needs of all participants so they emerge with the best case practice and skills. Self-defense is not "one size fits all" or unisex.

Some instructors feel that *kata* are a waste of time when training self-defense because they do not understand *kata*; but understanding the role of *kata* in fight applications has many benefits. One in particular is improved coordination, the ability to control the number of movement segments or body parts in a refined manner to produce well-timed and smooth motor outputs. Another is proprioception, which denotes the sense of how body segments are oriented in relation to each other through receptors in the joints and muscles. It enables the central nervous system to accurately identify movement onsets and determine the exact location of the limb at any time. Deliberate practice of *kata* produces precise movements that eventually become instinctive. Postural stabilization through stances and movement in those stances, comprehension of the importance of the center of gravity to maintain uprightness, and coordination of movements are all benefitted by *kata* training. Also, *kata* improve retention of techniques; focus, mental clarity, and calmness result. By practicing *bunkai* and various *oyo* with a more advanced training partner, self-defense strategies are rehearsed and memorized until they are instinctive. Thus, deliberate practice of *kata* empowers retention, increases flexibility, and develops *mushin*, a fully aware mind that is not controlled by emotion or thought.

In addition to *mushin,* women must understand *maai,* the use and penetration of engagement space, as essential for safety. While Westerners refer to this space as a personal bubble, personal zone, or proxemics among others, in the martial arts it is the distance of engagement and takes into consideration angles, rhythm of movement, and time. *Maai* can be closed by moving straight in, but the safest approach for women is to move at a 45° angle so they are on the outside of the attacker with several options including take-downs. Space can be closed with or without physical movement by both attacker and victim. It occurs psychologically when an aggressor disturbs the intended victim with words or looks. Demeaning or threatening discourse can create a fear and freeze response, whereas flattery or bribing can lure the victim closer. Both close space. For defense, space can be maintained with calmness, awareness, or de-escalation strategies, but women must also learn to control space using intuitive, deliberate "I am not your victim" messages that challenge male expectations of "feminine" responses.

The majority of women do not have the upper body strength of men, so they must approach actual defense situations differently, each with her personal, practical toolbox of skills. Women sometimes confuse strength with becoming masculinized. It is not the goal of karate training to masculinize women but rather to empower them with techniques that work. Forty-five degree movements were suggested above because standing face-to-face with a perpetrator is not the best option as it requires more complicated tools. To increase chances of success, women repeatedly rehearse striking and naming debilitating target areas, such as the liver, kidneys, eyes, lower mandible, brain stem, knees, diaphragm, and throat, to name a few. The groin is not always the best target because some men can ignore the pain temporarily and turn their anger back to the target, some men have learned to suck it up, literally, and others may wear protective gear. Instead women should consider that many men have bad knees, so low kicks can be effective, and "chopping at the trunk of a tree" helps distract them momentarily from other finishing techniques that follow. Defense is not upper body only but a whole-body response that moves in quickly to close distance and strikes immediately. Women must practice with the fundamental goals of "not on the run, not done" or "not down, not done" so that they can escape quickly and safely. In all cases, flight trumps fight if possible.

An andragogic approach to improve women's self-defense and to hopefully reduce violence against women requires both men and women to work together and to train women on the one hand in *jutsu*, combat strategies, and techniques that will effectively enable them to survive by quickly attacking male vulnerabilities. On the other hand, women need the opportunity to train together in a dojo environment where they can comfortably share their experiences, which is a facet of *Do*, thus transforming their perspective. Those communicative and peer-counselling aspects of training are essential because without a renewed inner spirit, all the *jutsu* in the world will not help them. Only with this combined approach women are able to create a toolbox of working self-preservation or survival techniques.

---

* Dr. Joyce Trafton is an educational researcher, author, and owner of the Crystal Coast *Seibukai Goju-Ryu* karate dojo in North Carolina, which is affiliated with International *Goju-Ryu Seibukai* in New York, USA, and in Okinawa, Japan. She lived in Okinawa for about twelve years and has trained men but mainly women and children over the course of more than forty years. Her admirable contribution of utmost importance to the karate world is that she works with women who have to deal with the severe psychological consequences of sexual violence (harassment, abuse, and rape). Dr. Trafton's teaching emphasizes self-defense strategies to include *kata* interpretation (*bunkai* and *oyo*), awareness and safety measures, movement sets, and others combined with adult education components to help participants regain and further strengthen self-confidence and self-esteem. Other Japanese and Okinawan cultural opportunities, such as *Ikebana* (flower arranging) and *Nihon Shuji* (calligraphy) are offered as well at her dojo. The above text is from emails I received on April 5, 2021; February 24, 25, and 27 of 2022; July 14, 2022; and August 15, 2022.

Summary of Chapter 4

After WWII, public attitudes changed in Japan from militarism toward peace-oriented values that further transformed karate from a combat art into a recreational, health-related, spiritual way with strong efforts directed at correcting the art's prewar misuse for militaristic purposes. Japan's national efforts to prove the country's significance and importance shifted from martial success to economic success. In this process, karate developed into a government-supported sports-business.

Consequences of this process included the loss of essential systematic knowledge about hitting vital points and techniques for utilize them in combat as well as a loss of knowledge caused by the transformation of offensive open-hand techniques into closed-fist ones and thereby suggesting their defensive use instead of the initial offensive one.

Understandably, the entire purpose of combat karate-jutsu had to be abandoned in sports-karate to avoid injuries while "playing games"; this refers to *kata* competition as well as to *kumite* competition. The initial unity of *kata* and *kumite* was separated into unconnected sport disciplines with separate scoring systems. As a result, there is no *kata* anymore in competition *kumite*, and there is no *kumite* anymore in competition *kata*. Creating impressions replaced fighting and led to the flimsy stances/positions in sports-karate *kumite*, which are quite different than the solid, grounded, toe-grabbing stances needed to deliver a fight-ending technique in karate-jutsu. Sports-karate *kata* competition, on the other hand, takes forms at face value, without understanding the hidden applications in these time capsules of combat knowledge, and often entirely misunderstands the true purpose of a move or sequence. *Kata* thus is no longer connected to the *bunkai* of its classic version, which transforms fighting applications into an athletic dance as a separate discipline of its own.

Japanese karatedo developed beginning in the 1950s—as planned—into a huge, multibillion business organized by JKF and WKF. In addition, Japanese governmental officials and mainland karate associations worked hand in hand to initiate and to heavily promote the installation of a new Olympic karate discipline—an effort that went on for decades and finally, though preliminary, succeeded with karate's inclusion as a new sport in the 2020/21 Tokyo Olympics.

Another consequence of Japan's general attitude shift from prewar militarism toward the rejection of violence and toward stressing the nation's contribution to world peace relates to karate's so-called "sacred" principle of *"karate ni sente nashi."* This not-to-attack-first-principle is, like so many other components of today's karate, a modern invention and not, as believed by many, a traditional and genuine moral code of Okinawan martial arts. Traditionally, martial arts were seen as "neutral," like a tool, and the early moral code for karate-jutsu was not pointed at "not to attack first," but at a "just cause" for attacking in order to maintain peace. The principle should be rephrased into "karateka aim at not attacking first, but they may move first" in case an attack is already underway as a clear intention for an immediately following use of physical force. Especially when teaching self-defense to women, this modification is of utmost importance as is the fact that women have a different understanding of self-defense than their male fellow karateka and that teaching women and girls requires a different and unique training approach; it needs an explicit combination of karate-jutsu with karatedo in the latter's specificity of communicative and peer-counselling aspects.

Though refraining from speculative exegesis, the possibility cannot be excluded that political reasons played a role in the 1920s to emphasize the principle's contorted "peaceful" version in support of karate's official recognition on the mainland and the art's approval by the Japanese police force. Socio-political intentions definitely impacted the positioning of martial arts as "peaceful" in postwar Japan.

Chapter 5:
The Path to Mastery in Karate: Growing into Higher Levels of Understanding of Karate-jutsu

Okinawan karate-jutsu may be called a multilevel system in terms of *kata* and *bunkai*. In its classic way, "Karate practice was based exclusively on *kata*, but this . . . consisted of the study with a partner of the applications contained in each movement. This could take several years considering the fact that *kata* included several layers appropriate to different levels of practice" (Ballardini, *Bugeisha* 2021 Issue #10, p. 8). In terms of these layers, there are obvious, *omote* (surface) applications for combat included in *kata*; these are offensive or defensive moves that can be recognized as such even with the untrained eye. Then there are *ura* (hidden) applications behind or underneath the obvious ones, which are only recognizable with deeper knowledge and understanding (some examples are given earlier in this text, as well as in Bayer 2020; and especially in Kane/Wilder 2005).

The more *bunkai* is advanced and hidden, the fewer students these concepts and their applications are shared with; because karate-jutsu's true application was a system of lethal techniques, it was "the art of killing" (Shimabukuro/Pellman 2022), which simply could not be taught to every student. Its most effective components were hidden and codified within *kata* and were taught, in complete secrecy, only to a few chosen students considered worthy by the headmaster of a school.

Image 18: Okinawan Masters of Shorin Ryu Shorinkan

These are the highest ranking and most senior Okinawan Yudansha under Nakazato Minoru, 10th Dan *Shorin Ryu Shorinkan*, who is Headmaster of this *Kobayashi Ryu* system.
(Right to left) Sakihara Chosei, 10th Dan; Kinjo Kenpo, 10th Dan; Buntoko Ifuku, 10th Dan (deceased); Gibo Giyu, 10th Dan; Genka Noritsune, 10th Dan.
In many karate systems the highest ranks of 9th Dan and 10th Dan wear a Red Belt. Depending on a system's tradition, ranks of 7th and 8th Dan, the two ranks sometimes called *Kyoshi* and sometimes *Shihan*, may wear a Red-White Belt or they may wear a Black Belt.

This fact is confirmed by contemporary witnesses, who explain how a karate-jutsu master chooses one individual or a small group of his students who are then secretly taught the deeper aspects of the art. "The selection criteria used by a headmaster to pick those special students who will receive high-level training is a personal matter and those selected have no way of knowing whether or not they will ever receive full *Okuden* level instruction" (Hayes 2018, p. 89).

The longer one earnestly trains under qualified sensei—and I am talking decades here, not years—the better one will see karate-jutsu moves as something to be understood in their fundamental functions, as concepts that can be used in a variety of different situations, rather than as a specific "technique" applicable only to a specific challenge. With deeper penetration and understanding on this learning path, based on one's own lifelong humility of a "beginner's mindset" and guided by sensei, knowledge and experience will increase and bear fruit, and over decades one may come closer towards "mastery."

However, a true practitioner of the art always is—at least should be—a humble person. True experts will not gloat and perhaps will not call themselves "master." This term is hardly to be found on Okinawa, but it is often used in the West, where we even find the accolade of "grandmaster," and not just "master," for the most competent head of a martial arts system.[1]

So, what does this term mean? First of all, it is not a term to coax someone's ego as shown in footnote 1, below. Secondly, in karate-jutsu it is not necessarily a rank or the color of the belt around a karateka's waist—especially not today, where we find an inflation of ranks, too often awarded based on training time and attendance rather than based on skills, and sometimes being awarded even for mediocre performance. Hence, belts and ranks are only interpretable within a specific school or dojo and don't mean much outside of the specific school.

Different colored belts and black-belt ranks did not exist in Okinawa (see the section "Milestones on the Path Toward Mastery" below). Instead, in karate-jutsu, *competency shows itself through successful application of concepts in* bunkai *and* kumite, *through control and superiority in fights, up to success in combat.* This is a difference of utmost importance between genuine Okinawan karate-jutsu and all other modern karatedo variations and their sports-karate derivations.

So, in order to further understand the term master, which is used in this text in its most general connotation to name the highest level on a continuum of skills, let us look at its three core components through a holistic-psychological lens.

---

1. On some websites I looked at, the headmaster of a system in the USA is actually called "great-grandmaster," believe it or not.

Three Core Components of Mastery

Generally speaking, *mastery in any art or skill is based on an advanced stage of holistic perception* (explanation below), *leading to a superior level of knowledge and insight, including all of its implications, its controlled applications, and its controlled outcomes.*

Dictionaries explain the last two components of this concept; namely, "comprehensive knowledge of or skill in a subject" and "control or superiority over someone or something." These definitions are of course not incorrect, but they are limited in the sense that they neglect broad or holistic perception as the prerequisite for stepping outside of the box of one's cognitive limits and thereby to overcome individual routine to actually gain new knowledge or skills, and to experiment with their applications.

The definition of mastery contained in the first sentence of this chapter is therefore more inclusive, and it definitely allows broader applications than the one typically used today, where the term is mostly applied to an educational environment as "mastery learning" and, within that context, primarily refers to intellectual capacities. However, *mastery in karate-jutsu is not just a question of education and intellectual capabilities; it inextricably includes the controlled and superior application of knowledge in* bunkai, bringing knowledge to life. Knowing *kata* and demonstrating it perfectly, even knowing dozens of *kata* and performing all of them flawlessly, as in some form-only Japanized karatedo styles, does not all by itself show mastery in karate-jutsu; only the flawless and superior application of *kata* concepts in *bunkai* and combat does.

With this in mind, let us look closer at the first component in our above definition of mastery, i.e., an advanced stage of holistic perception and insight.

Advanced Stage of Holistic Perception and Insight

Imagine someone in a forest—with his or her current perception and its limitations—trying to find a way to the next town. This situation would represent a beginner's level of understanding karate-jutsu. Now imagine this person climbing up the highest tree in that forest. This would represent a learning process. While climbing higher, i.e., learning more and understanding better, the related perception of our friend's surroundings changes continuously. Finally, there will be a moment, close to the tree top, when the view suddenly opens up, and the entire perspective completely changes. Our friend is now able to look across all the other tree tops, and he or she will have an entirely new perspective and new insight. He or she now can see "the big picture" of the forest, the "totality" of the landscape beyond the forest, and the many details close by as well. A new insight is gained that changes all the person's understanding irreversibly and completely. The revolutionary *change of perspective and related understanding* in this metaphor is an important facet of the first aspect of mastery. It represents a change of perception from detailed to holistic; i.e., from seeing parts of a whole to seeing the whole as more as the sum of its parts.

Let us now look harder at the implications of such a changed perspective and the options it opens up for new understandings. Everyone who plays a sophisticated board game, like chess or Go, knows that there are different levels of understanding the game. Beginners may think through one move, its implications, and an opponent's options for responding. More advanced players may be able to think through two, three, or even more moves. But there are chess-masters who play at the same time, simultaneously, with a dozen or more adversaries. These masters walk around a room from one opponent to another, briefly glance at the board, and make their move. A couple of minutes later all their opponents are either check-mate or give up.

How is that possible?

There is no way that these masters analyze "sequentially," i.e., step by step, and that they think through in detail all possible moves during the split-second they only need to react to the displayed situation. They must *process the information on the board differently* compared to less advanced players. And this they do indeed. Parallel to our forest-metaphor, the beginner perceives details more or less in close proximity to the pending move and processes this information sequentially, one step after another. In contrast, representing the view at the tree-top in the forest metaphor, a master's perception is "holistic," "total and at once," realizing the "totality," i.e., the entire big picture, its inherent patterns, and its possible developments.

This *holistic perception is the first core component of mastery*. Psychological theories help us to understand how an individual's perceptions are shaped by personal experience, by subjective thinking patterns, by social environments, by individual physiological conditions, and by circumstances (Schaffer/Kipp 2007). Humans do not just perceive, they *interpret their perceptions*, and they *"construct their individual reality"* (Berger/Luckmann 1966). Hence, individual perceptions amongst individuals differ; they are more or less narrow, constricted and shot through with emotions and attitudes, beset by stress, routine and habit, by anger, fear, ambition, by social-cultural components, and, last but not least, by ego.[2] The wider one's view, extending beyond what some call "comfort zones," and the less constricted by subjective impacts, the more an individual's perception approximates reality. Masters overcome most of these limitations; they widen their perception, and they have a clearer, less subjective awareness of reality. At its most developed stage, a master's perception becomes "total," "here and now," grounded in the complete calmness of an "empty mind." Thus, a master's holistic perception is completely open.

The result of such an open perception leads us to the *second core component of mastery*: *a master's mental store of cross-linked concepts,* which permits a master's advanced level of knowledge and understanding.

Advanced Level of Knowledge and Understanding

Developmental psychology explains how individuals organize and store their perceptions and experiences in order to find meaning in their surroundings, and in order to be able to act reasonably. Human perception can recognize a possible *inherent structure* within singular events, which makes it possible to *identify patterns* (Kretch et. al. 1969, pp. 98ff); e.g., "blocking-receiving" as one structure within many moves in karate-jutsu. Comparable patterns may now be detected, which allows us to *group* those patterns further; e.g. "blocking-receiving with an arm" in karate-jutsu. Within an array of groups, *similarities of a second level* may be identified, e.g., "arm-blocks as preemptive strikes" in karate-jutsu, allowing us again to cluster them. Within this selection of clusters, *parallels of a third level* may be identified, e.g.,

---

2. This led to the scientific finding that perceived "reality" in the eye of one individual is not necessarily the same perceived reality in the eye of another; but both "subjective realities"—which are in fact interpretations—are "individually real," hence personally correct. This social fact of utmost importance was already formulated in the early 1900s by the Austrian psychologist Alfred Adler, a colleague of Sigmund Freud's, who named it "individual logic." The concept was further elaborated by Adler's student Rudolf Dreikurs, who immigrated into the USA in 1937, and who called it the "private logic" of an individual (Dreikurs 1981, pp. 69ff).

"pre-emptive arm strikes as the preparation for a take-down" in karate-jutsu, and so on and so forth.

To organize and structure recognized patterns this way is "reduction of complexity" (Luhmann 1968) and represents a basic intellectual function allowing human beings to find the meaning and the sense in related events. A published karate-related example that illustrates this structure is Sensei McCarthy's description of himself "recognizing common principles" in defensive moves across a variety of Asian martial arts: "I compared and contrasted many of the ritualized practices utilized by a great number or Asian empty-handed defense traditions. I discovered a shared commonality in technique and defensive applications across all of these arts" (McCarthy 1998a, p. 38).

Reduction of complexity leads to an organized *hierarchy of cross-linked concepts,* a scheme with deeper penetration of the subject, where each higher level allows a more advanced understanding, just as our climber in the forest metaphor above gains a broader view the higher he or she climbs.

Within this hierarchy of cross-linked concepts, through a process of "creative synthesis," the *grouping or clustering of patterns leads not just to an array of elements but allows to us realize a completely new "whole"* (Werner 1980, p. 3)—just as the conjunction of several tones creates a melody, which is more than just an array of tones. At a certain level, referring once again to our forest metaphor, this allows to us see "the trees through the forest" as well as the big picture of "the forest through the trees"—as well as the even bigger, the total, picture of the entire landscape the forest is a part of.

The deeper the penetration and understanding of the subject, the more *the complexity of reality reduces itself into a limited number of constituting fundamentals.* As Sun Tzu had already written 2,500 years ago, "there are not more than five musical notes, yet the combinations of these five give rise to more melodies than can ever be heard. There are not more than five primary colors (blue, yellow, red, white, and black), yet in combination they produce more hues than can ever been seen. There are not more than five cardinal tastes (sour, acrid, salt, sweet, bitter), yet combinations of them yield more flavors than can ever be tasted . . . there are not more than two methods of attack—the direct and the indirect; yet these two in combination give rise to an endless series of maneuvers" (Sun Tzu n. d.; Chapter V; #7, #8, #9, #10; p. 27f).

Correspondingly, at the mastery level of karate-jutsu, it becomes obvious how the combinations of a handful of core concepts, or "fundamentals," to use Sensei Patrick McCarthy's term, explain all single actions—like all the countless hues of printed artworks are reducible to combinations of only four basic printing colors, blue, yellow, red, and grey.

The benefit of this theoretical explanation in understanding mastery in martial arts becomes clear when we match the term "totality" with "concepts used in *kata*," the term "big picture" with "moves used in *kata*," and the detail term "elements/patterns" with "techniques used in *kata*." *Advanced-level karateka understand concepts, including all their hidden options, and realize all big-picture aspects of combat[3] where these concepts may be applied*, whereas beginners narrowly see a technique as a mere technique to be used for only one specific application, or perhaps a limited few.

Humanistic-holistic theories in psychology[4] explain further how a mental core store of such overarching, all-embracing high-level wholes and totalities allows us to hear the melody instead of recognizing a collection of tones. With this kind of mental store, the initial process of "bottom-up creative synthesis" involved in creating the store (see above) can be reversed to become a "top-down analysis" for understanding single events as part of totalities, as part of big pictures.[5] In scientific language: "The elements are not precedent to the whole, but the whole, as a basic entity, is the precursor of its component parts" (Werner 1980, p. 9).

It is of course not easy to illustrate these complex theoretical explanations graphically and represent them with a helpful image. Science gives it a shot by creating schemata to visualize reduction of complexity within the neural network of the human brain, like the one in Image 19:

---

3. Interestingly enough, a completely different approach, i.e., *Cybernetics* (the science of communications and control) arrives at a comparable hierarchy of concepts and their constitutive fundamentals, when a "functionalist perspective" (Acutt 2012) is used to reduce the complexity of martial arts systems. "In order to define and to understand those variables, it is essential that we perform a 'reductionism' on the combat arts to attempt to deliver them back to their most universal definition; to remove all aspects which might serve to mask their basest existential value—to the use of the human body in physical conflict with another human body" (ibid. p. 4).

4. These are theories that stress that a whole is more than the sum of its parts; they stress the underlying structure, unity, and integration of individual perception, development, and action (theories were formulated, e.g., by Adler, Erikson, Freud, Pearls, Piaget).

5. In cybernetics terms, "Historical insight/knowledge becomes a vocabulary from which a new synthesis may flow" (this from Jamie Acutt's feedback on a draft of this text).

THE PATH TO MASTERY IN KARATE... 117

Image 19: A Model to Illustrate Pattern Recognition in a Neural System

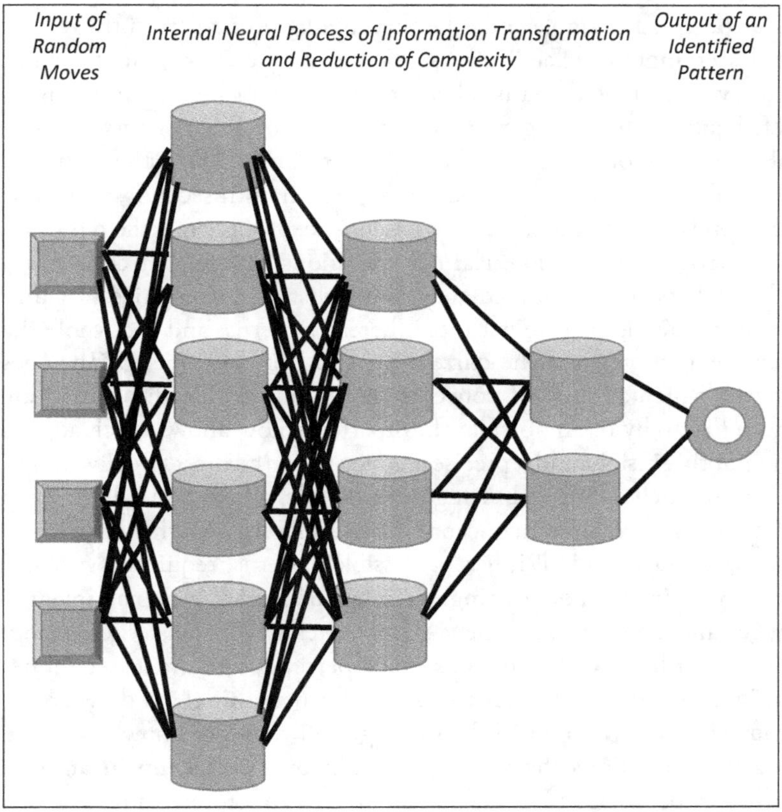

| Input of Random Moves | Internal Neural Process of Information Transformation and Reduction of Complexity | Output of an Identified Pattern |

The perception of random moves (quadratic symbols on the left) is immediately and holistically cross-checked in the core store (symbolized as drums in the model), which reduces the complexity of the initial input and results in the identification of one shared pattern (round symbol on the right) as common denominator of all perceived input moves.

As we see in this model, the karateka perceives some random moves (quadratic pictures on the left) as input. This input is immediately and holistically cross-checked with all stored clusters in the karateka's brain, his or her core store (symbolized as drums in the model). The check identifies one shared pattern (round symbol on the right) between all perceived input moves and thus reduces the complexity of the initial input, where all elements initially seemed to be unique and unrelated.

A practical example could be that in a fight one person throws several seemingly unrelated offensive punches and kicks (input), which, however, all show the same identifiable pattern of slightly dropping the left hand when moving forward. This result of holistic cross-checking all those random inputs in the opponent's brain allows the identification of the pattern (dropped left hand) within milliseconds, and allows the application of the specific counter concept that ends the fight.

Referring these theoretical considerations back to our chess example: a chess master immediately and holistically recognizes a game's totality, the big picture with its inherent patterns, and the whole that represents more than the current positions of chess pieces. The chess master's mental store of concepts in combination with a broad and deep hierarchy of all possible chess-patterns now allows quick application of this insight and a precise reaction with the most effective move.[6] Owning such an all-embracing mental store, a broad and deep hierarchy of core principles, concepts, and functions, together with chess-game totalities and all inherent possible patterns, requires a very long and extensive path of learning, training, analyzing, and experimenting to reframe one's own experience. It requires a chess master to step outside his or her own box of constricted perception in order to gain new insights. It requires him or her to try out new things, to draw correct conclusions beyond wishful thinking, and to apply knowledge in all practical situations that can be thought of—ending up in an automatic, subconscious but correct application of stored knowledge and insight.

"Automatic" Application of Insight and Knowledge

Continuing to use our chess example, chess masters read everything that was ever written about chess, they analyze countless games played by others, and they play countless games themselves and analyze those. Generally speaking, and in summation, masters know everything about their art it is possible to know. Specifically with respect to the

---

6. In cybernetics terms, "It might be said that the practitioner has reached a level of skill that provides "requisite variety. That means that the practitioner has sufficiently internalized the possible scenarios they might encounter" (Jamie Acutt's feedback on a draft of the text).

martial arts, *every concept, every move has to be repeated tens of thousands of times under all thinkable circumstances* so that the application of concepts in combat is not just understood but happens smoothly, efficiently, and effectively without thinking and without hesitation.

This end result on a path toward mastery is often called an "instinctive" or "intuitive" application of moves, but as our examples show, intuition is—at least in large part—the outcome of a lifelong path of learning and practice, a path of decades filled with hard work and sweat. "Practice makes perfect" as they say; though there is more needed than mere practice because practice alone as such can also lead to complacency in routine instead of mastery. Moreover, practicing the wrong thing only makes one a master of failure. "Practice does not make perfect; it makes permanent. Only perfect practice creates perfection in application" as Sensei Lara Chamberlain puts it on her Facebook page. Practice needs to be constantly double-checked and compared to benchmarks to avoid practicing something incorrectly. Practice needs to be guided by a sensei for a long time, it needs to supersede anger and ego, and it needs a karateka's dedication and stalwart commitment to continue on this never-ending path. During this journey, one achieves complete self-control of body and mind and the unconscious, accurate application of concepts becomes habit. Moves become reflexes and happen automatically, without thinking.

Such a cumbersome path to the top is inherent in every art, in every craft or skill, and not only in karate-jutsu or martial arts in general.

Mastery is the end point of a continuum, but there are of course intermediate competency levels, many of them achievable by devoted students of the art. Their competency in karate-jutsu shows itself through successful application of concepts in *bunkai* and *kumite*, and, above all, through survival in combat—though the vast majority of karate practitioners will never be in a situation where they have to protect their life or that of others. That does not change the fact that their karate-jutsu training has always to be serious, imagining combat situations and preparing for the always-looming challenge in reality. Kyan Chotoku Sensei's advice in this sense is that "you must practice with the same will and the same feelings as the moment when you are facing your enemy" (Shimabukuro/Smith 2020, p. 31).

As mentioned at the beginning of this chapter, the color of a belt around karateka's waists alone, however, tells us nothing about their combat skills in this sense.

Milestones on a Path toward Mastery

In the old days of Okinawan karate-jutsu a disciple's achievement of a milestone was not displayed and performance levels were not recognizable for outsiders. There were neither official ranks and belts nor specific training uniforms used in Okinawa. Historic photographs show students wearing whatever clothes were at hand (see Image 16 as an example), and *kata* was assigned individually to students per a sensei's judgement.

After introducing karate-jutsu to mainland Japan, Funakoshi Gichin Sensei adopted the belt/rank system from Japanese judo in 1924 to document levels of proficiency in his Japanese karatedo style, which was later named *Shotokan* by his students. This early belt/rank system initially had two general levels, white and black (Kane/Wilder 2022, p. 14), soon increasing to three general performance levels up to mastery, displayed as white, brown, and black belts, before it was again changed a decade later in Europe into an even more diversified *Kyu*-system of ten ranks with differently colored belts (Messner 2020).

The three-level structure of the early belt-system was helpful for many educational purposes and was adopted by the mid-1960s in all martial arts disciplines, including Okinawan karate-jutsu:
- White Belt (initially two, later three grades; these were lower level *Kyu* ranks)
- Brown Belt (three grades; these were higher level *Kyu* ranks)
- Black Belt (ten grades; these were *Dan* ranks used in the same way as today)

This first belt system shows an amazing similarity to the way craft and trade was taught in medieval times in Continental Europe. For instance, in Germany (Bonenkamp 2012) apprentices (equivalent to white belts) stayed with recognized masters for three to five years—like *uchi deshi* (live-in students) in martial arts—in order to learn the nuts and bolts of a trade. Their next qualification level was journeyman (equivalent to brown belts) who wandered all across the country for some more years to apply their skills in various projects and to learn from other masters. Thereafter, while still travelling and learning as senior journeymen (equivalent to black belts) they worked and honed their skills under experienced and renowned masters for many more years, until, perhaps, reaching own mastery (equivalent to the ranks of 9th and 10th Dan).

Image 20: In the mid-1960s Only Black Belts, Brown Belts, and White Belts Were Worn in Okinawan Dojos

This photograph shows Nakazato Shugoro Sensei correcting Sensei Noel Smith and other Okinawan *Shorin Ryu Shorinkan* students of different rank levels at the association's *Honbu* Dojo in Okinawa 1967. At that time only black belts, brown belts, and white belts were worn to show rank.

The inherent three-level concept—or curriculum, if you will—in these examples proved itself reasonable and useful for all kinds of personal and skills-development and therefore has parallels in various areas. Examples beyond trade education may be the three levels in academia, e.g., elementary, middle, and high schools and associate's; bachelor's, and master's degrees; the three main military ranks of private, non-commissioned officer, officer; and the three core levels in management (upper, middle, lower).

Each and every qualification level had to be, and still has to be, thoroughly and completely acquired and perfected for some years to develop the corresponding foundation at that level. It is like building a rock-solid stairway: if the steps are not sufficiently founded, the whole thing collapses as soon as weight is put on it—which means in karate-jutsu, as soon as an opponent is met in free fighting or in combat.

Today, belts are universally recognized as symbols of martial art achievements, a stairway of progress. The belt system in martial arts became so popular that industries and businesses have begun adopting them to show competency levels. Although achieving belts can be a good way of gauging a student's progress, in my opinion there are two distinct milestones of utmost importance during a karate-jutsu journey: the first white belt shows that a student has begun to train, and the first black belt indicates that a student has begun to understand.

Image 21: The Endless Stairway of Continuous Improvement

Staircase in London/England's City Hall

"Inductive" versus "Deductive" Learning in Karate-jutsu

During this learning process it is just as important to study one concept "deeply" as it is to study several concepts "broadly." However, it is a common occurrence—and a mistake—that someone who supposes his or her knowledge is insufficient chooses to study "broadly," i.e., to study another related subject, instead deeply penetrating the subject at hand. An example would be that martial artists, assuming that their art is not sufficient enough to succeed in a fight, start to study other styles instead gaining adequate proficiency with their own and thereby discover hidden *bunkai* in their style. We find a comparable mistake in form-only karatedo, where students assume they "know" *kata* as soon as they remember a pattern and execute the moves fluently, and then go on to train another *kata*.

Penetrating a subject deeper, called inductive learning, creates experts; it creates someone who knows everything there possibly is to know about a specific subject. This leads to advanced levels of insight and understanding—in contrast to learning broadly, i.e., deductive learning, which creates a generalist, someone who knows something about many subjects. The perfect combination would of course be an optimal synthesis of general and specialized capabilities.

Penetrating further into one subject allows one to discover new meanings and close in on the core components of the subject. The example of driving a car may illustrate. Let's say one person learns how to drive but knows nothing about how technology, physics, biological factors, or psychological factors may impact driving. Another driver acquires a deeper competence with driving by, for instance, learning how engines, transmissions, and brakes work; by learning about the impact of temperature, lubrication, and speed on a car's performance; by learning about human perception, reaction time; and so on and so forth. It goes without saying that there will be a substantial difference between these two drivers' skills and that there will be significantly different ways of driving their car, of steering, accelerating, and of hitting the brakes. The more our driver understands about background and underlying factors impacting how a car needs to be handled in various circumstances, the more this insight will consciously and subconsciously form his or her way of driving and the more advanced his or her driving skills will be. To penetrate the subject even deeper, our driver now studies how to control spinning cars and how to maximize traction on wet or frozen surfaces. Thus, hidden concepts about how to control challenging or dangerous situations now become accessible.

When we apply these thoughts to the inductive and deductive ways to study *kata*, their different outcomes are illustrated in the Image 22.

Inductive learning was reflected in the old days of Okinawan karate-jutsu by the fact that legendary masters were experts in just a few *kata* they practiced, and that their students worked on one single *kata* for years. Related to this approach, though a real comparison of today's practice to the old ways is not possible, some styles have a closed curriculum-based *kata* system with a limited number of *kata*, which are each studied for a long(er) time. Others have an open, non-curriculum based

Image 22: Inductive (left) vs. Deductive (right) Learning of Kata

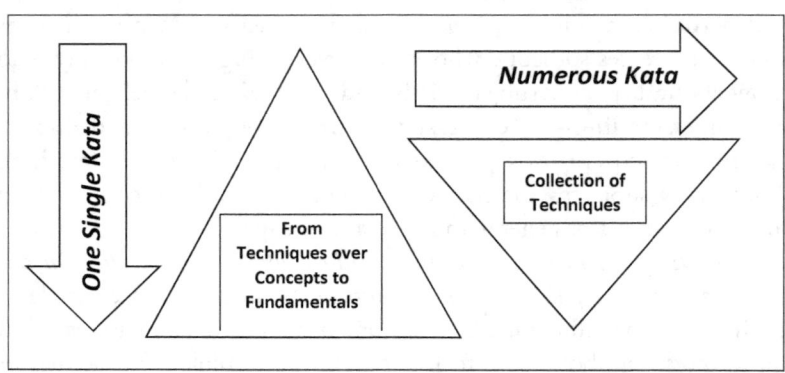

kata system and students learn dozens of *kata* without ever experiencing the deeper meaning of inherent *kata* concepts (Volume 1, pp. 105ff).

As an example of curriculum-related closed *kata* systems, Funakoshi Gichin Sensei introduced nineteen *kata* into his *Shotokan* karatedo with the argument that "it is not necessary to study indiscriminately large numbers of them . . . since the purpose of learning *kata* is not just for the sake of learning them but for tempering and disciplining of oneself" (Funakoshi 1973, p. 9). His understanding of the purpose of learning *kata* in Japanized karatedo, namely to "temper and discipline oneself," of course represents just a fraction of, and differs greatly from, the genuine intentions of learning self-defense and the protection of one's life in Okinawan karate-jutsu.[7] In the latter, self-control is a mean to the end of success in combat, not a goal in itself.

In contrast to the old ways, however, in many styles one single *kata* is today no longer practiced for years before another one begins to be practiced, and promotion to the next higher *kata* happens relatively fast, surely sometimes too fast. There are exceptions, though, even in the USA: Doug Perry, 10th Dan *Shorin Ryu, Okinawa Shorinryu*

---

7. The Okinawan *Shorin Ryu* karate-jutsu systems teach (beyond some basic drill forms) between fifteen *kata* in Chibana Choshin Sensei's *Kobayashi Ryu* (the style I practice), eighteen *kata* in Nagamine Shoshin Sensei's *Matsubayashi Ryu* (Nagamine 1976) and in Kyan Chotoku Sensei's/Shimabukuro Zenryo Sensei's *Seibukan* (Shimabukuro/Smith 2020), nineteen *kata* in Ueshiro Ansei Sensei's American *Matsubayashi Ryu* branch (Cummins/Scaglione, 2002), and twenty-three *kata* in Shimabukuro Eizo Sensei's *Shobayashi Ryu* (Hayes 2018).

Karatedo Kobudo Kensankai, told us at a training camp I attended that his son, Jason Scott Perry, now 8th Dan in *Shorin Ryu, Okinawa Shorin-ryu Karatedo Kobudo Kensankai,* practiced *Naihanchi Ichidan* exclusively for two years before he moved him to the next *kata,* an assignment Sensei Jason himself did not recall specifically when I contacted him for verification. He texted me: "I had been doing karate at some level since I was very little and more regular dojo training since I was probably six or seven with Bill Hayes [i.e., Sensei William Hayes, 9th Dan *Shobayashi Ryu, Shobayashi Kan*] and my dad. What I do recall is less *kata* and more basic drilling. Pretty mundane stuff but a lot of basic work." His statement confirms the superiority of the above-mentioned old ways of inductive karate-jutsu training by diving deeper into specific moves, a way that may be neglected today. In Sensei Jason's words, "Basic mechanics involved in creating speed and power in a balanced way."

Only deepening and honing skills at every level for years, not just for months, develops the needed persistence and resilience to succeed on the path to sustainable martial arts competence beyond all kippers and curtains.

Sensei Correct Errors and Blunders, Mistakes You Have to Correct Yourself

Learning is only possible as a combination of trial and error. Looking at it the other way round, learning is impossible without failure; and any kind of improvement is equally impossible without making mistakes while trying. Even worse, students need to accept the fact that they will experience more failures than successes as they are learning; as it is said, "The master has failed more times than the novice has even tried." It is, however, an unfortunate fact that in Western culture mistakes may be seen as personal disaster, as something bad, something to be avoided at all costs, which is expressed for instance in the common management principle of "failure is not an option." This widespread attitude is counterproductive to progress; it impedes learning, and it actually contrasts with some Asian philosophy where mistakes are seen as an unavoidable detour on one's way to achieve a goal.

Such an encouraging view of mistakes needs to be separated from the fact that Asian people do not like to "lose face." This cultural norm in Asia is not as different as one may assume from the attitude of Westerners who don't like to have their image damaged in public. Asian people do not try to avoid admitting failure, but they do try to save face while admitting failure. A whole school of etiquette evolved to accomplish this, and it represents a phenomenon that may be difficult for Westerners to understand or duplicate and as a result can lead to serious misunderstandings. For instance, Image 20 shows how an Okinawan karate master directly corrects students, openly pointing out incorrect moves or postures, which creates the risk that the student may lose face, one may assume, but which obviously does not contradict the cultural requirement of keeping face.

There are important differences between specific characteristics of incorrectness, namely errors, blunders, and mistakes. A sensei can correct two of these versions, errors and blunders, by pointing out the correct way in order to allow the student to eliminate them; the sensei, however, cannot correct the third version, mistakes, for karateka need to do this themselves. To understand these differences, a clarification of the three versions of incorrectness, as well as an explanation of the underlying neurological process involved in the learning process, is needed.

All three versions of error, blunder, and mistake imply that something has been done wrongly. Errors are made due to one's lack of knowledge or information. Hence, *errors usually are made only once and can be eliminated after the relevant information is understood* (Bayer 2005). Using the example of learning a new *kata*, errors occur right away at the beginning of the learning process and are unavoidable, because the student does not know some moves in this *kata*, meaning that some action is unavoidably wrong because the karateka does not have the needed knowledge yet. As soon as the knowledge is shared and all necessary information is known, errors can be avoided.[8]

Blunders on the other hand occur accidentally although the karateka does know the correct way. *Blunders are the accidental repetition of an error in spite of the fact that one should have known better* (ibid.). While learning a new *kata*, this often happens when the student progresses from a counted performance (each *kata* move is separately triggered as a response to a sensei's count) to a no-count performance (the

---

8. Hence, the modern management motto of "make your daily mistake" to increase risk-taking and thus creativity actually should read "make your daily error."

kata is uninterrupted and fluidly performed per the karateka's own timing). The karateka knows that something is wrong, but in this no-count setting the previous incorrect moves "slip back in." They can, however, be eliminated after sufficient repetitions of the *kata* while persistently being corrected by the sensei.

Mistakes are a completely different category. *These may be characterized as "permanent blunders," as incorrect actions contradicting the karateka's body of knowledge, as repeatedly occurring* (ibid.) and seemingly ineradicable. My sensei in the USA, Noel Smith, calls these permanent mistakes a karateka's "individual idiosyncrasies," which he cannot correct in the dojo whether through encouraging, explaining, offering feedback, or yelling. Karateka have to correct those mistakes/idiosyncrasies by themselves through home training or through working individually in front of the dojo mirrors. There are plenty of examples, e.g., not sitting down as low as possible in a position and thus unnecessarily limiting body-weight transfer power into a move (see Volume 1, p. 128ff); not looking at an opponent but instead looking up, down, or at one's own hands or feet; permanently placing a foot at a slightly incorrect angle after stepping; and so on and so forth. All these mistakes do sometimes look like a karateka stubbornly neglecting a sensei's correction and adhering to an individual interpretation of a move. This is not the case, though; the mistake is rooted rather in nerve cell connections in a karateka's brain, which have to be disconnected and "reprogrammed" (see below), but it jeopardizes these karateka in combat or *bunkai* settings and leaves them prone to being harmed.

Whereas the reduction and elimination of errors and blunders may be achieved in weeks or months, overcoming mistakes takes years. The reason for this is that it impacts the connections within the karateka's neural system.[9] This system is a relatively stable and unfortunately a relatively inflexible information-processing arrangement. Over the course of an individual's development and socialization, the system of neural connections were established, which provides an individual and personal pattern for how new information is integrated into this existing system, created early on, without changing the system as such. This makes the process of integrating new knowledge difficult and explains

---

9. The following explanations are based on "The Nervous System" (Krech et.al. 1969, pp. 72ff), "Lernen und Gedächtnis—Neurophysiologische Grundlagen" [learning and memory—neurophysiological fundamentals] (Lecturio 2020, n. p.; translation by author).

the rigidity of existing mental patterns (for example, of attitudes). Information processing "within the existing system without changing the system" means that the number and the intensity of already existing neural connections can be even more strengthened by new information; in other words, the new information is selected, unconsciously reinterpreted, and "forced" into the existing system, sometimes even bent to fit. Based on their existing neural connections, karateka will act subconsciously and automatically, and apply the very move they have always used before in their life to a new situation by using the application that has worked in their life up to now but that may be inappropriate for a new martial art move.

The neurological translation of the common phrase "Learning occurs outside our comfort zone" is that *learning something new means that new neural connections need to be created in one's brain.* This perhaps can be achieved within a couple of weeks or months but may just as well need quite a bit longer to be created. Such a process is scientifically called "tuning." Tuning is the basis of and illustrates how errors and blunders are corrected. In karate, learning to move with controlled C-steps (named as such because of a half-circle-shaped arc of the stepping leg) may serve as an example. Everyone starting to train karate assumes they know how to step. Everyone does this unconsciously by bending the torso forward, thus moving weight, in parallel moving a leg forward and falling into the step with an angled hip. If something is physically hindering the unconscious leg movement, one stumbles or falls. Learning the fundamental C-step means that a karateka has to create new neural brain connections that allows the hip to remain squared while moving a leg circularly forward and while simultaneously bending the back leg. This controls the travel of the center of gravity during the entire time at the same height while stepping—so this C-step can be interrupted at any time before its completion without losing balance, stumbling, or falling. It is quite astonishing how long it takes beginners to transform their everyday step into such a karate C-step, but it usually is achieved within a couple of months, and a new neural connection of nerve cells is established.

To correct mistakes, however, to eliminate individual idiosyncrasies, creating new neural connections is not enough. *It requires that existing synaptic connections in the neural system have to be disconnected before new connections can be established.* Something has to be not just modified but completely unlearned before something new can be learned.

This happens through a neurological process known scientifically as "reconstructing." During a reconstructing process habitual motoric patterns and routinized ways to process information, learned over a lifetime, need to be erased and "reprogrammed," to be substituted with new patterns and processes that better fit the new martial arts requirements. Reconstructing eliminates mistakes in the long run during a time-intensive and burdensome learning process which, in my own experience, takes years of cumbersome work directed at a seemingly unachievable objective and falling back into previous mistakes, a process very often accompanied by frustration and even desperation.

Tenacious persistence and self-discipline becomes the keys to eventually succeed. The higher we climb up the performance ladder, the smaller and harder earned the gains will be. Our passion will carry us only so far, and when passion wanes, all that remains to carry us forward is our mental discipline.

No More True Mastery in Today's Changed World?

Unfortunately, the way of patiently and solidly developing skills is no longer popular in many Western mindsets these days, neither in the business world, nor in trades, nor in the arts. "Aim for the highest quality possible" when creating, manufacturing, or repairing something is no longer the guiding idea for engineers, craftsmen, handymen, and other professions. This idea and its related mindset once represented the core of professional pride.

Unfortunately, the highest quality possible became economically obsolete in the view of many in an age with worldwide competition. A different mindset, preaching "only the minimum quality needed to ensure sales and with the lowest cost possible" substituted for old professional's aspiration, "Let us produce something with the maximum quality possible." The unfortunate results are in way too many cases sloppily cobbled-together products that even include predetermined breaking points to ensure replacement sales.

Within this general shift, a search for "quick wins" arose and dominates today; i.e., a search for quick rewards without the need to invest corresponding efforts and sweat. Sociological studies explain the subjacent profound change in values in this sense within just two postwar

Image 23: Only Years of Training, Not Months, Lead to Solid Basic Skills

There is no quick way to obtain solid skills. At the time of their *kobudo* promotion to 1st *Kyu* these karateka both held the rank of 3rd Dan in non-Okinawan martial arts systems; hence one may assume neither was starting from scratch. Yet it took them five years of regular and intensive training to relearn everything they did, to go through their—using the scientific term—neural reconstructing process in order to erase and to reprogram habitual patters, and thus to eliminate enough errors, blunders, and mistakes to finally achieve their new rank in a traditional *Shorin Ryu* dojo.

generations, and not just in the West, but in Japan and Okinawa as well, which completely changed how kids are raised these days. The unintended negative impacts on building up solid skills at a young age are expressed by many sensei who try to teach traditional martial arts but find that "the great majority of children are growing up with no boundaries, no expectations, no accountability, no discipline, and not knowing how to work hard for something" (Sanguinetti 2021, p. 43).

As an effect thereof, ego boosts, attention seeking, and tinsel and glitter are wide-spread, and the "entertainment" and rewarding of Karate Kids to keep them motivated often needs to substitute for their lack of internal self-discipline. Consequently, we find modern dojos where belts are awarded based on attendance or money paid rather than on competency, and where only a few weeks of training is needed to get promoted to the next level.

However, mastery is achieved differently. Karate-jutsu needs benchmark-masters "who are willing to train for decades to achieve a standard that equals that of the past and by which others will be judged in the future" (CFA 2020, p. 11). More than a few higher ranks in the martial arts are well underway in this sense and are dedicated to their path, as a new study fresh from the printing press found. "These folks aren't dipping their toes in the proverbial water, or dabbling in something that might be interesting for a moment or two, they have figured out exactly what they want and have a reasonable understanding of how to earn it. And, once identified, they are willing to pay the price" (Kane/Wilder 2022, p. 23).

Though the long lasting, arduous true path, the only successful way to mastery, is not highly valued in today's world, it does not change its verity. It simply means that only very few will endure its challenges, and every student of any art should be extremely thankful for the opportunity to learn from those few.

Summary

The core components of "mastery" were illustrated by the example of playing chess or another sophisticated board game with different levels of understanding the game. Beginners may think through one move, its implications, and an opponent's possible reactions. More advanced players may be able to think through two, three, or even more moves. But there are chess masters who play at the same time with a dozen or more adversaries, walk from one opponent to another, briefly glance at the chess board, and make their move. A couple minutes later all their opponents are either checkmate or give up.

Such a level of masterly performance is explained as the combination of three core components
1. A master's *broad holistic perception,* total and simultaneous, realizing the totality of an entire big picture, its inherent patterns, and its possible developments.
2. A master's *mental storage as a complex hierarchy of cross-linked concepts*, an organized scheme of deep penetration of the subject, which allows advanced levels of understanding and enables the master see the details as well as the whole thing in unison.
3. A master's *automatic, habitual, subconscious*, actions and reactions rooted in the *complete calmness of an "empty mind,"* honed through decades-long training of every move and concept in all thinkable circumstances.

The widespread use of a three-levelled system to assign qualification levels on a continuous path toward such mastery is introduced together with the explanation of why each of these levels has to be thoroughly and completely acquired and performed for many years to develop the needed foundation at that level before moving on to the next one.

It was pointed out why, in order to gain deeper insight, inductive learning with "deep" penetration of karate-jutsu moves and their combat applications beats "broad" deductive learning. Inductive learning creates experts who know everything that is to be known about their subject whereas deductive learning produces a generalist, someone who knows something about many subjects.

Since learning is only possible as a combination of trial and error, those errors, blunders, and mistakes are unavoidable. The important differences between these three specific forms of incorrectness is explained as:
- Incorrectness because of missing information (error).
- Incorrectness as accidental repetition of an error in spite of the fact that one should have known better (blunder).
- Permanent incorrectness contradicting the karateka's body of knowledge and occurring repeatedly (mistakes).

The "wiring" of the human neural system casts light on the different learning and teaching paths needed to correct errors, blunders, and mistakes and explains why a sensei can correct errors and blunders, but not mistakes, and why karateka need to do this themselves.

Based on changed mindsets in modern times, the necessary long, arduous path toward mastery by patiently and solidly developing skills seems no longer popular today, which does not change the fact that it is the only way to get there.

Chapter 6:

The Outlook—What Will Happen to Karate in the 21ˢᵗ Century?

It was mentioned earlier that postwar Japanese karatedo turned into a worldwide business the development of which followed the track of industrialization of other crafts and arts. This thought has to be further elaborated and supported, because if that is the case, the further market developments of those other arts and crafts should provide a historic blueprint we can use to shed some light on the most probable further developments of the art and craft of karate.

"Arts and Crafts Movement" Following Industrialization Offers a Historic Blueprint

To be able to do that, the gist of industrialization first needs to be understood, and to aid in gaining that understanding we illustrate the process with the example of how the handcrafted table became an industrially mass-produced commodity. Initially, individual fine carpenters built the tables they designed from beginning to end in one pass, and the path to finished table had its individual meanderings. One core method of industrializing a craft is breaking down a sequential construction process into its constitutive passes that then could be carried out separately, repeatedly, and independently from the following step, thus standardizing and rationalizing the manufacturing process.

So, the passes of cutting, ripping, dadoing, sanding, coating, etc., were separated and normed (i.e., standardization), then independently repeated in their most effective way (i.e., rationalization), while the parts were later assembled into similar end products with one design. This reduces the average cost per output unit (one table) quite considerably.[1]

A second core element of industrialization is reducing the cost of production to maximize profit. The industrialized manufacturing process aims to produce the minimum quality needed for the market instead of producing the highest quality possible. Thus, production is stripped of complicated and costly procedural components, which secured high quality and which are replaced with simpler techniques of lower cost (e.g., gluing or screwing parts together instead of dovetailing them). Mass production of the same product further reduces the cost per produced unit (i.e., multiplication), a phenomenon also called "economies of scale." This basic economics term refers to the fact that an organization's proportional cost when producing one unit declines as output increases. If that is the case, growing bigger provides an economic advantage to the organization, which carries increased profit opportunities. In addition, the use of cheaper raw material (e.g., plywood or core boards instead of solid wood) lowers the cost of production for our tables even more. The driving force behind all this is the evolution of a seemingly unlimited demand for goods and services (here, tables) on the one hand, and the money and the profit to be harvested by the owners of the industrialization process on the other.

The loss of traditional knowledge, the loss of product quality, and the loss of craft-specific values and skills through mass production provoked the rise of a counterculture in all those countries that went through their industrialization process about five decades later, a counterculture called the "Arts and Crafts Movement." "The Arts and Crafts Movement was fueled by anxieties about the quality of life in the industrial era and the rise of mass-produced goods. Arts and crafts designers sought to reform both decorative design and daily life,

---

1. Let's simplify for the sake of the argument and say that one fine carpenter can build one table in a week. That would be four tables a month. With a rationalized and standardized process, these four tables would be produced in, say, one day, which results in a time reduction of around 94 percent per table. "Time is money," as they correctly say.

creating objects that were beautiful and functional . . . The tenets of the movement—simplicity in design, honesty in materials, hand craftsmanship, and depicting the natural world—are still widely valued today" (AACM Museum, n.d., n.p.). As the quote shows, the American branch of this movement has its own museum as well as standing displays in exhibitions at other locations, like at The Henry Ford, where it is explained that "the Arts and Crafts Movement emerged in the 1860s and 1870s in England, then the most industrialized country in the world. Theorists and designers promoted a return to an idealized past where artists and craftsmen collaborated to create beautiful and useful objects. Many of the Movement's ideas spread to the United States by 1900" (The Henry Ford, n.d., n. p.), and into Japan in the 1920s.

Still using our example of tables, the overall result of industrialization and its follow-up developments is that today we have a large market meeting a large demand for mass produced tables. This large market supply satisfies the demand of most consumers in search for of a cheap table. In addition, we have a smaller market niche for consumers looking for tables with better quality materials and produced using better techniques but affordable though still industrially produced. Finally, there is a market niche for purists in search of genuine craftsmanship, of honest materials, of traditional skills and hand production. This market niche is small but stable and its craftspeople suppliers, the guardians of the craft, set an unmatched benchmark that mass production tries to copy and is sometimes quite successful on the surface in doing so. However, the difference remains, and though the end products may look almost alike at a first glance, a closer look always shows significant variances in materials and techniques used, and everyone will see, feel, and understand the quality difference between an IKEA table and one hand-crafted by an Amish fine carpenter.

From an economics point of view, the market for arts and crafts underwent a transformation from a supplier-driven structure to a demand-driven one during industrialization. Now many suppliers compete in the same markets; hence, these suppliers need to create a market niche for themselves to be profitable; they need to be able to point out criteria that set them apart from competitors to establish their unique selling position. The more unique the position in a market, the closer the selling organization comes to a monopolistic status, a situation where one vendor owns the majority of the market share, can set the price, and harvest exclusive profit opportunities.

The market transformation through industrialization applies to the art and craft of karate as well, as shown below. However, since tables and other craft products are used in everyday life, they are well-known to all people, and therefore the quality difference between handcrafted and industrially produced goods is common knowledge and does not create any misconception or dispute.

This is quite dissimilar from the art and craft of karate, the different versions of which are known solely to insiders. Yet, karate's development also follows the above pattern of industrialization, which led to industrially produced versions as well as to traditionally crafted ones.

Today's Karate-jutsu Movement Is the Countercultural Response to Karatedo's Industrialization

Let's apply the historic blueprint to the craft of karate. Industrialization here means that the initial "manufacturing process" of the craft, as an individually created nonphysical good for selected recipients on Okinawa, was transformed into the production of a mass product, delivered to as many customers as possible worldwide. The supplier-driven market structure of Okinawan masters transferring their art to a limited number of selected followers turned into a demand-driven market in search of a recreational product.

But how to profit economically from this process? How to turn the craft of karate into a global commodity and a global brand? How to transform the knowledge of local Okinawan fighting skills into a methodical, institutionalized Japanese product where copyrights and financial interests of involved parties are protected? Karate is, economically speaking, a "common good"; it is a nonphysical product that cannot be claimed as an intellectual property and that cannot be issued a letter of patent in a way comparable to the sport of "boxing." So how, despite the lack of legal protection as intellectual property, was it possible to establish *Shotokan*—representing in the 1950s the most common style of Japanese karatedo—as the world's most popular style in a competitive market, in spite of copying, appropriation, and plagiarizing?

Postwar Industrialization and Commercialization of Japanese Karatedo

At this point the sophisticated political and economic strategies of Japanese *Shotokan* officials come into play after the Japan Karate Association JKA was founded in November 1949 by some of Sensei Funakoshi's dedicated students. The new postwar commodity of Japanese karatedo was at that time in its majority represented by Funakoshi Sensei's *Shotokan*. It therefore embodied a specific characteristic within the range of karate systems and thus allowed the "common good" status to be overcome and move toward the status of intellectual property. "At least as far as acknowledgement goes, the true 'owners' of *Shotokan* karate are said to be Funakoshi and his first-generation disciples. This is a stepping-stone where a new version of karate was born. Funakoshi and his disciples toiled at the reproduction of a new, modern karate adapted to new audiences, and, later, on its introduction to non-Japanese audiences as well as its distribution worldwide" (Kotek 2016, p. 16).

The "new and modern karate" in the above quote was the modification of Okinawan karate-jutsu in its *Shorin Ryu* version (Noble 2019, 2020) into a recreational, health-oriented athletic activity, as explained throughout this text and in Volume 1. It created a new version of karate with its own characteristics apart from its initial specifications as a fighting art, which aimed at new groups of consumers who were interested in physical exercises and in personal improvement rather than in the attainment of fighting capabilities.

That this entire development is based on business considerations rather than on the desire to preserve an ancient fighting art is supported by the fact that "JKA was established mostly by persons from two different social avenues: one was characterized by its wealthy and aristocrat alumni of several universities. They favored non-commercialization. The other group was mainly comprised of Takushoku University[2] graduates, who majored in business-related subjects with international orientation. *The latter approach, that favored commercializing karate, prevailed*" (ibid., p. 60; italics are mine).

---

2. Takushoku University is an elite private school; it was and still is today a leading university of security studies with close relations to Japan's government, offering degrees in Commerce, Political Science, Economics, Foreign Languages, International Studies, and Engineering. https://english.takushoku-u.ac.jp/information/.

The commercialization of karate that followed was achieved through an admirably sophisticated process of business development that displayed all the earlier explained criteria of industrialization, i.e., rationalization, standardization, and multiplication into large-scale-production, by which Japanese karatedo's, and especially *Shotokan*'s, unique selling position was established as a dominant supplier with vast market power.

First, in terms of *standardization and rationalization*, the emphasis on non-combative personal benefits as goals of karate training converted the initially crafted *kata* and *tegumi* of karate-jutsu into a selection of techniques that were appropriate for these new consumers. The commodity was standardized by breaking the craft down into basic techniques to be assigned to specific learning objectives and to be exercised separately. As mentioned above, when talking about the "Loss of Essential Knowledge" in Chapter 4, "Karate techniques were developed into a complete system. For the first time there emerged a clear, scientific, and practical 'best' form for each *kumite* stance, posture, and movement. There also emerged a clear delineation between the 'correct' and 'incorrect' way to execute each stance, punch, kick or technique" (JKA, "History" tab; n.d., n.p.). These *kihon-waza* (basic technique) exercises of today were developed in the 1920s and 30s and did not exist earlier.

Second, in terms of *standardization and multiplication*, JKA-accredited instructors were sent all over Japan and soon thereafter all over the world to spread the art—not only to meet rising domestic and international demand but to generate further demand as well, which created nothing less than a worldwide karate inflation in the 1950s and 1960s. To achieve this remarkable success, JKA created an instructors' program in 1956, "the first-ever karate specialist instructor . . . training program at the headquarters dojo . . . This was the start of the finest karate instructor training program ever created, a program never matched or even approached by any other karate organization. It is through this program that the JKA has built up its unique cadre of distinguished karate instructors, all full-time salaried professionals" (ibid.), thus securing the spread of "JKA karate branches in towns, schools and as many as 40 prominent universities in Japan" (ibid.). Whether a one-year-long training program actually can produce "fine instructors" whose qualification matches that of Okinawan masters raises a flag, though many of those JKA instructors may have experienced previous years of training.

In addition, "The JKA . . . began sending (as early as 1958) some of its most highly-accomplished professional instructors overseas to America, Europe, and the Middle East to teach and establish dojo. Karate was becoming a big hit outside Japan too" (ibid.). JKA officials correctly realized the formation of a huge demand wave for karate, a wave that was greatly accelerated by new TV series and movies painting a picture of superhuman capabilities, by American service personnel returning home who had learned the art while stationed in Japan and who now opened their own schools, and by a new overall philosophic interest in "everything Oriental" in the West (Volume 1, pp. 33ff).

Japanese karatedo established and maintained its unique selling position through an effective "quality assurance system" of owners and guardians, both in charge of uniformity and consistency of what is being taught, which served as a substitute for patenting the art. Like all other karate systems, the JKA structure is pyramidal. "At the top of the system is the leader. The leader's direct students constitute the second level, which in all probability will provide the next leader. Each of them has his own students, who make up the next level, and this formation repeats itself in a recursive manner, creating a pyramidal structure" (Kotek 2016, p. 83). These core leaders are the "owners" of the karatedo system (the commodity); they are the ones securing the unaltered preservation of the style and the only ones allowed to change anything. Hence, they have exclusive control over knowledge and as such secure the style's purity. The pyramidal structure is not only repeated domestically but internationally through "guardians" too. "Not only do cultural products that become indisputably recognized brands and labels have alleged 'owners,' but in some cases, the product is claimed to need 'guardians,' who presumably maintain its defining features. To ensure that karate was taught in the spirit of JKA, the representative of *Shotokan*, top instructors were assigned to head *Shotokan* JKA clubs abroad. These senior instructors became recognized by the members of their own organizations as guardians of the 'true' *Shotokan*" (ibid. p 15f). "It was their mission to ensure that not only is karate preserved in the form it was taught in Japan, but also that the guardians of *Shotokan* tradition remain its Japanese owners. Thus, these individuals became a part of the product" (ibid. p. 25).

Slipstreaming JKA's benchmark of setting worldwide success, other Japanese karatedo styles (and Okinawan systems as well) established their presence in domestic and in international markets. But though the organizational structure of Japan's other karate systems resemble that of JKA, no other system came even close to the latter's monopolistic position, neither in Japan nor in other parts of the world. The aggressive sales strategy of sending out dozens of instructors as multiplicators and developing gatekeeper guardians bore fruit, as did the marketing strategy of exporting the art as a genuine Japanese martial art with all its Japanese *budo* ingredients of etiquette, dress code, rituals, and the use of Japanese terms in training, which together became an inherent component of today's definition of karate.

In the early 1980s, the market position of *Shotokan* as the self-acclaimed prototype of Japanese karatedo was well established and further JKA initiatives focused on stabilizing its existing market position and its organizational structure, an effort that was remarkably successful in both preserving the Japanese identity of *Shotokan* and protecting the copyrights and financial interests of the parties involved.

As a commodity, Japanese karatedo was irrevocably established worldwide, initially as *Shotokan* through JKA, and soon followed by the other mainland Japanese karatedo styles of *Shito Ryu*, *Wado Ryu*, and Japanized *Goju Ryu*—including their combined claim to be a genuine Japanese martial art. The industrialization of the craft was completed, manufacturing ran hot, and commercialization focused successfully on its initial core product of teaching standardized curricula.

To meet another specific demand of youths who prefer to fight in competitions, other and additional organizations were established to promote sports-karate and for the sole purpose of managing tournaments. These do not engage in teaching at all as the style organizations do. "This status quo seems to serve well both types of organizations. Obviously, there is much money to be made in any competitive sport, and sports karate is no different. Home organizations capitalize on educating and qualifying karate practitioners to levels of expertise. Providing karate competitors to competition organizations is not necessarily a wanted result by the guardians of karate traditions, but it is a tolerated byproduct" (ibid. p. 62).

The "Back to the Roots" Karate-jutsu Movement as Counter-cultural Response

Karate's development was looked at in comparison to the industrialization of other arts and crafts and the counterculture that was a reaction to it. The end result of their evolution always led to (a) small market segments of classic products for purists in search of quality and tradition, (b) large segments of industrially manufactured versions for mass demand, and (c) special segments for fashion and Zeitgeist. In all countries a rebound of traditional craft, intended to preserve the old ways, always followed one to two generations (about fifty years) after industrialization had kicked off and boomed.

Interestingly enough, about fifty years after Japanese karate's postwar industrialization, i.e., in the 1990s, we find signs of a parallel movement back to the origins, to the genuine forms of karate-jutsu, comparable to the historic Arts and Crafts Movement blueprint; a movement forming not just in Okinawa but also in the West called by some "the reality drive" (Bowman 2014, p. 1).[3] This countercultural response has grown stronger by the decade since the mid-1990s, heavily profiting from the new possibilities the internet offers to communicate and to connect with kindred spirits.

Today the countercultural back-to-the-roots karate-jutsu movement became a strong and influential voice pointing out not only possible misunderstandings in Japanized karatedo and in sports-karate but providing examples for and explanations of the old ways and offering learning opportunities, seminars, training camps, publications, and educational materials in printed, electronic, or online streaming forms. The declared purpose of this movement is elucidated in an exemplary way in the name of print magazines to this effect; e.g. *Bugeisha—The Traditional Martial Artist*, which started to publish in 1996, or *Classical Fighting Arts—The Authentic Martial Disciplines of China, Japan, and Okinawa*, which evolved from a newsletter into a full-color glossy publication around the same time. Both publications were able to secure a solid market position for their contributions about the old ways today, setting themselves apart from other main-stream-karate newsstand magazines.

---

3. The author, Dr. Paul Bowman, however, sees the invention of new "realistic styles" as the drive to reality in martial arts, instead of the move back to the origins within existing Okinawan karate systems, which we describe here.

Important back-to-the-roots research is also conducted by research societies publishing their findings in print format and, mostly, on the internet. To name a few of those:
- International Ryukyu Karate Research Society (https://www.koryu-uchinadi.com/), where Patrick McCarthy has compiled a comprehensive collection of historic documents, discussions, articles, and interpretations of *koryu* [traditional] karate.
- Ryukyu Bugei (https://ryukyu-bugei.com/), where Andreas Quast presents considerations on genuine karate and *kobudo* and discusses historic findings.
- The International Shudokan Research Society (https://www.toyama-book.org/research-society.html), where Christian Bellina shares his findings concentrated on the karatedo of Toyama Kanken Sensei and its historical roots.
- The Chibana Project (http://chibanaproject.blogspot.com/), where, some years ago, Terry Garret presented his findings about, Chibana Choshin Sensei, who organized *Shorin Ryu* (written as *Kobayashi Ryu*) as a tradition within the array of *Shuri-Te* karate systems.

Additional impact in the sense of spreading knowledge has come from social media groups where aspects and applications of authentic karate-jutsu is discussed amongst thousands of members and where historic findings are shared. To name a few of these member-restricted platforms:
- "Karate" by Ryukyu Bugei (Andreas Quast administer in Nov. 2022; about 24,800 members) (https://www.facebook.com/groups/709248329841056)
- "Okinawa *Te* : [All Lineages]" (Mark Wetmore administers in Nov. 2022; about 7,800 members) https://www.facebook.com/groups/OkinawaTeALL
- "The Society" (Patrick McCarthy administers in Nov. 2022; about 770 members) (https://www.facebook.com/groups/642448296886696)
- "Okinawan Karate" (Bruno Ballardini et.al. administer in Nov. 2022; about 970 members) (https://www.facebook.com/groups/423553994426689)
- "*Shuri-Te Bu-Jutsu-Kai*" (Troy J. Price administers in Nov. 2022; about 2,300 members) (https://www.facebook.com/groups/118925384821738)

- "Okinawan Karate Research & Discussion" (Sean Schroeder administers in Nov. 2022; about 600 members) (https://www.facebook.com/groups/ShorinryuShorinkanGroup)
- "Traditional Okinawan Karate & Kobudo" (W. Dan Hausel administers in Nov. 2022; about 200 members) (https://mewe.com/group/5ee3c4c6a07c9a6c7dee4f8e)

All these undertakings concentrate on efforts "to bring basics and foundation back into the limelight of martial arts" (*Bugeisha* 1996, Issue #1, p. 1) and thus unmistakably institute a back-to-the-roots countercultural movement against industrialized karatedo.

Mainstream official efforts on Okinawa itself seem to aim at a different objective: they focus on cementing the view of the island as the "birthplace of karate," as laid out in Volume 1 (pp. 50ff) and in Chapter 2 above, rather than on developing the art back to its roots. That is, many prefectural efforts are of socio-political character in order to preserve the subcultural heritage of karate from being completely swallowed by the culture of the mainland.

Though there are strong Okinawan endeavors to curate the three genuine Okinawan versions of *Shuri-Te, Naha-Te,* and *Tomari-Te* systems and to institutionalize these in an organization opposing mainland Japan's Karate Federation, a reconnection of the systems' modern versions with their ancient roots is not the obviously identifiable core of these efforts. This core is primarily to establish and to promote a specific interpretation of history with the assumption that what is practiced today is the authentic old ways, which, however, is not always the case. As a result, the versions of Okinawan karate offered in Okinawan dojos today may or may not be authentic karate-jutsu; overall there is a good chance that many karate tourists encounter Japanized and thus tempered karatedo instead of genuine karate-jutsu—keeping in mind, however, that Okinawan masters may be hiding true karate-jutsu from karate tourists as described earlier. In summation, that a dojo is located on Okinawa does not mean by itself that what is taught there represents a *koryu* (authentic) art.

Today, the authentic art is curated by a select group of elder instructors who were considered, character-wise, "worthy" by preceding Okinawan karate-jutsu masters to be taught genuine *bunkai* and therefore had the privilege to be taught the art's applications in authenticity. This group of instructors in Okinawa (and in the West) will preserve the knowledge, continue the lineage, and hand down their secrets after screening carefully those they select as their inheritors by using the same selection criteria they were chosen by.

The Resulting New Market Structure

When bringing it all together, the boilerplate example of how crafts were industrialized with their following countercultural Arts and Crafts Movement allows us to formulate the most probable path toward the ultimate market structure of the art and craft of karate in the 21st century. The tracks toward a parallel existence of three different variations (see Chapter 1) are well-established today, and the size of each of the three market segments will be defined by the demand for them in modern societies.

Sports-Karate Remains the Prevalent Type

Sports-karate's perspective, the prognosis for the largest karate-version in our days, is the easiest one to formulate. Sports-karate is demanded by kids, teens, and adults who are eager to compete. It is demanded by parents as physical—even quasi-therapeutic—exercise for their children. It is demanded by karate schools as a way to demonstrate the success of their training and to show off their athletes; and it is demanded by sports officials and their organizations to maintain their job. Sports-karate is, last but not least, the version of the art closest to today's competition-oriented values in market societies.

Hence, and overall, sports-karate will definitely have the highest impact on the view of karate in the public's eye. Sports-karate created its new and unique karate interpretation (see Chapter 4) through overtaking and altering many genuine Okinawan *kata*. Reinterpreting and manipulating those in terms of competition rules and regulations "bestowed Japan (including Okinawa) tons of gold medals, international fame, money, careers" (Quast 2020, n.d., n. p.) and cemented sports-karate and its competition-facilitating organizations as the karate branch with the greatest market power. The World Karate Federation (WKF), formed in 1990, which is the largest international governing body of sports-karate and the only karate organization recognized by the International Olympic Committee, reports in 2014 more than ten million members in 198 member countries, and "100 million karate practitioners worldwide."[4] These figures give an impression of the sheer size of the commercial market for sports-karate.

Karatedo Perpetuates Japanization's Lasting Budo Impact but Will Incorporate Some Rediscovered Karate-jutsu Elements

The role as the second largest karate version is held and will be maintained by karatedo as defined in Chapter 1 of this text. This includes not only the Japanized versions of Okinawan karate on the mainland and worldwide but a large part of karate as practiced today on Okinawan itself too. Karate being taught on Okinawa and being offered to karate tourists does not as such qualify as genuine karate-jutsu,[5] because the changes to the art, starting with Itosu Sensei's alterations and Funakoshi Sensei's interpretations thereafter to support its recognition as a Japanese martial art produced substantial and irrevocable changes to the old ways, as explained earlier. It gave birth to karatedo with all its new orientations and purpose, moving away from using the "craft of jutsu" toward perfecting oneself by following the concept of an individual *Do*.

To this point in this book, calling karate an "art" was tantamount to calling it a "craft." Here, it seems wise to pause and clarify these two terms and explain why karate-jutsu *could be seen as the "craft" component, the tool, and karatedo as the "art" component, the tool's scholarly, spiritual, and mental undergirding.*

First, referring to the *craft component*, the *jutsu*, one may reasonably assume that some centuries ago those Okinawans employed as law enforcement, as bodyguards, or as guards of warehouses, trade vessels, and caravans would be the ones most frequently needing and applying their empty-hand (and their *kobudo*) combat skills. This martial skill would have been one of the basic crafts of their profession. In this perspective, karate-jutsu appears as a value-neutral tool, the way martial arts were initially looked at, as a weapon, which in itself does not have any moral connotation, whereas the specific code or moral guidelines

---

4. https://olympics.com/ioc/news/five-things-you-need-to-know-about-karate.

5. We want to reiterate at this point the idea introduced in Volume 1 (p. 82f) and earlier in this text too that, in my opinion, only the members of the culture in question are in a position to rightfully deal with aspects of their cultural heritage. Since karate is a part of Okinawan (sub-) cultural heritage, no foreigner is in a position to decide on matters important to it, though there may be as outstanding karate experts outside of Okinawa as in Okinawa itself.

for how to use this tool, how to handle this empty-hand weapon, were developed separately and in a scholarly fashion, but not within the craft. Hence, in terms of hermeneutic-historic reasoning, it seems safe to assume that everyday guards and street police officers cared less about some possible noble conceptions of their everyday tool and that karate's craft aspect, i.e., that it work flawlessly when used, was of utmost importance to them.

Mainland Japan, on the other hand, beginning in ancient times, elevated its martial skills up to the level of an art, and it based martial "arts" study and practice on transcendental, spiritual, and philosophical conceptions to add specific meaning to the physical and bellicose aspect of a martial craft. This was explained in Chapter 3, and it seems to be related to the fact that samurai in ancient Japan constituted a high-ranking caste and that the core education of this caste (and other high classes) consisted of philosophy, especially Zen Buddhism, calligraphy, poetry, and other fine arts and did not focus exclusively on the craft of martial skills as such. The complexity of those components within a warrior's educational curriculum would *re-interpret a martial craft as a martial art*, and it seems reasonable in terms of hermeneutic-historic reasoning that this concept of mainland Japan's samurai education transferred to the education of Okinawan's gentry and upper classes as well.[6]

Thus, we find "martial craftsmen" in Okinawan history like street-level police forces, body guards, and warehouse or trade-vessel guards, and we find "martial artists," like royal guards, gentry, and aristocracy; both groups practiced the same fighting system with differing philosophical undertones.

The allegedly simple—yet in terms of purpose, significant—change in nomenclature from karate-jutsu to karatedo, and the related transformation into *budo*, paved the way for the integration of all the philosophical foundations of Japanese martial arts into Okinawan karate, and, contrasting with *dento* (genuine) Okinawan karate-jutsu, these *budo*-specific philosophical, Zen- and health-related superstructures

---

6. This statement harmonizes with what we know about Itosu Anko Sensei's upbringing, who was born into a scholarly-aristocratic family. Hence, his formal education "for the sons of noble families up to the age of 17 or 18 . . . [included] the advanced practice of writing and calculation . . . Chinese language, calligraphy, and the elementary texts of the Chinese classic . . . [as well as] Confucianism as the official state canon and the core of education" (Feldmann 2021, p. 72f).

Image 24: Modern Karatedo Training Group

This photograph illustrates several aspects of modern karatedo training, which all share the common denominator of making things easier for an exercising karateka compared to traditional karate-jutsu. The group seems to practice *Pinan* (or *Heian*) *Yondan*, a form created by Itosu Anko Sensei for the purpose of safely educating school kids. The usually wooden dojo floor of postwar Okinawan dojos is replaced with rubber mats to allow softer contact when stepping and to cushion the fall if thrown.[1] Different variations of the same move are accepted; we do not see just the genuine (and correct) move, i.e., an eye-high *shuto* block/strike with the right arm and a forehead-high block with the left arm, but we see higher right arm and left arm positions as well—and we see 90-degres foot positions of the left back legs pointing sideways instead of the genuine (and correct) 45 degrees pointing forward.

---

1. On a side note: a dojo visitor from a rubber-matted dojo told Sensei Noel Smith in 2021 that the wooden floor at Okinawan Budo Institute was actually hurting his feet too much when stepping. No further comment on this one. A visiting high-ranking guest instructor who wore his socks while instructing me and fellow karateka mentioned that the floor was too cold for him. No further comment on that one either. On another side note: *Doshinkan* karatedo groups train on all kinds of hard surfaces inside and outside too; rubber mats are definitely not used in this style either.

became more important than the art's original self-protection purpose.

Eastern martial arts hold special significance in the West for their seemingly esoteric nature and, as such, martial arts are not always considered to be sports but rather disciplines with fairly different mental and spiritual connotations for practitioners. For instance, when studying the values and attitudes of British martial artists, it was found that they, when "comparing themselves . . . to assumed, typical visions of Western sporting masculinity, such men draw upon the imagined uniqueness of their martial arts to construct a sense of moral superiority over other men. In so doing, they contribute to a rejection of what they believe to be 'mainstream' sporting Western masculinity, thus indicating the role that 'alternative' visions of physical culture can play in men's active constructions of gender" (Channon 2012, p. 111).

Based mainly on Funakoshi Sensei's recommendations, in Japanized karatedo the entire karate practice moved away from *tegumi/kumite* as its most important training component towards *kata* practice. "Why this change of 'Jutsu' to '*Do*' is so vital is due to the pedagogical shift towards *kata* as the principle form of training in most of these *budo* martial arts" (Dodd/Brown, p. 38). *Kata* training in itself becomes the center of practicing the Japanese version of a martial art. "*Kata* represents a pedagogy inextricably linked with spiritual cultivation, and may explain why Japanese culture has an alternative word for form, '*katachi*,' referring to a form devoid of meaning or purpose" (Dodd/Brown 2016, p. 33). Thus, *kata* instead of *kumite* became the core of Japanese karatedo.

> If the *Do* alone were the core of practice, we have to ask why use a *martial* art at all to achieve self-improvement? One could achieve the same goal by following the paths of ikebana or calligraphy. All relevant philosophical thoughts with their implicit components of devotion and character optimization are included in those fine arts too.

So, it seems that the use of a *martial* art to pursue an individual *Do* is inextricably associated with fighting and with combat, and not only with physicality and the philosophical component of personal development by pursuing the *Do*. If only philosophical implications of pursuing one's *Do* would be sought after, this could be achieved by practicing calligraphy instead of a martial art, as stated above. In other words, even in its Japanized version, karatedo remains a *martial* art, not only a gymnastics art or a fine art.

The widespread confusion created by using a martial art for non-martial purposes finds expression in Sensei Davey's statement: "What about the term 'art' as in martial arts and martial artists? Well, while I don't view my practice as particularly martial by definition, and while I've never been in the military, I do believe what I've devoted over fifty years to, is an art form. But I also think many people involved in *budo* are not clear about what art actually is, and I don't always see much of what they're doing that relates to art, especially in terms of how the Japanese founders of many *budo* thought about art and artistic concepts" (Davey 2022, p. 9). The difference between *jutsu* and *Do*, between crafts and arts, and between a Japanese *budo* version and the initial Okinawan combat version clearly shines through this statement, where today's practice is described as "not particularly martial by definition." We can easily find a parallel in this quote to Matsumura Sensei's distinction of "martial arts of scholars" versus "true martial arts"—and last but not least we can see the impact that the experience of violence, be it in the military or on the street, has on a karateka's understanding of their practice.[7]

It seems, however, that the genuine martial component regained significance in karatedo over the last few decades, beginning in the 1990s and early 2000s in many styles, and cannot be overlooked anymore. The voices of the countercultural karate-jutsu movement speak particularly loudly and clearly all over the internet today and find their way into the most combat-reluctant circles of karatedo. Important reminiscences of genuine karate-jutsu as hidden lethal concepts and combat applications were most successfully pointed out over the last two decades by the craft's countercultural movement against its industrialization. Consequently, practitioners of karatedo cannot avoid encountering these concepts and adding some of them to their up-to-now solely or mostly philosophically oriented interpretation of their art.

---

7. On a side note, perhaps shedding light on the relation between life experience and karate system chosen, it seems like a large number of US-sensei in the Okinawan *Shorin Ryu* system I practice served in the military (myself included) or in other security-related professions, whereas the majority of the same group in *Doshinkan* karatedo did not. This, however, is my impression based on in-person and social media communications; it is not an exact statistic evaluation.

This development of integrating karate-jutsu elements into karatedo has already started, as shown for instance in a publication about *Shotokan*'s secret as traditional hidden combat techniques underneath today's moves (Clayton 2020), and in publications that seek to reevaluate karate and the entire *Shotokan* system under a scientific hoplology (science of fighting arts) perspective (e.g., Wittwer 2014). Interestingly enough, the listed authors are *Shotokan* practitioners themselves, which makes it hard for me to understand all their arduous efforts to link *Shotokan* back to karate-jutsu when the original *Shotokan* root, which is *Shorin Ryu*, exists in parallel and is today practiced on Okinawa. Why not use *Shorin Ryu*'s current systems of *Kobayashi Ryu*, *Shobayashi Ryu*, *Matsubayashi Ryu*, *Matsumuro Ryu*, *Seibukan*, etc., to support arguments about combat originality? Why use *Shotokan*, the most Japanized and altered style, to establish a cumbersome link to genuine combat roots instead of using a less-altered Okinawan style that still exists all over Okinawa?

Nevertheless, the rollback of karatedo toward karate-jutsu is found within several karatedo styles in the form of an increasing number of YouTube clips as well, which demonstrate technique application in combat situations, and in the form of social media groups dedicated to *bunkai* applications. More contributions in this sense will appear and accelerate the reinvention of karatedo under its combat perspective as new insights are published and the internet continues to allow their broad spread. Already today the consequences thereof are clearly to be seen and support the most probable perspective for the future development of karatedo: *some rediscovered or reengineered reminiscences of genuine karate-jutsu will be dissolved into these versions, thus bringing the Japanized karatedo systems back closer to their martial origin.*

However, karatedo will never go completely back to the initial craft of karate-jutsu. The Japanization of Okinawan karate has had a lasting, irrevocable impact on karate, moving it away from its *jutsu* craft roots into *budo* and the art of *Do*.

From the most comprehensive view, karatedo in its Japanized version may even be seen as the only way to practice martial arts in postwar Japan, after everything militaristic became highly suspicious and undesirable—as well as the only commercially promising way to practice martial arts worldwide with regard to overall changed attitudes toward combat and violence. In this line of thought it is certain that after WWII, at the age of sixty, "when Master Funakoshi demonstrated a *kata*, he did this in a relaxed and less powerful way" (Wittwer 2007, p. 180, author's translation).[8] He demonstrated a relaxed and easygoing version in a way that cannot be explained as a result of his relatively advanced age. This is still an ideal age in *budo*, and I personally know many other adepts of hard styles who do execute their moves powerfully at an even greater age (myself, in my mid-seventies, included). Hence, Funakoshi Sensei promoted this relaxed, disarmed way of executing *kata* moves as an alternative valid way to interpret *kata*, which resulted in a split of *Shotokan* practitioners into substyles that focus on powerful moves and into others that took over Funakoshi's new soft approach and tried to understand their hidden meaning and pursued those as a new and correct application. This lead to some new, more relaxed, *Shotokan* substyles (ibid. p. 182).

"The philosophical shift of *bu-jutsu* to *budo* can be argued to be the saving grace of the Japanese martial arts, allowing the ancient/traditional martial arts [*koryu budo*] to develop into their modern forms [*gendai budo*], while maintaining a lineage to the past masters of the arts" (Dodd/Brown, 2016, p. 39).

Although I do not agree with this quote, because in my view traditional forms exist in parallel with their modern variations and the latter are not an evolutionary transformation of an earlier version into a later one but an alternative interpretation of them, which exist separately—but I concede that the modern forms of karatedo at least helped the art to get permission by the occupying US military after WWII to be continuously practiced as some kind of a "peaceful" art.

* * * * *

Doshinkan, the karatedo system I practice in addition to *Kobayashi Ryu* karate-jutsu, is a cogent example that illustrates the development of emphasizing karate-jutsu components in Japanese karatedo styles. Under new leadership since March 2019, *Doshinkan*'s return to its combat roots seems obvious to me. Since one component of this style's position is to keep all knowledge and components of training in-house, and not share it with non-members, I will only refer to evidence that

---

8. "Wenn Meister Funakoshi eine kata vorführte, tat er dies mit einer entspannten, wenig kraftvollen Art und Weise."

does not violate this rule and only use examples readily available to everyone.

Today it is stated on the style's website that "basic self-defense skills are taught from the beginning level in karatedo *Doshinkan*. These skills are gradually developed until self-defense is no longer a concern. Modernized sport-karate is of questionable value in providing effective self-defense skills because it has been stripped of these techniques, but traditional karatedo has always provided effectiveness in this area" (*Doshinkan* link, "Self-Defense" n.d., n.p.). And, to equally stress both components, self-protection and self-perfection, it says further that karatedo "is commonly thought of as a way to defend oneself from attack. Although self-defense skills are included in the training, the karatedo experience offers much more" because "karatedo is a form of traditional *budo* (martial way of life)" (ibid.).

Online training sessions nowadays show, as a new element of highest importance, that Sensei Fujimoto-Stock Masako does not teach or explain a complete *kata* to all students, which used to be how it was done. Now either only one single technique, or a limited sequence of techniques, are practiced, explained, and demonstrated as *bunkai*, depending on the qualification of students attending a training session. In my opinion, this new training concept maintains and supports the secrecy of specific concepts and pays tribute to the fact that each *kata* is a complete set of defensive and offensive applications. The system of *Doshinkan* karatedo *kata* is seen as the style's treasure to be protected and to be only shared and curated internally. Applications are shared that match the level of insight within a training group, and the most complete applications are shared only with select karateka.

* * * * *

Thus and overall, karatedo and karate-jutsu seem on track to converge to a certain degree, creating the opportunity for both paths to complement each other. Since all karate combines physical, spiritual, and mental development, the long-time contradiction between Okinawan karate-jutsu and Japanese karatedo may evolve into a new overarching unity—like night and day, yin and yang—not being mutually exclusive, but defining each other by contrast in order to constitute a new holistic entity. The chances that this may happen were never better in karate's history since today *both* approaches, not only the Okinawan

THE OUTLOOK—WHAT WILL HAPPEN TO KARATE... 153

Image 25: Example of Amplified Emphasis on Karate-jutsu Components in a Karatedo Style

Take-down with wrist manipulation at a training camp.

systems, come closer to maintaining the art's initial purpose of combat and lethality. On the other hand, the Okinawan systems integrate the way of *budo* too, as in the Japanized systems of the mainland. Hence, the synthesis of karate-jutsu and karatedo is no longer as unrealistic as it used to be some time ago—at least not for the hands-on efforts of practitioners; the political/organizational division between Japanese versus Okinawan styles and their associations remains unbridged.

In terms of such a synthesis, and parallel to the self-defense benefits of karate-jutsu, karatedo provides many lifelong physical and mental and spiritual benefits. Physical benefits are obvious, and beyond that, while learning and executing *kata*, practitioners constantly do what they call nowadays "brain exercise," especially when working on constant improvement, on learning new *kata*, and when thinking about *bunkai* and developing corresponding drills or partner *kumite*. When karate is interwoven with one's entire life, as it should be, practitioners gain spiritually[9] by developing patience, focus, persistence, ambiguity tolerance, and stress stability as well as self-control and, last but not least, humility.

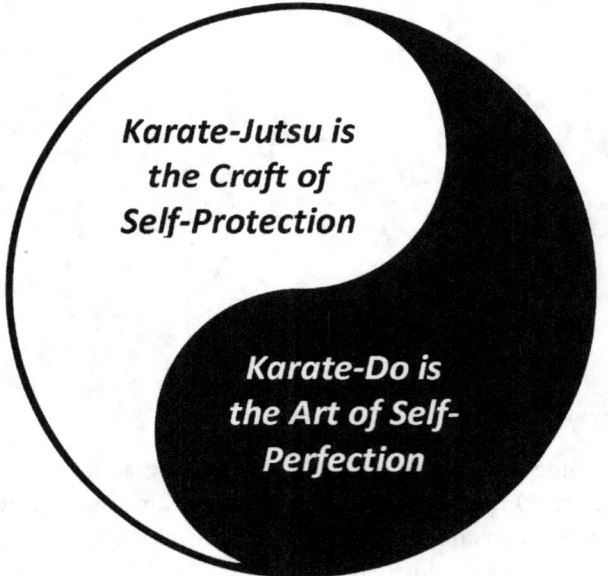

Image 26: Self-Protection and Self-Perfection
Both Constitute the Whole of Karate

Karate-Jutsu is the Craft of Self-Protection

Karate-Do is the Art of Self-Perfection

---

9. At the fringe of this karatedo market an outlier group of religious Zen- and Buddhism-based believers is found, which, though tiny in comparison, shall not go unmentioned. It is a group of esoteric believers and religious practitioners who integrate meditative components of a martial *Do* into their belief system. Representations of this group used to be Asian centers that were sometimes visited by Western *uchi deshi*. Their belief system of Zen-Buddhism and their approach has spread into the West over the last decades by Asian refugees and by Western scholars. The best-known ancient representatives of this group are supposedly the monks and lay people of the Chinese Shaolin monasteries, made famous by several contemporary movies (views about the connection of Fujian boxing and Shaolin monasteries with Okinawan karate-jutsu are looked at in in Clarke C. 2012b, pp. 51ff).

A Group of Dedicated Karate-jutsu Curators Secures the Art's Genuine Points of Reference

"To study the old is to understand the new" says the first verse of Funakoshi Gichin Sensei's poem introducing his latest-published book to describe his path (Funakoshi 1983). In this sense, pure karate-jutsu needs to be and will be preserved as an ancient blueprint, as a benchmark, and a point of reference by a group of dedicated custodians. These curators embody the cultural reaction against karatedo's industrialization that fundamentally and essentially altered the art and craft. It parallels a reaction that is found in the market for *kobudo* and its weapons as well, where a small but stable market niche is held by craftily skilled martial artists who handcraft weapons for their fellow practitioners using the traditional ways, philosophy, materials, and production processes and thus convey the genuine body of knowledge through its embodiment in classic and authentic weapons.

In karate, *kata*, *bunkai*, and *kumite* were handed down from a unique time and culture that does not exist anymore and cannot be reproduced. However, because *kata*, *bunkai,* and *kumite* are based on the timeless circumstances, distances, angles, and concepts of hand-to-hand combat, as well as on the equally timeless anatomy of the human body, *kata*, *bunkai,* and *kumite* are treasures that should be conserved. The art and craft of karate needs conservators more than innovators, and this effort is underway. In Sensei Jason Scott's words in a Facebook discussion, "There is a deliberate and concerted effort in Okinawa to not lose the distinctly Okinawan character of karate. Tournament karate [*kyougi* karate] is a potential threat to traditional karate. I think people can see where judo is going and they want to preserve the aspects of Okinawan culture . . . encapsulated in karate."

The need for and the benefit of unlocking the hidden secrets of *kata*, *bunkai*, and *kumite* and the need for and the benefit of bringing back the lost knowledge of the original art and craft were discussed throughout this text (see especially Chapter 4, the section "The Loss of Essential Knowledge") and will not be repeated here. It just has to be reemphasized that the authentic craft is today embodied in a small but stable group of headmasters and instructors who were selected as "worthy," character-wise, of being taught genuine *bunkai* and *kumite* by preceding Okinawan karate-jutsu masters. This group of instructors in Okinawa, who had the privilege of being taught the art's applications in their authenticity, will preserve the knowledge and continue the lineage. Sensei Dan Smith, US-chief-instructor in the *Seibukan* system (see footnote 7 in Chapter 1), is not sure whether those curators can be found outside of Okinawa. He wrote to me, saying, "I do not know of any outside of Okinawa. You would think there would be many based on the high *yudansha* grades. I think there are skilled karate men outside of Okinawa due to their long and continuing efforts in performing the techniques but their knowledge will come from what an application could be versus having been taught what it was" (email, April 27, 2022).

This group of Okinawan curators will hand down their secrets after screening carefully the ones they select as their inheritors while using the same selection criteria they were chosen by. Estimating the size of this group seems impossible, so I will not attempt it. But I do want to share that my conversations with masters suggest that there are indeed a few walking encyclopedias of their systems spread all over Okinawa and perhaps the USA and other places as well. This needs to be taken with a grain of salt, though, as Sensei Dan Smith points out: "I do not believe that any Westerns are 'custodians of the art' for two reasons. 1) I do not think the knowledge is deep enough by any Westerns to be a custodian of the entire art of *Uchinandi*. The effort of learning the entirety of *Uchinandi,* which would have included not only *Shorin Ryu* as it was named for political purposes but the *Udunte* (Palace Hands), *bo-jutsu, sai-jutsu,* and the many other combat weapons, would have been impossible. Even many of the current Okinawan teachers are not custodians of the comprehensive arts . . . By not having a qualified custodian for these many methods there is a need that has been filled by a few non-Okinawan to create what they think the combat method would be. I appreciate the efforts of these men but at the same time they should name it as what it is, as their opinions about possible applications"(ibid.). But, again, there is a chance of encountering true curators of the art and craft as well, though it is not easy. "Several dojo kept up the emphasis on preparing the body for combat, but by the time of the twenty-first century it was hard to find dojo that were operating in the 'old ways'" (ibid.).

As a dedicated karate-jutsu practitioner one may ask oneself how to find one of these true curators and master instructors. The answer is simple, though perhaps not satisfying: they find you! Karateka practicing for a very long time with different sensei and, regardless of their rank and assumed level of insight, always keeping up their humble attitude of a beginner's mind, may be selected later in their karate career by one of these curators. Then they may encounter concepts and applications they never assumed this instructor would know, because it has been hidden successfully from them for many years.

Hence, it looks like that the group of karate-jutsu custodians are compiled of an inner circle (perhaps a handful, perhaps a dozen, perhaps more) genuine curators of the art and craft most on—and some outside of—Okinawa, a group of older masters, at least seventy-five years of age and better, and an outer circle of serious Okinawan and non-Okinawan karateka worldwide who attempted to meet the need to decipher the initial *kata* concepts and get them to reveal what the combat applications would be, by re-creating, reinventing, and reinterpreting. The efforts of these latter traditionalists are commendable and are included in this text as guardians of classic karate-jutsu; but, as Sensei

Image 27: Four of the "Original Seven" Custodians of the Sakugawa-Matsumuro-Itosu-Chibana-Nakazato Tradition in the USA

Nakazato Sensei and his spouse are sitting in the front. Behind them, standing from left to right, are Noel Smith, Shiroma Jiro, Sid Campbell, Yamashita Tadashi.
The other three custodian members of the "Original Seven," not pictured here, are Eddie Bethea, Frank Hargrove, and Robert Herten.
Sensei Sid Campbell and Sensei Robert Herten passed away in the meantime, may they rest in peace. The other five are still teaching.

Dan Smith pointed out, they should characterize their *bunkai* examples and applications truthfully as their personal opinions and interpretations of what it could have been and not present them as "the inner truth" of classic Okinawan karate-jutsu.

The small market segment of dedicated inner-circle curators of the genuine art and of outer-circle cryptographers and decoders seems stable and its voice will become even more influential with the use of the internet as its most promising communications medium and vehicle for research. This allows the establishment of a helpful benchmark for the art and craft of empty hand and of *kobudo*, which is open to be used by individual karateka of all karate-jutsu and karatedo systems to cross-check what they are doing and to improve themselves.

Only time will tell to what extent this ancient treasure will actually transform the existing Japanized karatedo versions. The transformation process is underway nonetheless, as illustrated above, and will bear fruit. It will bring karatedo back closer to karate-jutsu; it will, however, not impact sports-karate at all.

LIST OF ABBREVIATIONS

AAU	Amateur Athletic Union.
CFA	Classical Fighting Arts magazine.
e.g.	Abbreviation for the Latin "exemplum gratis," meaning "for example."
et. al.	Latin, meaning "and others"; used to shorten a lists of co-author names when referencing.
FAJKO	Federation of All Japan Karate (predecessor of JKF).
f, ff	Abbreviations "folio" and "folios" respectively; used to signify that the discussion on one page continues on the next (f) or over the course of an indeterminate number of pages (ff).
GAISF	Global Association of International Sports Federation.
ibid.	Latin, meaning "same location"; used to reference an immediately before quoted source.
i.e.	Latin, meaning "that is."
JKA	Japan Karate Association.
JKF	Japan Karate Federation, aka. Japan Karatedo Federation.
MMA	Mixed Martial Arts.
NASA	National Aeronautics and Space Administration.
NACA	National Advisory Committee for Aeronautics.
n.d.	"No publication date available"; used when referencing (internet) publications.
n.p.	"No page numbers available"; used when referencing (internet) publications.
ODKS	Okinawa Dentou Karatedo Shinkokai; or "Okinawan Traditional Karatedo Association."
OKIC	Okinawa Karate Information Center within the Okinawan Karate Kaikan.
OPG	Okinawan Prefectural Government.
publ.	"Publishers"; used to distinguish authors from publishers in references.
sic	Latin, meaning "thus"; used to indicate that something unconventionally written is intentionally being left as it was in the original.

SMAA   *Shudokan* Martial Arts Association.
UNESCO   United Nations Educational, Scientific, and Cultural Organization.
WKF   World Karate Federation.
WWI   First World War 1914-1918.
WWII   Second World War 1939–1945.

EXPLANATIONS OF EAST ASIAN TERMS

Especially for our readers not familiar with karate and martial arts, the explanations of *East Asian terms for both "Analysis of Genuine Karate" books,* Volume 1 and Volume 2, are listed here alphabetically for your quick orientation. Explanations are focused on a term's connotation as referred to in the text.

B

Bo	Staff, about six feet long, used as a weapon in *kobudo*.
Bubishi	Name of an ancient Chinese work on martial arts and traditional medicine.
Budo	Japanese term for modern Japanese sports martial arts derivatives from *bu-jutsu*.
Bugei	Martial arts, military arts, arts of war
Bu-jutsu or jujutsu	"Warrior skills"; term for traditional martial arts on ancient mainland Japan.
bunkai	Application of *kata* moves and concepts in combat.
Bushido	Moral code for a samurai's attitudes, behavior, and lifestyle.

C

Ch'üan fa	Ancient term for traditional Chinese empty hand martial art.
Chi, Qi or Ki	Asian terms for the natural energy of the universe flowing through everything.
Chudan	Solar plexus level; often called "middle" in a karate move.
Chudan-uke	"Middle block"; in karate, a defending arm move using a forearm's radius bone.

D

Dachi	Stance/position in karate.
Daimyo	Feudal vassals of a Shogun in ancient Japan.
Dan	Ten black-belt ranks in martial arts; used to designate levels of proficiency.
Deshi	Student of an art.
Dento	Genuine, original.

Do	Never ending "way" or "path" of continuous improvement.
Dojo	Training hall.
Doriyoky	Hard work with total commitment.
Doshinkan	"Hall to study the way of the heart"; a Japanese karate style created by Ichikawa Isao in the 1960s based on the teachings of Toyama Kanken's *Shudokan* (around 1930).

E, F

Eku	Often used term for an oar, about six feet long, used as a weapon in *kobudo*.
Fukyu (kata)	"Something to be spread and shared"; in karate a "*Fukyu kata*" is a basic *kata* of a style.

G

Gaijin or gaigene	Non-Japanese foreigner; has somewhat negative connotations.
Gedan	Lower-body level; often called "low" in a karate move.
Gedan-barai (uke)	"Low block"; an arm technique in karate to block the lower part of one's body.
Gi	Martial arts uniform worn during training and performance, traditionally white in karate.
Goju Ryu	Officially recognized umbrella karate style in Okinawa; created by Miyagi Chojun around 1930 based on the teachings of Higaonna Kanryo around 1870; literally "hard-soft-style."
Gojushiho	Name of a *kata* practiced in Okinawan and Japanese karate.

H

Hachiji-dachi	"Natural stance"; an upright position in karate with feet shoulder-width apart and angled naturally.
Haito	"Knife-hand"; cutting move in karate with the edge of the hand at its thumb side.
Hanshi	Honorary title meaning "master, "most senior teacher," and "teacher of teachers"; used in many martial arts for the top few instructors of that style, sometimes translated as "Grand Master"; in many

	karate styles awarded to tenth Dan; in some styles to 9th Dan as well.
Heian	Name of a *kata* series in Japanese *Shotokan* karate created by Funakoshi Gichin as a modification of the Okinawan *Pinan kata* series.
Heiko-dachi	Comparable to *jigo-dachi*, "horse stance"; a karate position like riding a horse with feet set wide apart, knees bent, but feet parallel, not angled, and pointing forward.
Heisoku-dachi	An upright position in karate with feet placed parallel together; in some styles this is the "bow position."
Hiki	Ryukyu Islands' royal government organization under King Sho Shin in the 16th century.
Hojo undo	Physical conditioning and strengthening practices as a discipline of genuine karate-jutsu.
Honbu dojo	Martial arts style's administrative headquarters and central training hall.
Honto	"Real," "true"; here, essence of *kata* concepts.

I, J

Ichidan	See *Shodan*.
Ichigeki hissatsu	The martial arts ideal of killing with a single blow.
Ikebana	The Japanese art of arranging flowers.
Isshin Ryu	Karate substyle of *Shorin Ryu* in Okinawa (with considerable *Goju Ryu* elements); created by Shimabuku Tatsuo in the 1950s.
Jigo-/Jigotai-dachi	"Horse stance"; a karate position like riding a horse with feet set wide apart, knees bent, and feet pointing outward, angled in line with thighs.
Jo	Mid-sized staff up to 5 feet long, used as a weapon in *kobudo*.
Judan	Head-level; often called "high" in a karate move.
Jutsu	"Science of an art"; general Japanese term for combat martial arts.
Jujutsu	"Warrior skills"; traditional martial arts on ancient mainland Japan focused on grappling, pinning, joint locks, and throws, using attackers' energy against them.

K

Kado	The Japanese art of formal flower arrangement
Kakedameshi	Challenge match resembling a real fight setting in traditional Okinawan karate-jutsu
Kama	Sickle used as a weapon in *kobudo*.
Kamaete	"Get ready" or "in position"; a command used in karate.
Karate	Japanese martial art, created and developed in Okinawa as the renaming of *Te* and *Tode*, the genuine fighting arts of the Ryukyus; initially meaning "China-hand," to be altered later to "open-hand."
Karatedo	Path of continuously practicing karate to combine physical, mental, and spiritual development.
Karateka	Karate practitioner (singular and plural).
Kata or gata	Standardized series of defending and attacking moves; literally meaning "form."
Kenpo	"Fist method"; traditional Okinawan martial art related to Chinese boxing.
Ki	See *Chi*.
Kiai	Focusing all energy, e.g. into the application of a technique by combining body movement with breathing. The result may be a shout, or it can be done silently.
Kiba-dachi	"Straddled leg stance" in Japanese karate, comparable to *heiko-dachi*.
Kihon (kata)	"Basic"; in karate a "*Kihon kata*" is a combination of fundamental moves.
Kiko	Techniques for the development of internal energy as a module in genuine karate-jutsu
Kyusho (Jutsu)	Striking vital points as a discipline of genuine karate-jutsu
Kyoku	Name of a *kata* series in *Doshinkan* karatedo.
Kobayashi Ryu	Other word for the karate style of *Shorin Ryu*; created by Chibana Choshin in Okinawa around 1930 based on the teachings of Matsumura Sokon (around 1840) and Itosu Anko (around 1900).
Kobudo	Using everyday tools and trade equipment as extensions of the body in karate.

EXPLANATIONS OF EAST ASIAN TERMS

Kohai	"More junior student"; in this context, seniority refers to membership in the same organization, not to age.
Kokusaidori	Main street in central Naha, Okinawa, Japan.
Koryu	"Old school"; a Japanese term for any kind of traditional arts.
Kuchibushi	Literally "mouth warrior" used in the text as "time to talk through things."
Kumite	Partner exercises; used in karate as formal drills or as sparring or free-fighting combat.
Kung-fu or gongfu	Modern term for Chinese empty-hand martial art.
Kyogi or Kyougi	Game, match, contest.
Kyoshi	Honorary title meaning "polished senior teacher"; in some karate styles awarded to 7th and 8th Dan; in others awarded to sixth Dan and above
Kyu	Ten colored (initially all white) belt ranks below the ten black-belt Dan ranks in karate and other martial arts to designate various levels or degrees of proficiency or experience.

M

Maai	Martial arts term for the space between two opponents in combat; the "engagement distance."
Machi dojo	Privately owned dojo in Okinawa where traditional martial arts are taught and preserved.
Mae-geri	Forward kick; foot/leg technique used in karate.
Makiwara	Strong but flexible tapered wooden board, anchored to the ground and hit by karateka for hand, arm, foot, and leg conditioning.
Matsubayashi Ryu	Karate substyle of *Shorin Ryu* in Okinawa created by Nagamine Shoshin after WWII; the term is derived from kanji of *Shuri-Te* and *Tomari-Te* masters Matsumura/Matsumora.
Morote	Using one hand/arm to support the other one in a karate technique.
Mushin	Fully alert mind neither distracted by thoughts or emotions.
Musubi-dachi	An upright position in karate with heels together and feet open at a 45-degree angle; in many styles this is the "bow position."

N

Naihanchi	Name of a traditional Okinawan *kata* series that today has three forms.
Naihanchi-dachi	"Straddled leg stance" in Okinawan karate.
Naore	"Return to the starting position"; in some karate styles used as a command at the end of a *kata* performance.
Nekoachi-dachi	"Cat stance"; a position in karate with most of the weight on the back leg and bent knees.
Nukite	"Spear-hand"; a thrust move in karate with extended fingers tightly compressed together.
Nunchaku	String- or chain-connected short wooden pieces used as a weapon in *kobudo*.
Nunte Bo	Harpoon/boathook used as a weapon in *kobudo*.

O, P, Q

Obi	Belt worn by martial arts practitioners.
Okuden	A high level of advanced training in Japanese arts.
Omote	"Outside" or "surface" of something. Here, the obvious application of a *kata* concept.
Oyo	Application, practical use of a concept
Pangainun Ryu	Initial name of an Okinawan karate style later renamed *Uechi Ryu*. Created by Uechi Kanbun in the early 1920s based on Okinawan *Te* and Chinese martial arts.
Pinan	"Peaceful (mind) and (stay) safe"; name of a karate *kata* series of five forms created by Itosu Anko around 1900 for educational purposes in the public school system.
Qi See *Chi*.	

R

Rei	"Bow and show respect"; used as a command in martial arts ceremonies.
Renshi	Honorary title meaning "polished Instructor." Skilled or expert teacher. Awarded in karate to fourth Dan and above.
Ryu	"School" or "system"; term used when naming martial arts styles.

S

Samurai	Military nobility and officer caste of medieval and early modern Japan from the twelfth century until their abolition in the 1870s.
Sanchin (kata)	Basic *kata* in some karate styles representing the most important fundamentals to synchronize breathing, focus, conditioning, moves, and body-weight transfer.
Satsuma	Southern Japanese former province led by the Shimazu clan that increased its feudal domain by invading and occupying the Ryukyus in 1608.
Seibukan	Karate substyle of *Shorin Ryu* in Okinawa created by Shimabukuro Zenryo in the 1960s.
Senpai	"Senior student"; in this context, seniority refers to membership in the same organization, not to age.
Sensei	General term for "teacher," "mentor"; not reserved for teachers of a particular Japanese art; doctors, lawyers, and certain other professionals may receive this designation too.
Shima	A millennium-old form of Okinawan wrestling/grappling.
Shihan	Honorary title meaning "chief instructor." In some Japanese karate styles used as 9th Dan rank below Hanshi, in others it is not related to rank.
Shitei/seitei (kata)	Form/*kata* created in the early 1980s by JKF, based on traditional Okinawan forms as a prerequisite for karateka to qualify for JKF-facilitated tournaments. Used until 2013.
Shito Ryu	Officially recognized karate style on mainland Japan created by Mabuni Kenwa around 1935.
Shobayashi Ryu	"Small Forest Karate," a substyle of *Shorin Ryu* in Okinawa created and named by Shimabukuro Eizo around WWII.
Shogun	Historical term for Japan's military commander.
Shodan	First level; used to name a *kata* or rank level in karate.
Shomen	"Font"; in karate the dojo wall where symbols, flags, and sensei portraits are displayed
Shorin Ryu	Officially recognized umbrella karate style in Okinawa based on the teachings of Matsumura Sokon around

	1840, *Shuri-Te*, and Itosu Anko around 1900; literally "small forest style."
Shotokan	Officially recognized karate style on mainland Japan created by Funakoshi Gichin in the mid-1920s; named by Funakoshi's students sometime later as *Shotokan* Ryu.
Shudokan	"Hall to study the way"; a Japanese karate style created by Toyama Kanken in the 1930s.
Shuhari	Japanese martial arts concept that describes the stages of learning to mastery. In this context, used to explain individual training variances within an acceptable range of possible interpretations.
Shodo	The art of traditional Japanese handwriting
Shoshin	Attitude of openness and eagerness when studying a subject, even when studying it at an advanced level, just as a beginner would.
Shuto	"Knife-hand"; cutting move in karate with the edge of the hand below the pinky finger.
Soto-deshi	Student of an art who lives outside of a dojo.
Soto-uke	"Outside block"; in karate, a "middle" defending arm move using the forearm's ulna bone.
Suikendo	"Fists flowing like water"; a karate fighting style created by Yamashita Tadashi.
Sundome	Stopping before contact; today light contact in sports-karate

T

Tai Chi	A so-called "internal" Chinese martial art, having spiritual, mental, and qi-related aspects, practiced for defense training, health benefits, and meditation. An "external" martial art focuses more on physical aspects.
Tanbo	Short staff, about four feet long, used in *kobudo*.
Taikyoku	Name of a *kata* series used in several karate styles.
Te or Ti or Ti'gwa	Traditional Okinawan weaponless fighting art; literally meaning "hand."
Tekki	Name of a *kata* series in Japanese *Shotokan* karate created by Funakoshi Gichin as a modification of Okinawan *Naihanchi kata*.

tegumi	A form of grappling dating back to the 11th century in Japan which became a module of genuine karate-jutsu.
Tekko	Net-hauling tool or modified horseshoes used as weapons in *kobudo*.
Tichiki / tijiki	Term in Uchinaguchi, the Okinawan language, meaning "hands show what I do."
Tichikun / tijikun	Term in Uchinaguchi, the Okinawan language, meaning "use your hands like this."
Tode, Todi, Toudi	Renaming of "*Te*"; literally meaning "China hand."
Tonfa	Wooden handle used as weapon in *kobudo*.
Torite or Tuite	The method of seizing and restraining an opponent, which was used by law enforcement officials, security agencies and correctional officers in the Ryukyu kingdoms and Japan.
Tsuki	Fist strike, punch; attack move in karate.

U, V, W

Uchi deshi	Full-time live-in student of an art at a dojo; literally "inside student."
Uchinaguchi	Native language on the Ryukyu islands.
Uechi Ryu	Officially recognized umbrella karate style in Okinawa created by Uechi Kanbun around 1900 based on Okinawan ^and Chinese martial arts.
Uechi-Hachiji-Dachi	"Inward natural stance"; an upright position in karate with feet less than shoulder-width apart, toes pointing inward and knees bent inward.
Uke	"Receive", a defensive concept in Okinawan karate-jutsu using the forearm bones; often somewhat inaccurately expressed as "to block" in modern karatedo.
Ura	"Back" or "behind." A side that is hidden from view; here, the hidden aspect of *kata* concepts.
Wado Ryu	Officially recognized karate style on mainland Japan created by Otsuka Hironori around 1935.
Waza	Technique; e. g. Kihon-Waza means basic technique in karate.

Y

yakusoku — In the karate context used here it means "arrangement," "engagement," and, more specifically, "partner exercises" or "partner drills."

Yin / yang — East Asian concept of dualism, describing how opposite or contrary forces may be complementary and interconnected in the natural world, defining each other by contrast and thus creating an overarching entity of mutual interdependence.

Yudansha — Martial artists holding Dan (black belt) ranks in karate or in other martial arts. (Singular and plural.)

Yumaru — Spirit of caring and helping one another in Okinawa.

Z

Zanshin — In karate the state of awareness and of relaxed alertness. In other martial arts it may also refer to a posture after the execution of a technique.

LIST OF PHOTOS (P), TABLES (T) AND GRAPHS (G)

Title	P	G	Page
Image 1 *Jutsu and Do Are Both Inseparable Components of the Whole of Karate*		X	xvi
Image 2 *Naihanchi Ichidan as Practiced in Okinawan Shorin Ryu Shorinkan*	X		8
Image 3 *Derived Move in Naifanchi Shodan as Practiced in Japanese Karatedo*	X		11
Image 4 *Genuine Move in Naihanchi Ichidan as Practiced in Okinawan Shorin Ryu Karate-jutsu*	X		12
Image 5 *No Solid Stance/Position in Sports Karate But Bouncing Back and Forth When Fighting*	X		14
Image 6 *No Clear Combat Bunkai Detectable In Some Sports-Karate's Kata*	X		16
Image 7 *Did Karate Originate in Okinawa or in China?*		X	18
Image 8 *The US Explorer 1 Launch Team 1958: Integrating Foreign Skills into an American Idea*	X		23
Image 9 *A Bavarian Subcultural Heritage Is Misinterpreted as a German Cultural Symbol*	X		35
Image 10 *An Okinawan Subcultural Heritage Is Misinterpreted as a Japanese Cultural Symbol*	X		36
Image 11 *A "No-Surrender" Doctrine Provided Budo as the Spiritual Shield to Have Soldiers Fight to Their Dutiful Death*	X		41
Image 12 *Original WWII German Stick Hand Grenade*	X		46
Image 13 *Passai Sho Bunkai as a Hidden Nukite in Karate-jutsu versus Morote Uke in Karatedo*	X		67
Image 14 *Correct (left) and Incorrect (right) Photographs of Itosu Anko Sensei and Portrait of Itosu Anko Sensei Created by Sensei and Artist Lara Chamberlain from the New Photo*	X		78
Image 15 *Spectacularly Exaggerated Sports-Karate Moves Are Not Realistic Fighting Concepts*	X		80
Image 16 *Genuine Okinawan Karate-jutsu Kumite: Miyagi Chojun Sensei & Kyoda Juhatsu Sensei in the Early 1900s*	X		84
Image 17 *Considerable Violence Still Exists in Modern Societies; It Is Not At All Extinct ...*	X		99
Image 18 *Okinawan Masters of Shorin Ryu Shorinkan*	X		110
Image 19 *A Model To Illustrate Pattern Recognition in a Neural System*		X	117
Image 20 *In the mid1960s Only Black Belts, Brown Belts and White Belts Were Worn in Okinawan Karate-jutsu*	X		121
Image 21 *The Seemingly Endless Stairway of Continuous Improvement*	X		122
Image 22 *Inductive vs. Deductive Learning of Kata*		X	124
Image 23 *Only Years of Training, Not Months, Lead to Solid Basic Skills*	X		130
Image 24 *Modern Karatedo Training Group*	X		147
Image 25 *Example of Amplified Emphasis on Karate-jutsu Components in a Karatedo Style*	X		153
Image 26 *Self-Protection and Self-Perfection Both Constitute the Whole of Karate*		X	154
Image 27 *Four of the "Original Seven" Custodians of the Sakugawa-Matsumuro-Itosu-Chibana-Nakazato Tradition in the USA*	X		157

REFERENCES

Acutt, Jamie (2016). *The Cybernetics of the Martial Arts: A proposed application of Cybernetics to the study of the function of Martial Art.* IQ Journal—Journal of the Institute of Martial Arts and Sciences, Volume 5, Issue 2, pp.18-85.

Andriessens, Elsa (1985). *Nahziele.* In: Brunner, Reinhard / Kausen. Rudolf / Titze, Michael (Ed.) (1985), pp. 300-304.

Asato Anko (1914). *Die Kampftechniken aus Okinawa Parts I, II, III—Asato Anko spricht über Karate.* [Interviewed by Funakoshi Gichin supposedly 1902 and published in Ryukyu News 1914]. In: Wittwer, Henning (2007). *Shotokan: überlieferte Texte – historische Untersuchungen.* © Henning Wittwer: https://www.gibukai.de/buch-shop/; pp. 9-26.

Bayer, Hermann (2022). *Japan's Assertion of Okinawan Karate—How a Subcultural Intangible Heritage Was Converted into a National Cultural Symbol.* Paper I presented to the International Martial Arts Studies Conference in Lausanne/Switzerland on June 30, 2022.

Bayer, Hermann (2021a). *Analysis of Genuine Karate–Misconceptions, Origins, Developments and True Purpose.* Wolfeboro, NH: YMAA Publication Center, Inc. (quoted as "Volume 1").

Bayer, Hermann (2021b). *Did Genuine Karate Originate in Okinawa or in China? A Contribution to Historic Reasoning in Martial Arts History.* https://ymaa.com/articles/2021/09/did-genuine-Karate-originate-in-okinawa-or-in-china. Retrieved Oct 21, 2021.

Bayer, Hermann (2005). *Aus Fehlern lernen–Praxis-Erfahrungen eines Coaches mit Problemsituationen und Lösungen.* Zeitschrift Organisationsberatung Supervision Coaching OSC, Volume 12, pp. 63–74.

Bayer, Hermann (2000). *Coaching Kompetenz—Persönlichkeit und Führungspsychologie.* München, Basel: Ernst Reinhardt Verlag. 2nd Edition.

Ballardini, Bruno (2021a). *The Keys to Tode-jutsu—How to Unlock Kata, Which Really Are "Time Capsules" and to Extract from them the Precious Treasuries They Preserve.* Bugeisha, Issue#10, pp. 8-10.

Ballardini Bruno (2021b). *Karate Archeology.* Standing Rubric in: *Bugeisha*, Issue# 8, 9, 10, 11, and 12.

Bellina, Christian (2018). *Toyama Kanken—The Heritage of Shudokan.* Klagenfurt/Austria: © Christian Bellina. Limited edition.

Benesch, Oleg (2011). *Bushido: The Creation of a Martial Ethic in Late Meiji Japan.* Thesis submitted in partial fulfillment of the requirements for the PhD degree at the University of British Columbia. Vancouver/Canada: http://www.unterstein.net/nn/OB2011-bushido-creation-of-a-martial-spirit-in-meiji-japan.pdf.

Berger, Peter L. / Luckmann, Thomas (1966). *The Social Construction of Reality: A Treatise in the Sociology of Knowledge*. Garden City, N.Y.: Doubleday.

Bishop, Mark (1991). *Okinawan Karate—Teachers, Styles and Secret Techniques*. London: A & C Black Publishers Ltd. 2nd edition.

Bittmann, Heiko (2005). *The Teachings of Karatedō*. Ludwigsburg-Kanazawa: Verlag Heiko Bittmann.

Black, M.C. / Basile, K.C. / Breiding, M.J. / Smith, S.G. / Walters, M.L. / Merrick, M.T. / Chen, J. / Stevens, M.R. (2011). *The National Intimate Partner and Sexual Violence Survey: 2010 Summary Report*. Atlanta, GA: National Center for Injury Prevention and Control of the Centers for Disease Control and Prevention. Cited as "Black et. al. 2011."

Blumenthal, Eric (1984). *Der hohen Jahre Ziel und Sinn—es ist nie zu spät, aber immer höchste Zeit*. Luzern, Switzerland: Rex Verlag. German Edition.

Bohnenkamp, Anne (2012). *Mit Gunst und Verlaub! - Wandernde Handwerker: Tradition und Alternative*. Göttingen: Wallstein Verlag.

Bowman, Paul (n.d.). *How Traditional Are Traditional Asian Martial Arts?* https://www.academia.edu/ 39864235In_Authentic_Relations_Traditional_Asian_Martial_Arts_East_and_West_How_Traditional_Are_Traditional_Asian_Martial_Arts. Retrieved 9/12/2021.

Bowman, Paul (2010). *The Globalization of Martial Arts*. In: Green, Thomas A. and Svinth, Joseph R. (ed.) (2010). *Martial Arts in the Modern World*. Westport, CT: Praeger Publishers, Inc.; 2nd edition.

Bowman, Paul (2014). *Instituting Reality in Martial Arts Practice*. JOMEC Journalism Media and Cultural Studies Journal. Cardiff/UK: Cardiff University Press. https://www.academia.edu/6989680/Instituting_Reality_in_Martial_Arts_Practice. Retrieved 12/15/2021.

Brunner, Reinhard / Kausen. Rudolf / Titze, Michael (Ed.) (1985). *Wörterbuch der Individualpsychologie*. München-Basel: Ernst Reinhardt Verlag.

Bugeisha Traditional Martial Arts Magazine (diverse years and issues). Cited as "Bugeisha Issue#, page#.

CFA Classical Fighting Arts Magazine (diverse years, volumes and issues). Cited as "CFA Issue#, page#."

Channon, Alex (2012). *Western Men and Eastern Arts: The Significance of Eastern Martial Arts Disciplines in British Men's Narratives of Masculinity*. Asia Pacific Journal of Sport & Social Science. Vol. 1, Issue# 2-3, pp. 111-127.

Channon, A. / Jennings, G. (2013). *The rules of engagement: Negotiating painful and "intimate" touch in mixed-sex martial arts training*. Sociology of Sport Journal, 30, 487-503.

Chambers, David, Ikemiyagi, Taku, Dohrenwend, Robert (publ.) (2020). *Okinawa Karate—The Exquisite Art*. Naha/Okinawa: Dragon Associates.

Inc. & Ikemiya Shokai Co., Ltd. © Classical Fighting Arts. (Quoted as "Chambers et.al. 2020").

Chen, Yea-Wen & Lin, Hengjun (2016). *Cultural Identities*. Oxford Research Encyclopedia, Communication (oxfordre.com/communication), © Oxford University Press USA. Retrieved 01/24/2020.

Clarke, Christopher M. (2012a). *Okinawan Karate–A History of Styles and Masters, Volume 1: Shuri-Te and Shorin Ryu*. Huntington, MD: Clarke's Canyon Press.

Clarke, Christopher M. (2012b): *Okinawan Karate–A History of Styles and Masters, Volume 2: Fujian Antecedents, Naha-Te, Goju Ryu and other Styles*, Huntington, MD: Clarke's Canyon Press.

Clarke, Michael (2009). *The Art of Hojo Undo: Power Training for Traditional Karate*. Wolfeboro, NH: YMAA Publication Center, Inc.

Corcoran, John (2012). *History of Modern Sport Karate*. https://www.backkicks.com/history-of-modern-sport-karate/. Retrieved 03/17/2021.

Creswell, J.W. (1994). *Research Design: Qualitative and Quantitative Approaches*. Sage Publications: Thousand Oaks, CA.

Cummins, William / Scaglione, Robert (2002). *Shorin Ryu–Okinawan Karate Question and Answer Book*. New York, NY: Person-to-Person Publishing, Inc. 3rd edition.

Dailey, Walter (1996). *Karate in the U.S.A. (A Fruit Salad)*. Bugeisha, Issue#1, p. 3.

Da Luz, Miguel (ed.). Okinawa Karate News. Div. Issues. Okinawa, Japan: Okinawa Media Planning.

Davey, H.E. (2022). *Wabi-Sabi in Classical Japanese Martial Arts and Fine Arts*. SMAA Journal, Volume 27, Issue# 1, p. 8-15.

Davey, H. E. (2021). *What is Jujutsu?* SMAA Journal, Volume 26, Issue# 4, pp. 3-6.

Davis, Roger J. / Osamu Ikeno (Eds.) (2002). *The Japanese Mind: Understanding Contemporary Japanese Culture*. Tokyo, Rutland, VM, Singapore: Tuttle Publishing.

Dern, Harald (2010). *Heuristische Grundlagen der Fallanalyse*. Forensische Psychiatrie Psychologie Kriminologie Vol. 4, pp. 98–106. https://doi.org/10.1007/s11757-010-0042-y *Forensische Psychiatrie, Psychologie, Kriminologie*. Retrieved 12/12/2021.

Dodd, Simon / Brown, David (2016). *Kata—The True Essence of Budo Martial Arts?* RAMA (Revista de Artes Marciales Asiáticas) Volume 11, Issue 1, pp. 32-47.

Doshinkan (n. d.). https://doshinkan.com/. Retrieved 02/02/2022.

Dreikurs, Rudolf (1981). *Grundbegriffe der Individualpsychologie*. Stuttgart/Germany: Klett-Cotta. 4th edition.

Drucker, Peter F. (1981). *Behind Japan's Success*. Harvard Business Review January 1981. https://hbr.org/1981/01/behind-japans-success. Retrieved 10/20/2021.

Encyclopedia Britannica. https://www.britannica.com ; div. terms retrieved July 16, 2021.

Enkamp, Jesse (n. d.). https://www.karatebyjesse.com/ Content about *Kusanku kata* retrieved 03/21/2022. https://www.youtube.com/user/KARATEbyJesse. Diverse video clips retrieved 02/20/2021.

Feldmann, Thomas (2021). *Anko Itosu. The Man. The Master. The Myth. Biography of a Legend*. Self-published with Lulu Press. © Thomas Feldmann.

Feldmann, Thomas (2007). *Kultur als Determinante der Wirtschaft? Unternehmensphilosophien in Japan*. Munich/Gemany: Judicum Verlag GmbH.

Finney, Patrick (2011). *Remembering the Road to World War Two—International History, National Identity, Collective Memory*. London: Routledge.

Fuente, de la, Eduardo Gonzales / Niehaus, Andreas (2020). *From Olympic sport to UNESCO intangible cultural heritage: Okinawa Karate between local, national, and international identities in contemporary Japan*. In: G. H. Keum & Ch. H. Park (Eds.), *Traditional martial arts as intangible heritage;* University of Gent: ICHCAP / ICM; pp. 40–51; http://hdl.handle.net/1854/LU-8681889.

Funakoshi, Gichin (1914). *Okinawa No Bugi—Martial Arts Technique of Okinawa—Part #1 About Karate*. In: McCarthy, Patrick (2018), pp. 27-35.

Funakoshi, Gichin (1935). *Speaking about Karate-do*. In: McCarthy, Patrick (2018), pp. 95ff.

Funakoshi, Gichin (1973). *Karate-do Kyohan—The Master Text*. Tokyo-New York-London: Kodansha International Ltd.

Funakoshi, Gichin (1983). *Karatedo–Mein Weg*. Tokyo & Weidenthal: Kodansha Int. & Werner Kristkeitz Verlag. 1st German edition.

Giesen, Bernhard / Seyfert, Robert (2013). *Kollektive Identität*. Aus Politik und Zeitgeschichte Vol. 63, Issue# 13-14, pp. 39-43.

Gill, Michael J. (2020). *Phenomenological Approaches to Research*. In: Mik-Meyer, Nanna / Järvinen, Margaretha (Eds.) (2020). *Qualitative Analysis: Eight Approaches for the Social Sciences*. London: Sage, pp. 73-94.

Gilje, Nils (2020). *Hermeneutics: Theory and Methodology*. in: Mik-Meyer, Nanna / Järvinen, Margaretha (Eds.) (2020). *Qualitative Analysis: Eight Approaches for the Social Sciences*. London: Sage, pp. 113-133.

Haines, Bruce A. (1970). *Karate's History and Traditions*. Rutland, VM & Tokyo: Charles E. Tuttle Company, Inc. 3rd edition.

Haitani Kanji (1990). *The Paradox of Japan's Groupism*. Asian Survey. Volume 30, Issue# 3, pp. 237-250.

Hammitzsch, Horst (1957). *Zum Begriff „Weg" im Rahmen der japanischen Künste*. Nachrichten der Gesellschaft für Natur- und Völkerkunde Ostasiens, Issue# 82, pp. 5-14.

Hart-Davis, Peter ("Duff") (1986). *Hitler's Games: The 1936 Olympics*. New York: Harber & Row, Publishers, Inc.

Hasegawa, Yoko / Hirose, Yukio (2005). *What the Japanese Language Tells Us about the Alleged Japanese Relational Self.* Australian Journal of Linguistics. Volume 25, Issue# 2, pp. 219-251.

Hashimoto, Akiko (2015). *The Long Defeat: Cultural Trauma, Memory, and Identity in Japan*. Oxford, NY: Oxford University Press.

Haskett, Norman D. (2016). *The Daily Chronicles of World War II: 365 Days of Text and Images That Capture the Conflict in Every Theater, Volume 1*. Chandler, AR: © Norm Haskett Designs, LLC. Kindle version. Retrieved 02/15/2022.

Hayes, William ("Bill") R. (2018). *My Journey with the Grandmaster—Reflections of an American Martial Artist on Okinawa*. ©1997 by William R. Hayes. Kearney, NE: Morris Publishing. 8th printing.

Hein, Laura E., & Selden, Mark (1997). *Commemoration and Silence: Fifty Years of Remembering the Bomb in America and Japan*. In: L. Hein, & M. Selden (Eds.). *Living With the Bomb: American and Japanese Cultural Conflicts in the Nuclear Age*. London/New York: Routledge Publishing, pp. 3-35.

Hein, Laura E. & Selden, Mark (ed.) (2003). *Islands of Discontent—Okinawan Responses to Japanese and American Power*. Lanham, MD: Rowman & Littlefield Publishers, Inc.

Herbert, Wolfgang (2019). *Was hat Bodhidharma im Karate-dōjō verloren?* OAG Notitzen 05/2019, pp. 10-35.

Herbert, Wolfgang (2021). *Miszellen zum Thema „Karate, Zen und Meditation."* Toshiya Magazin für Karate, Kampfkunst & Kultur, Edition 90, pp. 12-21.

Hickey, Walt (2012). *Switzerland's Military Defense Involves Blowing Up All Roads Into The Country*. https://www.businessinsider.com/switzerlands-military-defenses-2012-6. Retrieved 12/15/2021.

Hokama, Tetsuhiro (2000). *History and Traditions of Okinawan Karate*. Hamilton, Ontario, Canada: Master Publications.

Horney, Karen (1937). *The Neurotic Personality of Our Time*. New York: Norton.

Imbrišević, Miroslav (2021). *Is there a Future for Olympic Karate?* idrottsforum.org. Malmö University, Sweden https://idrottsforum.org/feature-imbrisevic210818/. Retrieved 02/08/2022.

International Ryukyu Karate Research Society (n. d.).Diverse articles and content. Retrieved 09/10/2020. (Quoted as "IRKRS n. d.")

Itosu, "Ankoh" Yasutsune (1908). *Ten Lessons about Karate.* In: McCarthy, Patrick (2018), pp. 23-26.
Japan Karate Association (n.d.). https://www.jka.or.jp/en/. Retrieved 12/02/2021. Cited as "JKA."
Izumikawa, Carol (2020). *Being Related to Mr. Miyagi, My Father's Cousin—Kanki Izumikawa, Was Chojun Miyagi's Successor.* https://carolizumikawa.medium.com/kanki-izumikawa-%E6%B3%89%E5%B7%9D-%E5%AF%9B%E5%96%9C-3b2a26baad49. Retrieved 11/29/2021.
Johnson, Noah C.G. (2012). *The Japanization of Karate? Placing an Intangible Cultural Practice.* Journal of Contemporary Anthropology, Vol 3, Issue# 1, pp. 60-78.
Judkins, Benjamin N. / Bowman, Paul (2018). *Show, Don't Tell: Making Martial Arts Studies Matter.* Martial Arts Studies Issue#5, p. 2-14. Retrieved 11/02/2021 from https://mas.cardiffuniversitypress.org/6/volume/5/issue/0/.
Kane, Lawrence A. / Wilder, Kris (2022). *Martial Arts and Your Life. The Story of Us. What We Do and Why.* Seattle, WA: Stickman Publications, Inc.
Kane, Lawrence A. / Wilder, Kris (2005). *The Way of Kata: A Comprehensive Guide to Deciphering Martial Applications.* Wolfeboro, NH: YMAA Publication Center, Inc.
Kerr, George H. (2018). *Okinawa—The History of an Island People.* Rutland, VM & Tokyo & Singapore: Tuttle Publishing. Revised edition.
Kotek, Ruthie (2016). *What is so Japanese about Shotokan Karatedo? Protection of Cultural Identity and Economic Rights in the Global Sphere.* Master Thesis at the University of Haifa's Faculty of Humanities, Department of Asian Studies.
Krech, David / Crutchfield, Richard S. / Livson, Norman (1969). *Elements of Psychology.* New York: Alfred A. Knopf, Inc. 2nd edition (quoted as "Krech et.al. 1969").
Lind, Werner (1991). *Die Tradition des Karate—Meister und Stile der traditionellen Kampfkunst in Okinawa, China und Japan.* Heidelberg-Leimen, Germany: Werner Kristkeiz Verlag.
Lloyd, Henry M. (2014). *Philosophy as a Way of Life and the Practice of Martial Arts.* Draft in https://www.academia.edu/4914897/Philosophy_as_a_Way_of_Life_and_the_Practice_of_Martial_Arts#. Retrieved 01/03/2022. Published as *Philosophy and the Martial Arts: Engagement.* In Priest, Graham / Young, Damon (Eds.). *Philosophy and the Martial Arts.* London: Routledge/Taylor and Francis.
Luhmann, Niklas (1968). *Zweckbegriff und Systemrationalität.* Tübingen: J.C.B. Mohr (Paul Siebeck).

Maslow, Abraham H. (2013). *A Theory of Human Motivation*. Mansfield Centre, CT: Martino Publishing. Reprint of 1943 Edition.

Matayoshi, Masaharu / Trafton, Joyce (2000). *Ancestors Worship—Okinawa's Indigenous Belief System—A Traditional View of Ideal Family Relationships*. Toronto, Canada: University of Toronto Press Incorporated.

Matsumuro Sokon (2020). *The Seven Virtues of Martial Arts*. Translated and published by Andreas Quast. Self-published Düsseldorf, Germany. © Andreas Quast. 2nd Printing.

Meyer, Stanislav (2007). *Citizenship, Culture and Identity in Prewar Okinawa*. A thesis submitted for the Degree of Doctor of Philosophy at The University of Hong Kong January 2007.

McCarthy, Patrick (2018) *Legend of the Fist Vol #1—A Compilation of Japanese-to-English translations By Patrick & Yuriko McCarthy*. © 2018 by Patrick McCarthy. Middletown, DE.

McCarthy, Patrick (2018a). *Meeting of the Okinawan Masters—Meeting Transcript*. In: McCarthy, Patrick (2018), pp. 185-200.

McCarthy, Patrick (2018b). *The Dai Nippon Butoku-Kai*. In: McCarthy, Patrick (2018), pp. 258-280.

McCarthy, Patrick (2016). *Bubishi—The Classic Manual of Combat*. Rutland, VM & Tokyo & Singapore: Tuttle Publishing. Revised and expanded edition.

McCarthy, Patrick (1998a). *Tegumi Part 1*. Bugeisha, Issue#5, pp. 36-40.

McCarthy, Patrick (1998b). *Tegumi Part 2*. Bugeisha Issue#6, pp. 16-20.

Meissl, Walter (2021). *Many Kinds—Zur Kunst von 10. Dan Isao Ichikawa Gründer von Karatedo Doshinkan*. Vienna, Austria: edition thetis.

Messner, Nicolas (2020). *The Belt: Myth and Reality of an Essential Symbol* https://www.ijf.org/news/show/the-belt-myth-and-reality-of-an-essential-symbol. Retrieved 03/01/2021.

Motobu, Choki (2020). *My Art and Skill of Karate*. Edited, and translated by Andreas Quast and Naoki Motobu. Waldbronn, Germany: Ryukyu Bugei © Andreas Quast 2020.

Motobu Choki (2018). *Okinawan Kenpo Karate-jutsu: Kumite*. Translated and published by Eric M. Shahan. © Eric Michael Shahan.

Museum of the American Arts & Crafts Movement (n.d.). https://www.museumaacm.org/about.html. Retrieved 01/26/2022. Quoted as "AACM Museum."

Nagamine, Shoshin (1976). *The Essence of Okinawan Karatedo*. Rutland, VM &Tokyo: Charles E. Tuttle Co., Inc.

NASA (n. d.): https://www.nasa.gov/naca100/overview. Retrieved 02/23/2021.

Nitobe, Inazo (2014). *Bushido—The Soul of Japan*. CreateSpace Independent Publishing Platform. 1st illustrated edition.

Noble, Graham (2019). *Gichin Funakoshi's Exquisite Art*. Classical Fighting Arts Magazine, Vol 3, Issue# 57, pp. 33-51.

Noble, Graham (2020). *Gichin Funakoshi's Exquisite Art Part II*. Classical Fighting Arts Magazine, Vol 3, Issue# 58, pp. 43-51.

OKIC Okinawa Karate Information Center within the Okinawan Karate Kaikan (n. d.). http://okic.okinawa/en/. Retrieved 08/30/2020.

Okinawa Karate News (div years). Div. Issues. Okinawa, Japan: Okinawa Media Planning.

OPG Okinawa Prefectural Government (2003). *History of Okinawan Karate*. https://web.archive.org/web/20081011051605/http://www.wonder-okinawa.jp/023/eng/001/001/index.html. Retrieved 08/30/2020.

Park, Charles (2020). *An Inconvenient History—Japan's Dark Shadow on Asia*. East Asian History and Peace Institute. © Charles Park

Priddy, Jake (n.d.). *Fighting Like Girls: The Ethical Considerations for Multi-gendered Formats in Combat Sports*. Research Paper in WMST 6220 Dr. Weiss. Women's and Gender Studies at the University of Memphis. https://www.academia.edu/7543442/Fighting_Like_Girls_The_Ethical_Considerations_for_Multi_gendered_Formats_in_Combat_Sports. Retrieved 02/27/2022.

Quast, Andreas (2020a). *Matsumuro Sokon—The Seven Virtues of Martial Arts*. Self-published Düsseldorf, Germany. © Andreas Quast. 2nd Printing.

Quast, Andreas (2020b). *WKF Official Kata List—Development 2012 | 2013 | 2020*. Ryukyu Bugei, https://ryukyu-bugei.com/?p=8991. Retrieved 11/30/2021.

Quast, Andreas (2021a). *Okinawa Kenpo—Viewed from a different angle*. Ryukyu Bugei, https://ryukyu-bugei.com/?p=9748. Retrieved 12/28/2021.

Quast, Andreas (2021b). *Torite*. Ryukyu Bugei, https://ryukyu-bugei.com/?p=9696. Retrieved 01/10/2022.

Quast, Andreas (2022). *Okinawan Sumo (Shima)*. Ryukyu Bugei, https://ryukyu-bugei.com/?p=9938. Retrieved 03/10/2022.

Regan, Richard J. (2013). *Just War—Principles and Cases*. Washington D.C.: The Catholic University of America Press. 2nd Edition.

Rogner, Josef (1985). *Kompensation*. In: Brunner, Reinhard / Kausen. Rudolf / Titze, Michael (Ed.) (1985), pp. 230-232.

Sanguinetti, Franko (2021). *The Future of Traditional Budo*. Bugeisha, Issue#9, pp. 40-51.

Seidenfuß, Josef (1985). *Gemeinschaftsgefühl*. In: Brunner, Reinhard / Kausen. Rudolf / Titze, Michael (Ed.) (1985), pp. 159-165.

Seiffert, Helmut (1971a). *Einführung in die Wissenschaftstheorie 1—Sprachanalyse, Deduktion, Induktion in Natur- und Sozialwissenschaften*. München/Germany: Verlag C.H. Beck. 5th edition.

Seiffert, Helmut (1971b). *Einführung in die Wissenschaftstheorie 2—Geisteswissenschaftliche Methoden: Phänomenologie, Hermeneutik und historische Methode, Dialektik.* München/Germany: Verlag C.H. Beck. 3rd edition.
Sells, John (1997). *Gusukuma Shimpan.* Bugeisha Issue# 3, pp. 62-63.
Shaffer, David R. / Kipp, Katherine (2007). *Developmental Psychology—Childhood and Adolescence.* Belmont, CA: Thomson-Wadsworth Higher Education. 7th edition.
Shimabukuro, Masayuki / Pellman, Leonard J. (2022). *Karate as the Art of Killing—A Study of Its Deadly Origins, Ideology of Peace, and the Techniques of Shito Ryu.* Berkeley, CA: Blue Snake Books an imprint of North Atlantic Books.
Shimabukuro, Zenpo / Smith, Dan (2020). *Shorin Ryu Seibukan: Kyan's Karate.* Kindle Edition.
Standley, Melissa J. (2008). *Aiming for the Moon—A New Age of Hope.* 1968 Retrospective: Conference at UMPI. Introduction for Science of 1968 Session, page 5.
Sun Tzu (n. d.). *The Art of War.* Middletown, DE: Filiquarian Publishing, LLC. Published due to its public domain status on 03/08/2021.
Swennen, Filip (2009). *The Evolution of Karate: From Secret Martial Art to Worldwide Cultural Sport.* Thesis at International Budo University, Japan. Supervisor: Professor Matsui Kantaro.
Swennen, Filip (2006). *The Creation of the Myth of "Traditional Japanese" Karate under the Pressure of Pre-War Nationalism.* Thesis for a Licentiate in Japanology at Katholieke Universiteit Leuven, Belgium. Academic year 2005-2006. Faculteit Letteren TAAL En Regiostudies.
Swift, Charles Joseph (2019). *Itosu Anko. Savior of a Cultural Heritage.* Tokyo: Self-published with Lulu Press. © Charles Joseph Swift.
The Henry Ford (n.d.). https://www.thehenryford.org/collections-and-research/digital-collections/expert-sets/105303/. Retrieved 01/22/2022.
Werner, Heinz (1980). *Comparative Psychology of Mental Development.* © Heinz Werner 1948. New York: International Universities Press, Inc. 3rd revised edition.
Wittwer, Henning (2014). *Karate Kampfkunst Hoplologie.* Niesky, Germany: Self-published. © Henning Wittwer.
Wittwer, Henning (2007). *Shotokan:* überlieferte Texte ~ historische Untersuchungen. Niesky, Germany: Self-published. © Henning Wittwer.
World Karate Federation (2020). *Karate Competition Rules. Effective from 1.1.2020.* https://www.wkf.net/pdf/WKF Competition%20Rules_2020_EN.pdf. Cited as "WKF."

INDEX

1936 meeting 3, 4, 9, 33
abused women and girls 99, 100
aligning foot-knee-shoulder 8, 11
Ancestors Worship 31, 51
Arts and Crafts Movement 133, 134, 144
Asato Anko 96
athletes create an impression 85
beginner's mind 111, 157
belt system 120, 121
big picture 113, 115, 116, 118, 132
birthplace of karate 143
blunders 126, 127, 128, 132
Bodhidharma 21
body-weight-power-transfer 8, 11, 15
Buddhism 21, 31, 50, 51, 52, 146
Budo 1, 38, 39, 42, 44, 49, 52, 53, 61, 82, 146, 148, 152
Bujutsu 1, 25, 39
Bushido 39, 41, 42, 50, 53, 55, 92
business considerations 137
calligraphy 146, 148
character development xvii, 10, 50, 52
chess 113, 118, 131
Chibana Chosin 33, 34, 68, 97, 124, 142
combat application 89
commercialization 137, 138, 140
commodity 58, 136, 137, 138, 139, 140
compensation 75
competency levels 119
concept of self-protection 50
Confucian-based thought process 31
Confucianism 50, 52, 94, 146
copyrights and financial interests 136, 140
corporative economic structure 57

countercultural movement 143, 149
counterculture 134, 141
craft-component 145
create maximal damage in the most effective way 8, 11, 56
cross-linked concepts 114, 115, 132
cultural heritage 7
culture of conformity 6, 31, 47
curators 7, 155
Cybernetics 116, 118
Dai Nippon Butoku-Kai 38, 40, 42, 43, 53
deductive learning 123, 132
dialectic thinking xix
dichotomy of culture and citizenship 30, 31, 52
domestic violence 98, 100
Doshinkan xvi, 51, 70, 147, 151, 152
economic success 57, 107
economies of scale 134
emphasize athletic performance 79
errors 126, 127, 128, 132
FAJKO 59
fighting system of percussive impact 9
Fujimoto-Stock Masako xvii
Funakoshi Gichin 2, 38, 59, 66, 68, 69, 91, 120, 124, 155
fundamental functions 111
fundamentals 115, 116, 127
genuine *Bunkai* 143, 155
grappling 20, 24, 25, 57, 62, 65, 71, 88
Groupism 47
group of dedicated curators 155
guardians 70, 135, 139, 140
hermeneutic historic reasoning 26, 146
heuristic-hermeneutic 21, 26
hidden concepts 4, 12, 86, 152

hidden lethal concepts 149
hidden secrets 155
hidden take-down 12
highest quality possible 129, 134
holistic entity 152
holistic perception 112, 113, 114, 132
Ichikawa Isao xvi
idiosyncrasies 127, 128
imperial armed forces 42
improving an existing idea 24
individualism 33, 47, 48
inductive learning 123, 132
industrialization 36, 58, 133, 134, 135, 136, 138, 140, 141, 149
inherent patterns 113, 118, 132
intersubjective verifiability xviii
Itosu Anko 35, 66, 68, 72, 146
Japanization of Okinawan karate 36, 53, 150
Japanized karatedo 2, 9, 56, 68, 69, 70, 112, 124, 141, 148, 150
JKA 50, 65, 69, 97, 137, 138, 139, 140
JKF 59, 60, 89, 107
journeyman 120
just cause 44, 94, 95, 98, 108
karatedo's industrialization 155
karate inflation 58, 138
karate-jutsu 2, 3
karateka's character 6
karate ni sente nashi 90, 91, 108
karate tourists 143
kata competition 15
kiai 15, 87, 88
Kobayashi 68, 81, 124, 142, 151
kumite 79, 80, 81, 82, 83, 85, 86, 107
kumite competition 14
Kusanku 24, 82, 87, 88
Kyan Chotoku 20, 33, 34, 119, 124
kyosho 69
kyusho 69, 70, 71, 72

large-scale-production 58, 138
learning objectives 62, 138
loss of knowledge 65, 69, 107
market niche 135, 155
martial arts in name only 93
martial arts of scholars 93
mass product 133, 136
mastery 79, 111, 112, 113, 114, 116, 119, 120, 131, 132
Matsubayashi Ryu 81, 124
Matsumura Sokon 69, 76, 93
mental patterns 128
mental store 114, 116, 118
militarism 38, 42, 55, 73, 90, 92, 107, 108
militarization 46, 73
minimum quality needed 134
mistakes 125, 126, 127, 128, 132
moral code 91, 94, 108
Motobu Choki 33, 91, 97
multiplication 58, 134, 138
Naihanchi kata 7
national cultural symbol 35
nerve strikes 50, 65, 71, 72
nerve suppression 57, 63
neural network 116
no-surrender doctrine 40
nukite 66, 68, 88
occupation of Southeast Asia 36
Okinawa is the birthplace of karate 19
Okinawan karate-jutsu xvi, 5, 7, 9, 10, 24, 50, 51, 57, 59, 69, 72, 81, 89, 90, 93, 109, 111, 120, 123, 124, 137, 143, 146, 152, 155
Okinawan subcultural heritage 30
Okinawan subcultural symbol 34, 50
Okuden 5, 6, 70, 110
Olympic Games 14, 58, 59, 61
omote 89, 109
overarching unity xix, 48, 152

Passai 66, 68, 71, 82, 86, 87, 88
peaceful art of meditative athletics 92
perceived gender roles 100
performance levels 120
physical education learning outcomes 13
pre-emptive strikes 96, 115
pressure points 50, 71
qualitative research xviii
quantitative research xviii
rationalization 134, 138
recognized patterns 115
reconstructing 129
reduction of complexity 115, 116
samurai tradition 49, 60, 61
Seibukan 81, 124
self-actualization 75
self-control 92, 119, 124, 154
self-perfection 9, 35, 50, 152
self-protection 3, 10, 24, 27, 34, 53, 56, 93, 97, 148, 152
senpai/kohai system 31, 48
Shaolin 21, 24, 154
Shintoism 31, 51
Shito Ryu 60, 90, 140
Shobayashi Ryu 124
Shorin Ryu xvi, 7, 10, 24, 68, 71, 81, 82, 96, 124, 142
shoshin 70, 90, 124
Shotokan 3, 59, 66, 68, 120, 124, 136, 137, 138, 139, 140, 150
Shudokan 33, 142
silent protest 34
spectacularly exaggerated moves 79
speedy, fencing moves with tagging contact 14, 56, 85
spiritual mobilization program 40
sports derivatives 1, 13, 19, 60, 69

sports-karate 3, 13
standardization 58, 134, 138
subcultural heritage 7, 35, 143
subcultural identity 29, 32
subcultural symbol 35, 52
Suikendo 82
Sun Tzu 115
superstructures 56, 146
taken at face value 87, 88
Te 20, 21, 24, 29, 52
tegumi 20, 24, 62, 63, 81, 82, 83, 138
telegraphing 97
there is no first attack in karate 90, 98
there is no *kata* anymore in competition *kumite* 107
there is no *kumite* anymore in competition *kata* 107
Tomaya Kanken 59, 142
torite 24, 62, 63, 69, 70, 71
totalitarian regimes 42, 43, 45
totality 113, 116, 118, 132
true martial arts 93, 96
tuite 20, 62, 63, 71
tuning 128
UNESCO 19
unique selling position 135, 138, 139
unity of *kata* and *kumite* 107
unity of *kata* concepts and their application in *kumite* 79
ura 109
US-American space program 23
warrior spirit 36, 38, 39, 40, 41, 42, 43, 44, 52, 92
WKF 80, 83, 89, 107, 144
yin and yang xix, 48, 152
Zen xvii, 2, 21, 42, 50, 51, 52, 53, 56, 146

ABOUT THE AUTHOR

Hermann Bayer, PhD Biography
Hermann holds degrees in economics, sociology, psychology, and business administration. He worked in German and US universities for eighteen years as a scientist, professor, campus dean, and multi-site dean. For another twelve years Hermann served as the CEO and executive coach of a German coaching and consulting firm. In addition, he had ten successful years of self-employment, another  nine years working in the manufacturing industry, and two years serving in the (West) German army's corps of engineers. He immigrated to the USA in 2005.

The author of several books and numerous articles on industrial relations, coaching, and consulting, Hermann now publishes on karate-jutsu's and karate-do's socio-cultural roles and their development.

Hermann started to train and to study the art of karate—including its historical and socio-cultural development—in 1981. His experience covers traditional (non-sports) Japanese *Shudokan-Doshinkan* karate-do as well as classic Okinawan *Shorin Ryu* karate-jutsu. In 2016 he completely changed his life priorities from academics to "full-time-karate." To broaden his karate development beyond its Japanese form and to better understand today's misconceptions about the art's original orientation toward protecting and preserving life, he restarted from scratch with classic Okinawan *Kobayashi Ryu* karate-jutsu and kobudo. In addition, Hermann studies *suikendo*—meaning "the art of fists flowing like water," today's most advanced karate fighting system. Over the years, he has spent considerable time with renowned Japanese, Western, and Okinawan karate teachers, all the while researching the core essence of the style they represent.

Today, in his mid-seventies, Hermann is still training hard, practicing karate daily and attends at least three, but mostly four, two-hour empty-hand and kobudo training sessions every week. To make a point about combining (not to be confused with "integrating") traditional karate-jutsu and sports karate, he successfully competes in martial arts tournaments and secures first place in his age bracket.

BOOKS FROM YMAA

101 REFLECTIONS ON TAI CHI CHUAN
108 INSIGHTS INTO TAI CHI CHUAN
A WOMAN'S QIGONG GUIDE
ADVANCING IN TAE KWON DO
ANALYSIS OF GENUINE KARATE
ANALYSIS OF GENUINE KARATE 2
ANALYSIS OF SHAOLIN CHIN NA 2ND ED
ANCIENT CHINESE WEAPONS
ART AND SCIENCE OF STAFF FIGHTING
THE ART AND SCIENCE OF SELF-DEFENSE
ART AND SCIENCE OF STICK FIGHTING
ART OF HOJO UNDO
ARTHRITIS RELIEF, 3D ED.
BACK PAIN RELIEF, 2ND ED.
BAGUAZHANG, 2ND ED.
BRAIN FITNESS
CHIN NA IN GROUND FIGHTING
CHINESE FAST WRESTLING
CHINESE FITNESS
CHINESE TUI NA MASSAGE
COMPLETE MARTIAL ARTIST
COMPREHENSIVE APPLICATIONS OF SHAOLIN CHIN NA
CONFLICT COMMUNICATION
DAO DE JING: A QIGONG INTERPRETATION
DAO IN ACTION
DEFENSIVE TACTICS
DIRTY GROUND
DR. WU'S HEAD MASSAGE
ESSENCE OF SHAOLIN WHITE CRANE
EXPLORING TAI CHI
FACING VIOLENCE
FIGHT LIKE A PHYSICIST
THE FIGHTER'S BODY
FIGHTER'S FACT BOOK 1&2
FIGHTING ARTS
FIGHTING THE PAIN RESISTANT ATTACKER
FIRST DEFENSE
FORCE DECISIONS: A CITIZENS GUIDE
INSIDE TAI CHI
JUDO ADVANTAGE
JUJI GATAME ENCYCLOPEDIA
KARATE SCIENCE
KATA AND THE TRANSMISSION OF KNOWLEDGE
KRAV MAGA COMBATIVES
KRAV MAGA FUNDAMENTAL STRATEGIES
KRAV MAGA PROFESSIONAL TACTICS
KRAV MAGA WEAPON DEFENSES
LITTLE BLACK BOOK OF VIOLENCE
LIUHEBAFA FIVE CHARACTER SECRETS
MARTIAL ARTS OF VIETNAM
MARTIAL ARTS INSTRUCTION
MARTIAL WAY AND ITS VIRTUES
MEDITATIONS ON VIOLENCE
MERIDIAN QIGONG EXERCISES
MINDFUL EXERCISE
MIND INSIDE TAI CHI
MIND INSIDE YANG STYLE TAI CHI CHUAN
NATURAL HEALING WITH QIGONG
NORTHERN SHAOLIN SWORD, 2ND ED.
OKINAWA'S COMPLETE KARATE SYSTEM: ISSHIN RYU
PRINCIPLES OF TRADITIONAL CHINESE MEDICINE
PROTECTOR ETHIC
QIGONG FOR HEALTH & MARTIAL ARTS 2ND ED.
QIGONG FOR TREATING COMMON AILMENTS

QIGONG MASSAGE
QIGONG MEDITATION: EMBRYONIC BREATHING
QIGONG GRAND CIRCULATION
QIGONG MEDITATION: SMALL CIRCULATION
QIGONG, THE SECRET OF YOUTH: DA MO'S CLASSICS
REDEMPTION
ROOT OF CHINESE QIGONG, 2ND ED.
SAMBO ENCYCLOPEDIA
SCALING FORCE
SELF-DEFENSE FOR WOMEN
SHIN GI TAI: KARATE TRAINING
SIMPLE CHINESE MEDICINE
SIMPLE QIGONG EXERCISES FOR HEALTH, 3RD ED.
SIMPLIFIED TAI CHI CHUAN, 2ND ED.
SOLO TRAINING 1&2
SPOTTING DANGER BEFORE IT SPOTS YOU
SPOTTING DANGER BEFORE IT SPOTS YOUR KIDS
SPOTTING DANGER BEFORE IT SPOTS YOUR TEENS
SPOTTING DANGER FOR TRAVELERS
SUMO FOR MIXED MARTIAL ARTS
SUNRISE TAI CHI
SURVIVING ARMED ASSAULTS
TAE KWON DO: THE KOREAN MARTIAL ART
TAEKWONDO BLACK BELT POOMSAE
TAEKWONDO: A PATH TO EXCELLENCE
TAEKWONDO: ANCIENT WISDOM
TAEKWONDO: DEFENSE AGAINST WEAPONS
TAEKWONDO: SPIRIT AND PRACTICE
TAI CHI BALL QIGONG: FOR HEALTH AND MARTIAL ARTS
THE TAI CHI BOOK
TAI CHI CHIN NA, 2ND ED.
TAI CHI CHUAN CLASSICAL YANG STYLE, 2ND ED.
TAI CHI CHUAN MARTIAL POWER, 3RD ED.
TAI CHI CONCEPTS AND EXPERIMENTS
TAI CHI CONNECTIONS
TAI CHI DYNAMICS
TAI CHI FOR DEPRESSION
TAI CHI IN 10 WEEKS
TAI CHI PUSH HANDS
TAI CHI QIGONG, 3RD ED.
TAI CHI SECRETS OF THE ANCIENT MASTERS
TAI CHI SECRETS OF THE WU & LI STYLES
TAI CHI SECRETS OF THE WU STYLE
TAI CHI SECRETS OF THE YANG STYLE
TAI CHI SWORD: CLASSICAL YANG STYLE, 2ND ED.
TAI CHI SWORD FOR BEGINNERS
TAI CHI WALKING
TAI CHI CHUAN THEORY OF DR. YANG, JWING-MING
TRADITIONAL CHINESE HEALTH SECRETS
TRADITIONAL TAEKWONDO
TRAINING FOR SUDDEN VIOLENCE
TRIANGLE HOLD ENCYCLOPEDIA
TRUE WELLNESS SERIES (MIND, HEART, GUT)
WARRIOR'S MANIFESTO
WAY OF KATA
WAY OF SANCHIN KATA
WAY TO BLACK BELT
WESTERN HERBS FOR MARTIAL ARTISTS
WILD GOOSE QIGONG
WING CHUN IN-DEPTH
WINNING FIGHTS
XINGYIQUAN

AND MANY MORE ...

VIDEOS FROM YMAA

ANALYSIS OF SHAOLIN CHIN NA
ART & SCIENCE OF STAFF FIGHTING
ART & SCIENCE OF STICK FIGHTING
BAGUA FOR BEGINNERS 1 & 2
BAGUAZHANG: EMEI BAGUAZHANG
BEGINNER QIGONG FOR WOMEN 1 & 2
BEGINNER TAI CHI FOR HEALTH
BIOENERGY TRAINING 1 & 2
CHEN TAI CHI CANNON FIST
CHEN TAI CHI FIRST FORM
CHEN TAI CHI FOR BEGINNERS
CHIN NA IN-DEPTH SERIES
FACING VIOLENCE: 7 THINGS A MARTIAL ARTIST MUST KNOW
FIVE ANIMAL SPORTS
FIVE ELEMENTS ENERGY BALANCE
HEALER WITHIN
INFIGHTING
INTRODUCTION TO QI GONG FOR BEGINNERS
JOINT LOCKS
KNIFE DEFENSE
KUNG FU BODY CONDITIONING 1 & 2
KUNG FU FOR KIDS AND TEENS SERIES
LOGIC OF VIOLENCE
MERIDIAN QIGONG
NEIGONG FOR MARTIAL ARTS
NORTHERN SHAOLIN SWORD
QI GONG 30-DAY CHALLENGE
QI GONG FOR ANXIETY
QI GONG FOR ARMS, WRISTS, AND HANDS
QIGONG FOR BEGINNERS: FRAGRANCE
QI GONG FOR BETTER BALANCE
QI GONG FOR BETTER BREATHING
QI GONG FOR CANCER
QI GONG FOR DEPRESSION
QI GONG FOR ENERGY AND VITALITY
QI GONG FOR HEADACHES
QI GONG FOR THE HEALTHY HEART
QI GONG FOR HEALTHY JOINTS
QI GONG FOR HIGH BLOOD PRESSURE
QIGONG FOR LONGEVITY
QI GONG FOR STRONG BONES
QI GONG FOR THE UPPER BACK AND NECK
QIGONG FOR WOMEN WITH DAISY LEE
QIGONG FLOW FOR STRESS & ANXIETY RELIEF
QIGONG MASSAGE
QIGONG MINDFULNESS IN MOTION
QI GONG—THE SEATED WORKOUT
QIGONG: 15 MINUTES TO HEALTH
SABER FUNDAMENTAL TRAINING
SAI TRAINING AND SEQUENCES
SANCHIN KATA: TRADITIONAL TRAINING FOR KARATE POWER
SCALING FORCE
SEARCHING FOR SUPERHUMANS
SHAOLIN KUNG FU FUNDAMENTAL TRAINING 1 & 2
SHAOLIN LONG FIST KUNG FU BEGINNER—INTERMEDIATE—ADVANCED SERIES
SHAOLIN SABER: BASIC SEQUENCES
SHAOLIN STAFF: BASIC SEQUENCES
SHAOLIN WHITE CRANE GONG FU BASIC TRAINING SERIES
SHUAI JIAO: KUNG FU WRESTLING
SIMPLE QIGONG EXERCISES FOR HEALTH
SIMPLE QIGONG EXERCISES FOR ARTHRITIS RELIEF
SIMPLE QIGONG EXERCISES FOR BACK PAIN RELIEF
SIMPLIFIED TAI CHI CHUAN: 24 & 48 POSTURES
SIMPLIFIED TAI CHI FOR BEGINNERS 48
SIX HEALING SOUNDS
SUN TAI CHI
SWORD: FUNDAMENTAL TRAINING
TAEKWONDO KORYO POOMSAE
TAI CHI BALL QIGONG SERIES
TAI CHI BALL WORKOUT FOR BEGINNERS
TAI CHI CHUAN CLASSICAL YANG STYLE
TAI CHI CHUAN THEORY OF DR. YANG, JWING-MING
TAI CHI FIGHTING SET
TAI CHI FIT: 24 FORM
TAI CHI FIT: ALZHEIMER'S PREVENTION
TAI CHI FIT: CANCER PREVENTION
TAI CHI FIT FOR VETERANS
TAI CHI FIT: FOR WOMEN
TAI CHI FIT: FLOW
TAI CHI FIT: FUSION BAMBOO
TAI CHI FIT: FUSION FIRE
TAI CHI FIT: FUSION IRON
TAI CHI FIT: HEALTHY BACK SEATED WORKOUT
TAI CHI FIT: HEALTHY HEART WORKOUT
TAI CHI FIT IN PARADISE
TAI CHI FIT: OVER 50
TAI CHI FIT OVER 50: BALANCE EXERCISES
TAI CHI FIT OVER 50: SEATED WORKOUT
TAI CHI FIT OVER 60: GENTLE EXERCISES
TAI CHI FIT OVER 60: HEALTHY JOINTS
TAI CHI FIT OVER 60: LIVE LONGER
TAI CHI FIT: STRENGTH
TAI CHI FIT: TO GO
TAI CHI FOR WOMEN
TAI CHI FUSION: FIRE
TAI CHI QIGONG
TAI CHI PUSHING HANDS SERIES
TAI CHI SWORD: CLASSICAL YANG STYLE
TAI CHI SWORD FOR BEGINNERS
TAI CHI SYMBOL: YIN YANG STICKING HANDS
TAIJI & SHAOLIN STAFF: FUNDAMENTAL TRAINING
TAIJI CHIN NA IN-DEPTH
TAIJI 37 POSTURES MARTIAL APPLICATIONS
TAIJI SABER CLASSICAL YANG STYLE
TAIJI WRESTLING
TRAINING FOR SUDDEN VIOLENCE
UNDERSTANDING QIGONG SERIES
WATER STYLE FOR BEGINNERS
WHITE CRANE HARD & SOFT QIGONG
YANG TAI CHI FOR BEGINNERS
YOQI: MICROCOSMIC ORBIT QIGONG
YOQI QIGONG FOR A HAPPY HEART
YOQI:QIGONG FLOW FOR HAPPY MIND
YOQI:QIGONG FLOW FOR INTERNAL ALCHEMY
YOQI QIGONG FOR HAPPY SPLEEN & STOMACH
YOQI QIGONG FOR HAPPY KIDNEYS
YOQI QIGONG FLOW FOR HAPPY LUNGS
YOQI QIGONG FLOW FOR STRESS RELIEF
YOQI: QIGONG FLOW TO BOOST IMMUNE SYSTEM
YOQI SIX HEALING SOUNDS
YOQI: YIN YOGA 1
WU TAI CHI FOR BEGINNERS
WUDANG KUNG FU: FUNDAMENTAL TRAINING
WUDANG SWORD
WUDANG TAIJIQUAN
XINGYIQUAN
YANG TAI CHI FOR BEGINNERS

AND MANY MORE . . .

more products available from . . .
YMAA Publication Center, Inc. 楊氏東方文化出版中心
1-800-669-8892 • info@ymaa.com • www.ymaa.com